AF580677

AVID
READER
PRESS

ALSO BY MATTHEW QUICK

We Are the Light

The Reason You're Alive

Every Exquisite Thing

Love May Fail

The Good Luck of Right Now

Forgive Me, Leonard Peacock

Boy21

Sorta Like a Rock Star

The Silver Linings Playbook

Dad, Love, Me

Matthew Quick

AVID READER PRESS
New York Amsterdam/Antwerp London
Toronto Sydney/Melbourne New Delhi

Avid Reader Press
An Imprint of Simon & Schuster, LLC
1230 Avenue of the Americas
New York, NY 10020

First Avid Reader Press hardcover edition July 2026

Interior design by Carly Loman

Manufactured in the United States of America

1 3 5 7 9 10 8 6 4 2

Library of Congress Control Number: 2026931282

ISBN 978-1-6680-9175-3
ISBN 978-1-6680-9177-7 (ebook)

With love, to my father, Michael Martin Quick, who—here in 2025—
often instructs me to "make the world a better place."

This has been going on for thousands
Of years! It doesn't change. Something
Happened to me, and I can't tell
Anyone, so it will happen to you.

—ROBERT BLY,
from his poem "Keeping Quiet"

Only a fool is interested in other people's guilt, since he cannot alter it. The wise man learns only from his own guilt. He will ask himself: Who am I that all this should happen to me? To find the answer to this fateful question he will look into his own heart.

—CARL JUNG,
from the Collected Works, Volume 12, *Psychology and Alchemy*

Author's Note

This memoir is a long overdue letter to my father. It's also how I remember parts of my life after getting sober and doing more than seven hundred hours of Jungian analysis.

I feel obliged to say:

Others might remember parts of my life differently. A few family members have told me so. I took their conflicting memories into consideration. I've changed some names and disguised a few identities. Long exchanges of dialogue are only my best effort at re-creating what was said weeks, months, years, and decades ago. Arranging my life into a narrative arc, of course, means the sequencing of events in this memoir—as well as what was put in and what was left out—were creative choices made in service of turning my personal history into a readable manuscript. Sometimes multiple events occurring on different dates were compressed into one event, same with conversations. I interviewed family and friends. When I asked to hear accounts more than once, small details in the interviewees' recollections often changed and—in some cases—conflicted. I pulled from all the many versions I heard. Memory is fallible; no way around that. At the end of the day, I chose to put the "me" in memoir and trusted my own memory and intuition.

All that said, I've done my absolute best to tell the truth as I now see it.

As I wrote and edited what you are about to read, dementia continued to turn my father's brain into mashed cauliflower. Odds are—by the time of publication—Dad will have lost the ability to read these words himself.

Prologue

Shortly after his ninety-first birthday, my grandfather decided to die.

He informed me of his decision during one of our weekly phone calls. Pop Pop Quick wasn't diagnosed with any specific disease. He was just tired of living. He'd seen many people succumb to death at the Brethren Village Retirement Community in Lititz, Pennsylvania, where he had spent his last years. So he knew what to expect. Once he stopped actively fighting the Grim Reaper, he figured he'd be gone in a matter of weeks, certainly no more than a few months.

I had recently turned thirty-eight and was drinking heavily.

"You survived the Great Depression," I argued with him. "The Nazis couldn't kill you in World War II. You still have a lot of fight left in you. Who will I talk to every Sunday night if you go to heaven?"

It was no use.

"Matthew," he said, "I want to make peace with your father before I go."

Suddenly, Harry Chapin's song "Cat's in the Cradle" was playing in my mind.

Pop Pop had repeatedly asked my dad to visit the old folks' home so they could have a long overdue father-son talk. Dad was coincidentally working near Lititz at the time, staying in a hotel on the weekdays. For five days and nights every week, he was only a ten-minute drive from his parents, but he insisted he had no time to visit them.

On the phone with me, in a shaky voice, my grandfather said, "I just want to know why Michael's been so angry with me for his entire life. I really have no idea. *Do you?*"

I did, but I wasn't about to tell my dying grandfather all of the horror stories I had heard. My father's miserable tales about growing up under Harry Quick's roof didn't match my experiences with my grandfather. Not even a little. Pop Pop's big love for me, his first-born grandson, probably saved my life when I was a teenager. But I also suspected that the man who liked to be called "Big H" was at least partially responsible for my father's often disagreeable nature.

"You're the glue of the family, Matthew," Pop Pop said to me, like he always did. "Maybe you can get your father to come see me. Would you at least try? I don't have a lot of time."

A few days later, I asked Dad if he might reconsider visiting his dying old man to clear the air.

"Matthew, you have no idea how busy I am growing the bank," my father said. "And you don't know the full extent of what went on between your grandfather and me. *Stay out of it.*"

When I reported back to Pop Pop, I could feel his heart cracking.

Then my grandfather's health began to go downhill fast.

Dad eventually did visit his father before he died. But when Pop Pop said, "I just want to know what I did to make you so angry. *Please*," Dad crossed his arms and pushed his lips together until they turned white.

Then—from the very recliner in which Pop Pop would ultimately die—he said, "Michael, with your brains and my personality, we could have ruled the world," which made my dad storm out of the room, leaving Pop Pop mystified.

"What did I do wrong?" he asked me, during one of the last Sunday night phone calls we ever had.

I said I didn't know.

My grandfather died in March 2012 without ever understanding why his second son was furious with him.

A few years later, when Dad was once again ranting about his late father's mistakes, I asked him why he hadn't confronted his father while he still had the chance. Dad shouted back at me, "What would have been the point? Your grandfather was a dying old man. It wouldn't have changed a thing. *I'm not a sadist.*"

The lies in that statement almost got *me* to confront *my* old man, but—as he seemed too wounded and self-absorbed to hear my pain—I too continued to say nothing.

Twelve years after Big H died, my father and I were taking one of our long walks in the Lowcountry of South Carolina, here on Lady's Island. This time it was Dad who was dying. In a boyish voice full of regret, he said to me, "I really wish I had told Father why I was so mad at him."

I didn't know what to do with that information, as I still hadn't directly confronted Dad—at least not in any constructive manner—about all he had done to make me furious with him for a half century. And now that he was losing his mind to dementia, unburdening myself felt too cruel.

What would be the point? My father was a dying old man. It wouldn't change a thing.

But I had so much anger and I didn't know what to do with it. I was pretty sure I wouldn't ever be able to truly love until I dealt with the tornado-like fury that had been secretly—and not so secretly—swirling in my chest since I was very young. And I had reached a place in my life where I really *wanted* to start loving again.

I'd even come to believe—here in midlife—that loving was the key to staying alive.

In an effort to love again, I'd already purchased a house just a block from my parents' home on Lady's Island and moved there so I could help care for Dad and support my mom. My father hadn't asked me to air my grievances with him, and I hadn't aired them. But when he told me he regretted sparing his own father's feelings, it seemed like a nudge. And yet, I didn't want to be a sadist.

I was in a double bind.

If I kept my mouth shut and swallowed my worst paternal memories, I would feel resentful and regretful for the rest of my life, just like Dad.

Since my father had dementia, he was no longer capable of having a productive conversation about the past. As you'll soon see, such a conversation would have been even *more* difficult before his cognitive decline.

Writers write. But I worried that documenting all that my father had done to me would take me down a dark, score-settling path. To be perfectly honest, there was a young and angry part of me that wanted to exact revenge. If I yielded to that temptation, would I be any better than my father had been to me at his worst?

I talked endlessly with my analyst about all of the above, but while talking helped, it didn't resolve the issue. For a long time, I didn't know what to do with my most troubling memories of Dad.

But then one day, a single ray of sunlight fought its way through my clouds.

Aim upward, it seemed to say.

"What does it mean to aim upward?" you might be asking now.

Well, I hope my humble memoir will answer that question.

Early readers have told me there is transformative magic ahead, so be forewarned. I, myself, wept in the most healing ways while writing the hardest parts of this memoir. But, as I type these introductory words to you now, I'm feeling at ease.

For a long time, I was terrified of putting this book into the world.

Now I'm inviting you—who are most likely a stranger to me—to look at some of the most intimate, painful, and beautiful parts of my life.

I trust your soul to know what to do with my memoir.

1.

Dad, when I was in elementary school and Mom was putting me to bed—often after you had screamed at me and made me tremble—I'd ask her why you didn't like me.

Mom would say, "Your father *loves* you very much."

"Then why is he always yelling at me? Why doesn't he ever want to play with me?" I'd ask.

Here's a summary of what Mom always said in response: Whenever the Philadelphia Eagles played in 1973—the fall I was born, back when you were twenty-five—you'd hold me on your lap while you watched your beloved Birds play on TV. Apparently, you'd rub my bald little head like a genie's lamp, thinking I could grant wishes. You believed I could make your team win.

"Your father never put you down during those games, Matthew," Mom would say. "He loved watching with you. He still does. *He really does love you.* He just doesn't always know how to show it."

The tale of you holding newborn me during Eagles games, rubbing my head for good luck, was my nightly medicine. Mom would go on to repeat the anecdote throughout my entire life, especially whenever I would complain about your surly ways. And I now think Mom's story was and still is lifesaving. Because it is the only evidence I have of you voluntarily touching me in any way even remotely resembling a loving manner for the first half century of my life. I don't know exactly just how conscious Mom was of what she was doing. Not to take any credit away from her, because she deserves a lot. But God works in mysterious ways and through all of us. And the medicine in that old head-rubbing, Eagles-game-day story seems more like a God thing than a Mom thing.

A big part of my little-kid brain refused to believe Mom's story was true. Or maybe it's more accurate to say the image of you holding me and actually enjoying it just clashed too hard with my lived experiences. The huge cognitive dissonance required to believe and thereby benefit from the tale was a lot to surf with any sort of confidence. I'd already wiped out too many times on the treacherous shores of you and me. But Mom just kept telling her hopeful story for decades and with the tenacity of a mother who feels just how badly her boy is hurting. In this way, the myth of you holding baby me during Birds games got into my bones and kept me surfing your unpredictable breaks forever and ever.

Here's something else Mom used to tell little me when I was feeling anxious in bed: She would say, "God has a plan for you, Matthew. He told me you were special. And that you would do something important with your life."

"God spoke to you about me?" I'd ask. *"Really?"*

"When you were in my belly," Mom would say, "God promised me you would do something truly wonderful and help many people. And on the day you were born, I looked in your eyes and could tell God had told the truth. You were sent here for a very specific purpose."

It was hard to believe that God was so interested in me when you, my own father, seemed indifferent at best.

"What's the purpose?" I'd ask.

And she would say, "God hasn't told us that yet."

"How will I know?"

"God will tell you when you need to know. Trust your Heavenly Father," Mom would say.

And I would try.

But God was in a place called heaven, and you were in our home at night and on the weekends, filling it with gloom, anger, and, occasionally, violence, so—back when I was a kid—I often used to close my eyes and will myself to remember what it felt like to be a newborn baby in your lap, because, again, I had no memory of you ever lovingly touching me at all, which seemed strange.

As I got older, I noticed how my friends' fathers—who were not exactly touchy-feely men by any stretch of the imagination but worked jobs like plumber and printing press operator and bartender and local shop owner and bookie and truck driver—often lit up whenever their sons walked into a room. You didn't do that with me. You usually didn't even seem to notice. When you did notice, you often screamed until I fled. I couldn't remember you ever once *smiling* at me. I couldn't remember a time when you seemed happy to see me. I was pretty sure you hated me and were just doing your best not to come right out and say it.

When I became an adult—after we'd had a few screaming matches and then drifted further and further apart—I told myself that Mom definitely invented the Eagles-game-day, baby-head-rubbing story. Maybe I needed that as a kid, but I had become a grown man, and I was done with make-believe.

However, whenever I'd get really sad about the lack of a connection between us, I'd still find myself fantasizing about being a newborn baby dressed in Kelly green. I'd see you making my baby hands clap so I'd appear to be rooting for the "Iggles" while nestled in your lap. I'd savor the imaginary warmth of your touch and approval and attention. You seeing any utility whatsoever in your first-born son. I indulged in this fantasy more times than I feel comfortable admitting.

At some point each go-around, a dark part of me would eventually rise up and shout, "I have *real* memories of Dad and me going to Eagles games at The Vet, back when I was a child. He'd ignore me and frown through the whole thing. And get angry when I had to use the bathroom. And shame me for not knowing the players' names and for rooting the wrong way. Later—when I'd go to The Linc as an adult with Micah and Megan and I'd get so drunk before noon—Dad would only coldly visit our tailgate parties for ten minutes at the most. And then he'd sit as far away from his three children as possible in his bank's luxury box. At the opposite end of the field. He'd text me ugly, pessimistic messages about the games. He'd even try to pit me against my siblings, using his ownership of the seat license and the tickets as a weapon, asking me—*in the middle of the games*—to collect owed money from Megan and Micah, and blaming me for their alleged delinquencies. And on the packed subway rides home, he'd barely grunt at my attempts at conversation. When the drunken crowds of subway riders rushed in and pushed our standing bodies together like sardines in a can, with Dad's face inches from mine and our torsos smashed together, I'd drunkenly fantasize about how he had once held me and rubbed my head and even allegedly enjoyed it; and I'd think, *How did I lose something so important? What unforgivable crime did I commit? What monstrous repulsive thing have I allowed myself to become?* And then I'd want to knee my father in the balls. And I'd also want to wrap my arms around him. And I'd want to scream curses into his face. And I'd also want to kiss his forehead. But I would just stand there doing nothing, as we both waited for people to get off at stops so that there would be more room in the subway car, and our bodies would cease touching. And I'd think, *Why do I even come to these games anymore? What is the point of this torture?*"

And after the dark voice in me had had its say, I would end up where I began—thinking it was best to dismiss Mom's Eagles-game-day, head-rubbing story as well-intentioned make-believe. It was far less painful to have never had your love than to have somehow lost it.

But I often flip-flopped.

I'd even do research.

For example, the internet says our first five Eagles seasons together were losers.

The first winning Birds season I lived through was also the first year that they made the playoffs during my lifetime. The 1978 season. I turned five that fall. We'd moved out of the city and just over the Ben Franklin Bridge to Oaklyn, New Jersey. We had a postage-stamp-sized plot of grass in the front yard and another in the back, where I'd eat lunch with Mom on a small wooden picnic table. You had your first mortgage on a little green house, located in a South Jersey town that was even less prestigious than the one in which you had grown up. And you were always either working or complaining about work, constantly underscoring how stupid your bosses were. That's where my conscious recollections mostly begin. You were not holding me on your lap then. You were not rubbing my head. You were cold and distant and often angry and worried about money and furious with your family of origin—to the point of madness. And I can't help wondering if you had been disappointed by my inability to make the Eagles win. Maybe you saw that it was better for the Birds when you kept your distance from me. Our Philadelphia Eagles' flight wasn't always pretty through the next forty years, but, overall, the Birds continued to trend upward as you and I drifted further apart.

Our team finally won a Super Bowl when you and I were hardly speaking at all. Super Bowl LII. February 4, 2018. You were almost seventy. I was forty-four and trying to quit alcohol. Completely sober in Alicia's and my Outer Banks home on the Albemarle Sound in North Carolina—so far away from you and Mom and Megan and Micah—my wife and I watched Philly win the biggest game there is. And when Nick Foles was named MVP and the Eagles were handed the Lombardi Trophy, I sat there unable to understand why—after following this team for almost half a century—I felt nothing at all. When Alicia went to bed, I kept sitting on the couch, powerless to get up. I flashed on George telling Lennie about the mythical farm and rabbits they'd someday own in *Of Mice and Men*. I saw Gary Sinise and John Malkovich locking eyes over a campfire. Then I tried to remember—as I had tried so many times before—the warm weight of your hopeful hand on my infant head as I sat swaddled in your lap, Dad. But I couldn't locate the old comfort. Instead, I felt a great and all-powerful void open up inside my chest, which horrified me. I worried that I would never experience the magic of Mom's story ever again. That time had run out. That the brokenness of my soul had become permanent. That maybe I had murdered the innocent child deep inside of me. That God never had a plan for me. That maybe God had never even existed at all.

Then I was sobbing and I couldn't stop for more than an hour.

2.

On the summer night that would alter my life forever, Alicia and I were eating alfresco on our second-story deck, which overlooked the Albemarle Sound. We were seated in the tall white chairs at the tall white round table. It was August 21, 2020. I was forty-six years old.

Osprey were dive-bombing the water and then flapping their wings doubly hard to lift fish up out of the black liquid and into the robin's-egg-blue sky. Once these magnificent birds were entirely free of the water, they made beelines for their nests, clutching their wriggling prizes in their talons.

"What are you thinking?" Alicia asked.

I looked out across the sound and saw a sailboat in the distance, racing toward the setting sun. Then I said, "Do you ever feel like we're still the kids we were when we met twenty-seven years ago? Like we tricked the world into letting us pretend to be adults? And someone from the government is going to knock on our front door and say, 'Our records indicate that you two are actually children. You need to be supervised, so we're seizing all your property and assets.'"

"Do *you* worry about that?" she asked.

I turned to meet her eyes before I said, "All the time."

"Maybe you should bring that up later tonight."

We started clearing the table, as our Scottish terrier, Desi, soaked up the last of the day's sunrays and enjoyed the cool breezes that used our thirty-foot-high, three-tiered bulkhead as a sort of ramp off the water to the second-story deck, which lined the entire back of our house.

I slid the sliding glass door open and walked into the air-conditioning.

The hardwood floor in the open concept living room, dining room, and kitchen always made me think of a basketball court. But the ridiculous number of windows and the vaulted ceiling—which formed several gigantic white triangles high above—almost made our home into an artsy cathedral. No matter how many years passed with us waking up every morning in this place, it was hard to believe that we lived here.

I took a quick shower and then put on a plain black T-shirt. I often wear a plain black T-shirt, but I had decided that I wanted to give the man we'll call Zeus a clue, regarding the suicidal feelings I'd been experiencing with increasing frequency. I would wear nothing but black until he asked me why. It was a little experiment I wanted to run.

I walked out of our bedroom, past the leather couch in front of the fireplace, and stuck my head back out through the open sliding glass door that led to the porch. Alicia was sitting out there with Desi on a white bench, watching the big orange ball of fire slowly falling through the sky toward the mainland on the other side of all that black water.

"I'm headed up to my office," I said. "Making it official."

My wife turned toward me. The magic-hour light lit her face perfectly and tinted her long curly brown hair with waves of gold.

"I'm proud of you," she said, as she smoothed Desi's black fur.

I closed the sliding glass door, turned around, and walked toward the open hardwood staircase. I climbed it to the platform hallway that looked over the rest of the house and reminded me of a catwalk in the sky. I walked past the third-floor bathroom and entered the small bedroom I had transformed into my office. I closed the door behind me, sat down at my big brown wooden desk, clicked the Zoom link Zeus had sent, and then waited for his face to fill the screen.

It was 6:59 p.m.

My heart was pounding.

My palms were sweaty.

I felt like I was being strangled by an invisible hand.

Then Zeus's face was right in front of mine.

He didn't look like the few pictures I'd seen of him on the internet. In all those—at least to my eye—he had appeared approachable and lively and straight-up fun. Like a big friendly elf. Or maybe like Shrek. On the Zoom video conference call, he looked formidable—like he could destroy me with his mind. Like even his unspoken thoughts could hurt me. I was Dorothy Gale staring at the Great and Powerful Oz—before Toto has pulled back the curtain.

"Tell me what your fantasy is," Zeus said.

"What do you mean?"

"About you and me. And Jungian analysis. What's your fantasy?"

I knew that Jungians used the word "fantasy" in a way that might make it interchangeable with the word "daydream" or "hope." But I bristled at the sexual connotations that "fantasy" brought up for me. Then I was saying, "I don't think I have a fantasy about analysis or you."

"Sure, you do," he said, flashing a disarming smile. "All first-time analysands fantasize. It's okay. You can tell me. That's why we're here. Right?"

I took a deep breath and began by talking about my Hollywood career imploding and getting sober all alone without any help whatsoever and my ensuing writer's block and losing sixty pounds and becoming addicted to long-distance running and feeling so lonely all the time and now needing a mentor. Maybe I even used the words "father figure." I told him that you, Dad, had dementia and were disappearing a little more every day—and all that was happening so far away from where I was currently living. I also told him how angry I had been with Mom and you over the years. I said I felt like I was uninitiated, that no one had ever taught me how to be an adult, let alone a man. I wanted to be a student of Jungian thought. That I hoped Zeus would be able to get me feeling mentally well without my having to use any drugs or alcohol. Maybe he could help me start writing again and get my career back on track. Maybe he'd also help me feel a little better about myself. I wanted to be a more stable husband. And I really wanted to attract better people into my life.

"What do you mean by *better people*?" he asked.

"I don't know," I said. "People who are going to push me toward health. People who aren't abusing alcohol and drugs, for sure. People who give as much as they take."

"What would you have to offer such people?" Zeus asked. "What would these people—*who give as much as they take*—what would they be getting from *you* exactly?"

I found myself feeling a little pissed off here, like this was round one of a long sparring session and my new analyst was already unloading nose-breaking punches, going for the knockout.

Maybe it's true, but come on, I thought. *You could let me ease into this.*

"Did my question offend you?" Zeus asked.

"I don't know," I said. "Was it wrong of me to say what I did? I thought this was a fantasy."

"It is," he said. "I'm just trying to understand your particular fantasy."

"I'm a good friend," I said, and then immediately thought of all the ways in which I hadn't always been a good friend. "Maybe, I guess, I want to be a *better* friend. That's why I'm here. To get better."

"And to attract people who give as much as they take," Zeus said. "Because *you* give as much as you take?"

"I don't know," I said again and then looked at the wall.

Next, he asked if I knew what active imagination was.

Since I had listened to Jungian podcasts, I actually did. I told him it is when you put yourself into a light trance and allow yourself to have a dream while you are awake. Almost like daydreaming, but with a more specific intention. And the active imaginer consciously interacts with the images that pop up in his mind, like he's in a play no one else can see.

"To connect with the unconscious," Zeus said.

"Right," I answered, even though I didn't really understand what that meant.

"Good," Zeus said. "You're a novelist. This should be easy for you. Close your eyes."

"Seriously?"

"Yes."

"Do I have to?"

"Yes."

I closed my eyes and then immediately felt infantilized. I flashed on mandatory nap time in kindergarten. *Was I seriously paying money to rest my eyes?*

I wondered what you, Dad, would have done in this situation. You'd have said active imagination was stupid. You would have demanded your money back and turned off the computer. Then you would have yelled and ranted at your family about how you had been tricked out of your hard-earned cash, and you would have barked about how everyone was out to get you, and how there was no one in the world you could trust when it came to getting well. Then I flashed on something your father used to tell me all the time. He'd say, "Whenever anything good happens in your life only two people will be happy about it: you and your wife." And here I was daring to trust a third person. *The audacity.*

I heard Zeus talking me through breathing exercises, making me inhale for a long amount of time, before exhaling in short, punctuated bursts. I heard him talking me into a relaxed state, telling me to fall deep inside of myself, to "drop down."

I kind of intuitively knew what he meant. I allowed myself to find the thing deep inside of me that is other and can take me to a place that feels sacred and more peaceful. I often felt this when I was in church as a young man. Sitting right next to you, I'd stop paying attention to whatever the minister was going on about, and I'd just stare at the light coming through the stained-glass windows. I would kind of trance out, and then, before I knew it, my feet and hands would be tingling, and I'd feel as though God were talking to me. God didn't say what the minister said. God didn't even use words. He just made me feel His warm, overwhelming intensity. And it was like anxiety and stress and fear and hatred and guilt and shame were just mud stuck to my skin, and God was a fantastic waterfall cascading down over my head and washing me clean.

Then—in the analytic session with Zeus—I was somehow narrating what I saw in the darkness of my mind. I was describing bright white lights set against a pulsing purple background—and then I was somehow falling through it all.

Or was I flying?

And Zeus was asking me what the lights and colors meant to me, telling me not to think, but to just answer, saying whatever popped into my head. There was no right or wrong, and everything was permitted in the unconscious.

So I told him I could kind of feel the lights and the colors speaking to me, only they weren't using words.

He said I should talk to the color purple and the bright white lights—everything I was seeing as I moved through it all. That I should ask what it was trying to get me to understand. That I should present myself as nonthreatening and curious so that whatever I was interacting with might respond in kind. So I did, saying, "What is it that you'd like me to know? Why am I here?" And then I began hearing a common male name emerge from the darkness and the purple and the light.

"Joseph," it kept saying.

I told Zeus I had known several men named "Joe."

"Do you feel any intensity when you think about any of these men?" he asked.

"No," I said. "Not at all."

I opened my eyes.

"Close your eyes," he commanded. "Stay with it."

I obeyed.

Then he asked, "What's the first thing that pops up in your thoughts when you hear the word *Joe*."

With my eyes closed again, I said "Joe" over and over in my mind—like an incantation.

And then I was very young.

"I'm on Furley Street. In the Olney section of Philly," I said. "Where I lived before my brother and sister were born. Great Oma's row home. She let my parents live there for free. I'm on the front stoop. I'm a toddler."

"What does it look like?" Zeus asked.

"It's a little porch. Under my feet is cement. There are black bars between the floor and the railings. The area's maybe seven by four feet. There's an iron gate blocking the steps, making it seem like a giant crib. My mother used to leave me out there, I think."

"How do you feel?"

"Scared," I said. "I'm all alone. I've been out there for a long time. All by myself."

"What do you want?"

"I want to be picked up. I want to be held."

"Tell the unconscious that you want to be held."

"What?"

"Just do it."

"I want to be held. Please hold me."

"What happens next?"

"Our next-door neighbor comes home from work. *His name was Joe!* My parents called him Joe the Scoop. Because they always asked him what the daily scoop was. Why am I thinking about *him*?"

"Describe Joe the Scoop. How does he look to you now?"

"He's older than my dad was at the time. Joe the Scoop is late thirties or early forties. He's Polish-looking. A worker. He's smiling. He looks kind."

"What does your neighbor do next in the active imagination?"

"He reaches over the railing of his stoop and picks me up. He carries me inside of his house and gets a beer can out of his fridge. Then we go back outside and he sits down on the steps of his front porch. He holds me on his lap. He calls me his 'little buddy.' He pops the tab of his brewski and bounces me on his knee. He drinks his beer and gives me tiny sips. He kisses my head. He tells me about his workday. He smells like sweat and cigarettes. The beer tastes warm and cold at the same time."

"How do you feel?"

"So much better."

"Why?"

"Because I'm no longer alone. Because I'm being held."

"Thank the unconscious for showing you these things."

"What?"

"Say thank you."

"Thank you."

"Open your eyes."

When I opened my eyes, Zeus was smiling at me.

"That was a real memory, I think," I said. "My parents used to say Joe the Scoop always bounced me on his knee when he came home from work. He'd just scoop me up. He really used to let me sip his beers. Do you think that's related to my alcoholism?"

"No."

"What's it related to then?"

"I want to tell you something," Zeus said. "And you probably aren't going to want to hear it."

I swallowed, braced myself, and said, "Okay."

Through the internet, using the cameras on our computers, Zeus looked deep into my eyes. It felt like he was literally in the room with me.

Then he said, "I love you."

If he had reached out through my laptop screen and smacked me across the face, I wouldn't have been more shocked, nor would I have felt more disturbed.

"I love you," he repeated more forcefully.

I swallowed and looked away.

"I love you," he said once more.

"Stop."

"Does hearing the words *I love you* make you feel uncomfortable?" Zeus said.

"You don't even know me," I said, and noticed that my voice was quivering.

"Your neighbor, Joe the Scoop, didn't know you. He just saw you on the stoop all alone and needing someone to love you. So he picked you up and he loved you. And you loved him. And that was meaningful."

"You don't know me," I repeated.

"You wrote a lot in your introductory email. I could feel your pain. I believed that you truly want to get better. It made me want to work with you. It made me feel love for you," Zeus said. "I'm here to pick you up again. That's a good thing."

"You *really* don't know me."

"I'm going to say it one more time, and then we'll finish for the night," Zeus said. "I love you."

Fuck you, I thought. *Why the fuck are you doing this to me? I didn't sign up for this mindfuck bullshit. Fuck you! Fuck! You!*

"That was hard for you, wasn't it?" Zeus said.

Again, I looked away.

"But you're still here," he said.

My fists were clenched off-screen.

"I really think I can help you. I *want* to help you."

My knee was bouncing up and down.

"How are you feeling right now?"

"Okay, I guess." *Fuck you.*

Zeus nodded a few times, smiled, and then said, "See you next week," just before he disappeared from my computer screen.

I looked at the clock.

Hours had passed since the start of my first analytic session. I had only paid for the agreed-upon fifty minutes.

I wondered why we had gone so far over the allotted time. I wondered if I'd be billed extra. I wondered if Zeus was running some sort of money-making scam on me.

I wondered why exactly I had internally screamed *Fuck you* so many times after Zeus had merely said, "I love you."

Then I said, "What the hell have I gotten myself into?"

3.

Dad, even when parts of me hated you, I never quit studying you. I never stopped listening. I never stopped trying to figure out what made you the way you were.

For the first four and a half decades of us, we never really had conversations.

Occasionally, you would trap me in some corner of your house, or ask me out for lunch, or we would go for a long walk, and you'd rant at me while I listened silently. If I ever dared to express an opinion, or tell you how I felt, or offer a counternarrative, your face would turn red, and then you'd scream, "Excuse me! You don't understand *anything*!" When you'd continue your rant, I'd listen silently, swallowing down equal portions of rage and shame—both yours and mine. Oh, I'm sure I put out a powerful—albeit passive-aggressive—fuck-you vibe from time to time. Every so many years or so I would actually scream back at you. But I'd mostly avert my eyes, slump my shoulders, and make myself submissive, as I sponged up the worst you had to offer. I heard and internalized every spit-laced word of every angry sermon you have ever given me. My heart dutifully recorded all of your many grievances and disappointments and pains. In some ways, the story of your life is written on my soul. I'd even go so far as to say I am the living bible of Michael Martin Quick. Like in that Dan Fogelberg song you love so much, "Leader of the Band." Your blood runs through my writing.

The immensely talented novelist Ron Currie once wrote this to me in an email:

How unlucky are our fathers? They thought they were just muddling through fatherhood anonymously, never suspecting their sons were writers.

When you first said to me—in your best Eeyore voice—"I know I'm the dad in *The Silver Linings Playbook*," you were referring to the very-you father in my novel and not the much more likable Robert De Niro patriarch in David O. Russell's crowd-pleasing Hollywood adaptation. And there was a dark score-settling part of me that enjoyed the hurt you were expressing after having looked into the very public mirror of my first major publication, if only because it meant that you at least *finally* got the fucking message.

When teenage me told you that I wasn't going to take your advice about becoming a lawyer and wanted to major in creative writing as an undergraduate, you said, "I'm not paying for a useless degree, so pick again. I know you won't pick any major I approve of, because you don't respect me. You *should* be a lawyer. But you're at least going to get a degree in something that will eventually provide health insurance and a pension." So I reluctantly became a secondary-education slash English major, thinking teaching would be easy and I could write during my summers off.

After I graduated, I quickly discovered that—if one actually cares about their students—teaching literature and writing is one of the most demanding jobs in the world. Grading essays and research papers often makes English teachers into round-the-clock, seven-days-a-week employees. I had a good, ball-busting, gym-teacher friend, and whenever he'd see me at my classroom desk slumped over a giant stack of student writing, he'd say, "Hey, Quickie, I scored three goals in floor hockey today and hit a home run in softball. Did a great workout in the gym during my prep period. And I have the weekend all to myself. Just remember, you picked English teacher. I even make more money than you do. Be a gym teacher in your next life." I've never in all my years on this planet worked harder for less money than I did when I was a high school English teacher.

I needed every second of the summer break to psychologically recover from the school year—not only teaching, but chaperoning and coaching, and doing my best to counsel troubled teenagers, and dealing with their willfully ignorant parents, and the soul-crushing politics of the town. I loved my students. I loved teaching writing and literature. But *boy oh boy*, did I hate working in public education. I wanted to change the world, but I was being paid to serve a system that I felt often did not prioritize the best interests of the kids. I youthfully clung to my ideals and tried to make teaching into an art form—naively expecting to be rewarded for such green narcissism—but the system relentlessly beat me down like it does almost everyone. A more grizzled special-education teaching buddy used to say, "When you leave, this place will go on just fine without you," and even though the young idealistic parts of me wanted to claw the skin from his face for having voiced such a dreary conclusion, he was absolutely right.

When several exhausting, grossly underpaid years of teaching went by in a blink and I wasn't writing at all, I started hearing this little song whenever I walked into Haddonfield Memorial High School. The singsong jingle went like this: "Put the gun to your head and pull the fucking trigger." Just that one-line advert on repeat, for weeks, months, years. I pushed that deep down inside of me. Even as the one-line song repeated in my brain, I'd wear a smile in the building. I'd give the kids everything good I had. Then I would come home and drink. The number of drinks I was consuming started to rise, especially on the weekends, when I didn't have to worry about how alcoholic my breath smelled in the mornings. Which is when I started talking to your older brother, Peter, about my dream of becoming a fiction writer.

Pete spent a lot of time at what he called "the fuckin' VA" palling around with and looking after war veterans suffering from PTSD. He talked about checking up on his Vietnam brothers when they all came home stateside. And he loved speaking with younger vets from the more current wars. Pete was an unlikely—camouflage-wearing and weapon-carrying—mental health advocate. He recognized that I was suffering. He'd check up on me. Drop by my house. Ask me how I was feeling. Listen to my hopes and dreams. Encourage me to create a livable future. He told me I couldn't hold everything inside. I couldn't hole up. I had to let it out, which I took to mean writing about everything. Then he encouraged me to take a big leap. "Risk and reward," he said to me a billion times. "No risk. No reward. That's how the fuckin' world works."

I was also telling my students that they should pursue their passions, even if that led to exploring fields that were not always the highest paying. I found myself zealously encouraging young creative types to pursue lives in the arts. And I was more and more feeling like a gigantic hypocrite.

A total fraud.

Once, when I was talking about the successes I had as a teacher, a family friend said to me, "Those who can do; those who can't teach," and I instantly felt like I was in a tub of boiling oil and my flesh was being fried right off my bones. When I told that same family friend I wanted to write a play, this person asked me if I was a homosexual in a way that made me understand why some of my gay students were afraid to come out. The comment was laced with hatred.

But Uncle Pete spoke with love when he said to me, "You're a good teacher. My next-door neighbor tells me that. Her kids took your little classes, so you must have done something right, pretty boy, if they're singin' your praises to their parents. That don't happen when you fuck up. You do one thing right, you can do something else right too. But you need balls. Risk and reward," which I knew was his way of saying, *If you are depressed doing this thing at which you are clearly succeeding, you should probably take a chance on doing something else. You have to save yourself in one way or another. Because the world is always going to be hard, but it's hardest on people who quit believing in a positive future.*

One spring night, Alicia and I sat down on the concrete steps of the back entrance to our little rancher starter house on the outskirts of Haddonfield, New Jersey, and we had a heart-to-heart. She was worried about me. She could see how much pain I was in. How mentally unstable I was becoming. How burned out I was from counseling young people with mental health problems far beyond my training. I was dealing with student pregnancy scares, serious drug addiction, rampant alcohol abuse, kids coming out as gay to me in their essays back before that was widely accepted, parental deaths, alcoholic parents in denial, kids who were being psychologically and emotionally abused, to name a few. I did what little I could for all who sought me out. The administration quietly encouraged my efforts. But I wasn't taking care of my own mental health, and the damage from that was accruing. My colleagues began pulling me aside and asking if everything was okay. Instead of telling them what was going on inside of me, I'd rant about what I perceived to be the ills of the system that employed me.

On those concrete back steps of our first home, my wife asked me, "What would you do right now, if you could do anything at all?"

Without hesitation, I told her I would enroll in a creative writing MFA program and begin writing fiction full-time.

And she said, "Well, then you should do it."

I reminded her that our bank account was empty, *and* we were carrying ten grand in credit card debt.

Which is when she reminded me that I had bumped into our real estate agent at one of the high school sporting events. I had coached and taught his daughters. And he had let me know that our modest house had miraculously doubled in value since we had purchased it. I had also previously told Alicia about the tax breaks Pete outlined for me—the ones that covered first-time homeowners who had made a profit on the sale of their house. Pete had already helped us refinance our home, taking advantage of money-saving banking-world information that you, Dad, had neglected to share with me, even though you too were a banker.

"Let's sell and use the money to pay for your MFA degree. You can write," Alicia said.

"But where will we live?" I asked.

Which is when Alicia called her parents in Massachusetts and asked if we could stay with them for a few years. To my great surprise, they immediately said they would welcome us into their home, and we could live there for as long as we liked while I attempted to become a fiction writer, whatever that meant. They missed their daughter, and I think they would have done just about anything to get Alicia to move back to the Bay State. They had never before allowed themselves to dream I would leave Philadelphia.

Then Alicia said to me, "Now you don't have any more excuses. You're free. You can do the thing you most want to do."

It was like my wife was a sorceress.

But I had been raised not to take handouts, to believe that accepting charity was a sign of weakness. And I was too broken to accept love as love back then. So I just sat on the steps frozen with fear, shame, and ignorance.

When I didn't say anything, Alicia said, "We're doing this. You need to get happy again."

I swallowed.

I was pretty sure we'd make enough on the house to cover my MFA tuition and our health insurance for a few years, but I would have to rely on my in-laws for pretty much everything else and would be moving back into a family structure. I'd be living with parents again, which felt like a major regression at almost thirty years old. And I knew that pretty much everyone in my life would think I had lost my mind when I told them I was quitting a tenured position at perhaps the best high school in South Jersey and selling my house to write a novel in the self-inflicted solitude of my in-laws' cold, musty, unfinished basement, far away from my Philadelphian friends and family. Kids who grew up in Oaklyn, New Jersey, didn't write novels. *Who did I think I was?* If I had told people in my life that I was building a rocket ship out of Popsicle sticks and would soon be living on Jupiter, most of their responses would have been the same.

Risk and reward, I heard Pete's voice say.

"I need you to do this," Alicia added. "For you. For me. For our marriage."

When I nodded, I felt an overwhelming amount of relief—like I had gotten myself out of an eddy and was now once again flowing in the great stream of life.

The suicidal feeling vanished. I no longer heard the self-slaughter ditty when I walked through the doors of the high school. I felt like I had a future with which I could live.

For the first time in forever, I slowly began to feel hopeful.

"Fuckin' badass," Pete said when I told him my plan.

But when I told you that I was going to use the profits from the sale of our home to get an MFA degree in creative writing and was quitting a "real" job with good benefits to pursue my dream of becoming a fiction writer, you screamed, "Idiot! How are you going to pay for food and lodging?"

I told you my in-laws had kindly agreed to let us live with them in Massachusetts.

Which is when you screamed, "I will *not* pay for your health insurance!"

"Dad," I said. "We already looked into that. We're using the money from the house sale to pay for our own health insurance out of pocket. And it will cover my tuition too. We've budgeted for a few years. Ultimately, Alicia will get a job, but we're going to take a little time to backpack around southern Africa and maybe hike the Grand Canyon and—"

"I will *not* pay for your dental!" you screamed.

I thought, *I just told you I had been feeling mentally unwell, Alicia had found a legitimate way for me to pursue my lifelong dream, and that—during the gap between the end of my employment and the start of my graduate school—we were even going to take a few life-changing hiking trips on a shoestring budget. But you're worried about* my teeth*?*

I was only twenty-nine at the time. You were fifty-five.

Mom—who was fifty-two—tried to lube the situation, saying, "Mike, he's always wanted to write. He's chasing his dream."

But you only screamed at Mom—repeating yourself—saying, "I will *not* pay for his health insurance! I will *not* pay for his dental!"

The great irony is this: For the next three years, Mom gave me a trip to the dentist for Christmas, so you actually *did* end up paying for my dental. Thanks for that, Dad. I'm glad to still have teeth.

But how did we get here?

I started this chapter saying I had listened to you and was trying to understand why you were the way you always were. But then I took a page out of your book and ended up talking about myself.

Let's remedy that now.

I want readers to see you as a three-dimensional human being. I want readers to understand how I found a way to make peace with and love you. I want readers to know how, after trying to cut you out of my life for so many years, I found my way back to embracing you as an integral part of my existence here on Earth. You've told me so many things that have helped me understand—in retrospect, because

I was often too angry with you to see clearly in the moment—what tormented you into acting the odious ways you did.

I know that one of your earliest memories—before the dementia—was crying helplessly in a high chair as your older brother, Peter, stuffed peas up your nose. By the time your mother discovered what was going on, your nasal passages were entirely clogged. You said you remembered feeling as though you couldn't breathe. You were traumatized. And it took a long time for Grandmom to get all of the green mush out of your nostrils. I wonder whether Pete completely stuffed your nose or simply put one or two peas up there. Being three years older than you, he would have been four or five when you were a toddler. Pop Pop had been killing Germans only a few years previously, and, of course, he was in Europe fighting the war when Pete was born.

Your father would never talk to me about his time under the command of General Patton. When I was a teenager, I asked a few probing questions about his tour, and I even asked how many Nazis he had killed. His eyes went dark. I thought of dead-eyed sharks swimming through a cold, pitch-black ocean. I saw his hands begin to shake. "Matthew, I will *never ever* talk to you about what I did in Europe. Don't ask me again. *Understand?*" he roared and then got up off his porch rocker and went into his house, leaving me outside alone and feeling quite guilty about my misstep. I thought I had been giving him a chance to brag. My high school history teacher had told me Pop Pop was a hero. But he certainly didn't act like a hero on the day I tried to talk to him about his World War II experience. That was the only time Pop Pop ever raised his voice at me.

Pete once told me Pop Pop had a drinking problem during the war and maybe even got men killed while searching for alcohol. Based on the shadow that fell over his face whenever World War II came up, I'm pretty sure he saw and did horrific things while wearing a US Army uniform. And no one goes from literally killing people while abusing alcohol to being father of the year just by crossing the Atlantic Ocean.

If five-year-old Pete was torturing you, Dad, someone had to have put that darkness in him. I suspect cruelty was the coin of your childhood realm. Little boys who are properly loved don't abuse babies, unless they are born psychopaths. Pete was a lot of things, but he wasn't a psychopath. He empathized with me often and showed me love in many ways. I saved the phone message he left me after Alicia and I had to put our elderly greyhound, Stella, down, and I replayed his words for years afterward, just to know that there was an older man related to me by blood who was looking after my emotional well-being. The message was partly an insane and racist rant about the people of Vietnam—as almost everything was with Pete—but it was also an *I love you* that moved me greatly, mostly because he didn't want me to feel bad about making the decision to end our first dog's life. "If the dog is in pain, there is no question. You did the right thing, pretty boy," he said. "There's no need to beat yourself up about it."

Dad, you've told me so many times about living on Lawnside Alley in Collingswood, New Jersey. It's actually called Lawnside Avenue, but you always call it Lawnside Alley for some reason. You said there were so many boys living on your block. Enough to easily fill out both sides of a baseball game—and even a football game. You said all you boys would ride bikes together like a giant gang, roaming the street and going down to the river. A boy only had to live on Lawnside Alley to be a member of the gang. That was it. And sometimes all of your parents would drive the entire gang to a swimming lake for gigantic picnics that went on all day and into the night. Whenever you speak of Lawnside Alley, your voice softens; you get this faraway look in your eyes; and the child hidden deep inside of you comes up to wave hello to me. Then you'll talk about moving away from Lawnside Alley to 403 Park Avenue, which is the house where

I mostly interacted with your parents, the place where your mom and dad would always throw their big Christmas Eve party with the 7UP and rainbow sherbet punch; and Philadelphia Cream Cheese and Lebanon bologna rolls held together with toothpicks; and hundreds of holiday cookies; and Grandmom's famous home-fried doughnuts covered in so much sugar that it rained white crystals with each bite, so much so that our footsteps crunched when we walked through the kitchen on Christmas morning. And you always get sad whenever you talk about the move to Park Ave—which was only a few blocks away in the same town—because the old Lawnside Alley boys didn't consider you a part of their gang once you were a Park Ave boy, so you lost access to your old Neverland. And there weren't any boys your age on the new block. Whenever you talk about this, I can always feel what a loss that was for the young you, and I think of Dylan Thomas's poem "Fern Hill."

You often tell me stories about the few times you broke your arm. One time, you were riding a bike that was too big for you. The details often change. But the story that has coalesced in my mind is this: Your friend wanted to ride your new bike and you let him, which meant you had to ride your friend's bike, which was too big for you. While you were riding, you lost control, crashed, and snapped the bone in your forearm. You said you went home cradling your deformed limb and your mother stabilized the break by tying your arm to a wooden breadboard before she took you to the hospital.

Another time you were out with your mother, headed back to her car, when you were struck by a sedan. The driver turned out to be an off-duty police officer who scooped you up off the street and rushed you to the hospital. Sometimes you say the accident broke your arm, and sometimes you say it didn't. But you always say how upset Grandmom was with the police officer who hit you and then rushed you to the hospital without even consulting her.

When you tell these two stories, I get the sense that you still feel guilty about the accidents, like you had put your parents out. I imagine having your arm set and cast cost money, which your Depression-era and previously poor parents valued more than just about anything. Your father often didn't have food as a child. He used to talk about eating nothing but a soft pretzel for lunch and then guzzling water, just to make the bread swell to fill his stomach. He sometimes had to move to a completely different neighborhood in the middle of the night because his parents couldn't make rent. His two older sisters had to drop out of high school and work to support the family. He was the only one of his siblings to get a high school diploma. His sisters sacrificed for him because, as a man, he had the greater earning potential. And he felt guilty and ashamed about his sisters' sacrifices for the rest of his life. But he never was able to shake his poverty mindset. He died clinging to it at ninety-one years of age. The last thing he ever said to me was by phone. He said, "The world is very hard. But I love you. The family loves you. And God loves you." I know he didn't use the word "love" with you when you were young, Dad, and surprise medical bills definitely would not have been welcomed in the house where you grew up. I also get the sense that you are still ashamed of having been breakable as a boy. Learning that your bones could actually snap was like knowing that your body, your manhood, your DNA could betray you. Like you were weaker than you should be. Like the world could break your body at any moment in time, and then you would be punished for it with screaming and a big heap of guilt and shame. "We don't have the money for you to keep breaking your arm every week," I can hear your father yelling at you. "Dough don't grow on trees. Drink your milk. Toughen up. Peter never snaps any bones. You keep breaking your arm and we're gonna start questioning whether you're a boy or a girl."

The third (or maybe second) time you broke your arm, you were playing high school football. Pete had been a star athlete, and the coaches had hoped that you would follow in his footsteps. You never told me what position Pete played. I imagine he might have been a ferocious linebacker for the defense. You played offensive line. And in the rough and tumble of a game, your arm snapped once again at the bottom of a pile of young men, and then you were sidelined, where you could do nothing at all to get yourself out of your older brother's large shadow.

You had a cousin at the school, and you paint him out to be a picaresque figure. Maybe the Ignatius J. Reilly of your childhood. According to you, our picaro was comically unathletic, but his father would brag about his son's athleticism all the time. You repeatedly tell this one pivotal story. It takes place at a family or church picnic. Your uncle grabs you and forces you to stand next to your cousin. Without irony, your uncle points to his son and declares to the entire picnic, "*This* is a man." Next, he points to you and declares, "This is *not* a man." Then you see your father shake his head and turn away from you. You were so humiliated that—more than sixty years later—you never once fail to tell me this story whenever we take a walk here on Lady's Island. You tell me the story every single time you and I are alone. Even with your dementia, you never forget a beat. I've heard it hundreds of times in the past year alone, and I cringe on your behalf with each retelling. I feel how wounded you still are by your public shaming and having been forsaken by your dad. You always end the story by saying, "My mother was so angry with my father that day. She yelled at him later that night. She told him he should have defended me. *But he didn't.* Can you imagine what that felt like? *Can you?*"

Not feeling like your father has your back.

Story of my life, Dad.

But I never say that to you. Instead, I say, "Maybe your father thought what your uncle said was so laughable that no one with any brains whatsoever would take him seriously. Maybe your father thought your uncle was embarrassing himself. That the situation spoke for itself."

"My father should have defended me!" you'll yell. "You don't understand what it felt like. When it came to football, my cousin was a joke. And everyone at the picnic was thinking I was less than a joke. And my father just turned his back. It made my mother so angry. She was furious with him. I'll never forget that day. *Never.*"

At this point, I'll switch gears and simply empathize with you, saying something like, "I bet that was really hard for you, Dad. I think you are a man. You've accomplished many things. Put three kids through college. Was a named executive at a publicly traded bank. Got that big payout at the end of your career. I bet your father is looking down from heaven and is proud of you. Pete too. And your mother."

"My father should have defended me," you'll say again, but without the exclamation point at the end of the sentence this time around, which lets me know that my efforts are at least somewhat placating.

I'll fight so hard to swallow the following words: *Dad, you've often made me feel like I'm not a* human being, *let alone a man. You should have defended me from yourself.*

Your dementia has made swallowing easier somehow. So I swallow. Then I swallow again. And again, and again, and again. Reversing the father-son flow. And I have to admit, I hardly even notice the swallowing these days.

You hated high school and talk often about finally cracking the starting varsity football lineup during your senior year, only to be shocked by the macho bravado of your varsity captains, who would throw you against the lockers without warning during the school day, and yell, "Are you ready, Quick? Are you tough enough? Do you have what it takes?" I imagine that the football captains were only trying to get you psyched for the upcoming game and were most likely roughhousing with everyone on the team, but you felt singled out and remain to this very day personally offended by their actions.

"Why are you throwing me into the lockers?" you'd ask them with an earnestness that makes my analyst question whether you might be undiagnosed neurodivergent.

To me, you say, "I told them, 'Stop throwing me into the lockers. I'll give everything I have on the field, but this is school. I don't want to be thrown into lockers while I walk down the hallway!"

Sometimes I try to engage your imagination, asking maybe if your teammates might have only been trying to include you in rituals that everyone else was participating in, and—with so much desperation in your voice—you say, "They told the coaches I was soft. And the coaches asked what was wrong with me. They said I needed to get with the program. But I learned all the plays. I played hard on the field. Why did I have to get pushed into the lockers during the school day? Why did people have to scream in my face? How did that help anything? I didn't like being pushed. *I didn't like being screamed at!*"

Oh, the irony, I always think, but we'll get to all that later.

When I first moved to Beaufort to help you battle dementia, you started telling me that one of your college professors helped you overcome a speech impediment. I'd never known that you used to stutter. You said you stuttered so much, it kept you from speaking to people. You said it had been an almost insurmountable problem for you. I'd never before heard about Professor Meyers, whom you used to meet in a place called White Chapel on the campus of Albright College.

"Why didn't you ever tell me about this before?" I'd say, but you'd always completely ignore my question.

Instead, you'd tell me that Professor Meyers was the most important man in your life, that he had seen something good in you when no one else did, that he used to counsel you in White Chapel, which you explained was an old church that was also used as an office. And you'd say that Professor Meyers helped you start making sense of all the noise that was going on in your head—all the competing voices. When I'd press you on this, asking what exactly Professor Meyers had done for you, you'd say things like, "He believed in me. He saw the good in me. He made me think that maybe I could have a future. He got me to organize my thoughts and direct them toward problem-solving. He got me interested in computer programming. The machines were gigantic back then. He got me to tutor other students. Put me in charge of important things. We all developed a computer program together and did statistical analysis. It was great. I'd teach the underclassmen. *I taught them.* They respected me. And then I just didn't stutter anymore."

"How *exactly* did you stop stuttering?" I'd ask you.

"I just stopped," you'd say.

"But how?"

"Professor Meyers was a great man," you'd say. "I wrote him a letter. Before he died. I think I did. Ask your mother. She'll remember. And I think I told him thank you for being such an important part of my life and that I wouldn't have ever become a named executive at a publicly traded bank if he hadn't helped me when I was so ashamed of myself. I didn't use to be as confident as I am today. Before you were around, Matthew, I wasn't such a great man."

It would always be hard for me to resist saying that you weren't always a great man when I *was* around, but, instead, I'd usually say, "Dad, do you think Professor Meyers initiated you into manhood?"

You'd think about it for a few seconds, and then you'd say, "I'll put it this way: I don't think you'd be here if Professor Meyers hadn't taken an interest in me. *I might not be here.* Okay?"

"Do you mean you would have killed yourself?" I'd ask.

"I don't want to talk about all that," you'd say. "I just wanted to tell you about Professor Meyers and what a great man he was."

"You really loved him, didn't you?"

"He was a great man."

"And you loved him."

"If you say so."

"I think *you're* saying so, Dad. It's okay to love people. Especially father figures. You know that, right?"

But you'd continue your rant, saying, "My college wrestling coach was a piece of work. We'd travel to away matches in an old stretch limousine because the college wouldn't pay for a bus. And if we lost a match, our coach wouldn't give us our meal money, so we'd have nothing to eat as a punishment. Because we'd all cut weight before matches, we'd be starving before we even got there. By the time the wrestling match was over, we were ready to eat our hands. And when our coach wouldn't let us eat anything, we'd get so angry. When he stopped for gas—while he was distracted by filling up the tank—we'd hit the vending machines, and we'd eat as many calories as we could before he called us back into the old limousine. It was awful. And after my junior year, I said to my coach, 'Hey, I'm not wrestling for you anymore. I'm going to enjoy my last year of college.' *And I did.*"

"What was so great about your senior year?"

"I got a good draft number. Guys sitting right next to me during the draft on TV got bad ones and had to go to Vietnam right after college. But my number was so good, I knew I'd never have to go. And that maybe saved my life. I'd seen what Vietnam did to Peter. He came home different. Motivated. He got his college degree right away and started making big-time money in the banking world. But he was different. Off. Not right. And I didn't want any of that. Guys who got bad draft numbers, they just got so drunk that night, and I felt bad for them, because I knew they might die. They knew they were maybe going to die. Some of them did."

"Why else was your senior year of college so much fun?" I'd ask.

"Well, don't tell your mother this, but I had this really great girlfriend."

"What did she look like?"

"Petite. Long blonde hair and blue eyes."

"So exactly like mom when you met her."

"Your mother is prettier."

"Well played, Dad. But you had a type, didn't you?"

"Margie was fun. We had a great time together."

"Why did you break up?"

"She was just a freshman when we were dating."

"You were robbing the cradle, Dad."

"No, I wasn't. She was in college. She was at least eighteen."

"But you graduated and she stayed behind at Albright College."

"Yes. Don't tell your mother about any of this, okay? This is just between you and me."

"Do you think Mom believes she was the first woman you ever dated?"

"Maybe. I think so. Yes."

"You never talked about your past with her?"

"About old girlfriends? Are you crazy?"

"I really don't think Mom would be upset about this. She probably already knows."

"You told her?"

"How could I?" I'd say. "You only just told me right now."

"I'm trusting you, Matthew," you'd say, which made me—who was planning on publishing this very conversation—feel extremely guilty.

"But I really think that people would find these secrets charming, Dad. They make you seem human. It's okay to be human, you know."

"I don't think you know very much about women."

"Would you be mad if I wrote about this in my book?"

"Will your mother be reading your book?"

"Without a doubt."

"She'll get mad at me! She'll put me in a mental institute! You have to be careful!"

"Dad, she can't put you anywhere without me getting a say."

"I worry about that. My grandmother was in one of those places. I used to have to go every Sunday after church. My mother would visit her mother. Father made us play football outside, but we could hear people screaming. From the electroshock therapy. And Mother was always crying when she came back out. I don't want your mother to put me in a place like that."

"Those places don't exist anymore."

"Oh yes, they do. And if my brain keeps getting worse, your mother might—"

"She won't, Dad, I promise."

"You'll stop her?"

"If I have to, but I don't think it will come to that. What did you do after college? Didn't you major in sociology? How did you end up a banker?"

"Father said, 'Michael, I got you a job at this bank,' and then I was a banker."

"So you didn't have a choice."

"I worked in this computer room at first. Sometimes overnight. And then I worked my way up from the bottom. It took me almost fifty years. But when I first graduated college, my father made me give the car I paid for with my own money to my younger brother, Jon. It was a Camaro. I loved it. Did you know Father used to call me Michelle? Because my mother always wanted to have a girl. So Father used to say Michael can be Michelle."

"How did that make you feel?"

"Not good."

"Pete used to call me a girly man and pretty boy—and much

worse—all the time. I always thought he was being affectionate. He only really teased the people he loved."

"I didn't like being called Michelle."

"Dad, I'm going to put all this in the book. You know that, right?"

"Just don't show it to your mother."

"She's going to read it. She reads everything I write."

"Your mother is a good woman. She loves you."

"I know."

"Peter is writing a book about us, I think," you'd say, because you mix up your older brother and me all the time now.

"Do you think Pete will write about this conversation in his book?"

"You can't ever tell Peter what to do. He's a wild man. He does whatever he wants."

"Are you okay with that, Dad?"

"I love my brother Peter," you'd say, even though you were furious with him for much of your life and often acted like you hated him.

"Even if he writes a book about us?"

"Isn't he in heaven?"

"Yep."

"I hope I see him when I get there. But I'm in good health other than my brain, right?"

"That's right."

"Good."

"I'm glad we had this talk."

"I hope we have pizza for dinner."

"I'll tell Mom."

"Only about the pizza, nothing else, right?"

"Yep. Only about the pizza."

So yeah, Dad.

I've been listening to you.

4.

A few months into my Jungian analysis—on a Friday night in the fall of 2020—I put on my black T-shirt, entered my office, sat down at my writing desk, logged into Zoom, and waited for Zeus's face to fill my laptop screen.

Maybe, I thought, *this will be the night he comments on my always wearing black to analysis.*

But when Zeus showed up for our session—fifteen minutes late—he only looked into my eyes and said, "Where would you like to begin?"

"I like your shirt," I hinted.

His was a light-colored button-up. He'd rolled the sleeves to his elbows and left the top few buttons undone so that a deep V of his chest was exposed.

"Thank you," he said blank-faced. "*Where would you like to begin?*"

He really did *not* want to discuss my black T-shirt.

I word-vomited at Zeus that night—cycling through various topics—but I kept coming back to my drinking and my rocky relationship with you, Dad.

Zeus interrupted, saying, "I'd like to tell you a story."

Then my analyst started talking about the Greek god Zeus.

The below is how I began calling my analyst Zeus.

Here's the story I heard that night:

Zeus the ancient god had an affair with the goddess of the underworld, Persephone, which produced a son named Dionysus. When Zeus's jealous wife, Hera, found out, she sent the Titans—badass giants—to kill the young child. They tore the boy apart limb-by-limb, roasted his dismembered parts over an open fire, and ate him. Thinking that the heart would not be tasty, the Titans threw Dionysus's ticker aside. When Zeus found out, he killed the Titans with lightning bolts. Then he cut open his own thigh, inserted his son's heart, and stitched the wound closed. Inside of Zeus, Dionysus regrew and was born again, emerging whole from his father's thigh.

"Do you know why I told you this particular story tonight?" my analyst asked, once he had finished.

"You think I've been metaphorically torn apart by the Titans," I said. "Symbolically, the Titans are my childhood traumas."

"I'm stitching you into my thigh," he said.

"So you are my Zeus and I am your Dionysus."

"I'm going to re-father you through the analytic process. You are going to be born anew on the other side of it."

"Are the Titans my father complex?" I asked. "And Hera my mother complex?"

Dad, a complex is a group of memories, associations, and ideas clustered around a central unconscious theme, which can often make a person neurotic or worse.

"For now," Zeus answered, "let's just say I'm here to rescue your heart, to protect it, and help it grow back into the whole complete thing it was before the Titans of your childhood psychologically dismembered you."

"Do you really think stories can heal us?"

"You're a writer who doesn't believe in the awesome medicinal power of stories, and you wonder why you are creatively blocked."

"Okay. Fair point."

"You need to start believing again. *Really believing.* Not just for your career. Your mental health depends on it."

"But wasn't Dionysus the god of drunken madness?"

"*Divine* madness, which was often acquired through the ritual intake of wine."

"Maybe for the sake of my sobriety, I shouldn't be Dionysus."

"I think you were worshipping at the altar of Dionysus for most of your writing career. You relied on alcohol to put you in touch with creative genius. You got creatively blocked when you stopped worshipping."

"So you're saying I should start drinking again?"

"Absolutely not."

"Then what *are* you saying?"

"Well, we're talking about two different things now. First, you have to allow me to regrow you in my thigh. That's the analytic process. You have to allow yourself to fall in love with me as a father figure. You have to merge with me for a time. Use my knowledge and strength to put yourself back together again. We have to reorient your soul to the positive sides of fatherhood and masculinity. That's work we'll be doing together. In that way, the Zeus-Dionysus metaphor works for this stage of the analytic process. It's very good medicine."

"Until we get to the part where Dionysus becomes the god of drunken madness."

"Many creative types have sacrificed themselves on the altar of Dionysus, who was also androgynous. I often think of pretty Jim Morrison with his long hair. He made divine madness his god and—through his worship—could whip audiences up into a Dionysiac frenzy. But the old gods, they don't care about human life. Humans are just logs for their fires, which is why so many artists who make divine madness their god tragically die young. Through ritual drug and alcohol abuse, Dionysus gives them access to the divine. And they gamble with their lives for access to what Dionysus offers. Your dance with Dionysus took you to the Oscars and made you a *New York Times* bestseller. But there is a cost for dancing with the old gods. You, Matthew, ultimately paid up when your body began to break down and you had your health scares. You paid for it with your depression, anxiety, paranoia, alcoholism, and everything else that drove you into analysis."

"So you're saying that I *used* to worship Dionysus, but now I shouldn't?"

"I'm saying you had no idea what forces you were playing with. You now need to put yourself in proper psychological relationship with your past, and then you need to choose a better god to at least symbolically worship. Because if you continue to worship Dionysus, you are going to die."

"So I need to be in your thigh as Dionysus now—*metaphorically*—but I also need to stop worshipping Dionysus in my day-to-day life."

"I'm trying to give you a narrative that you can use as a road map. And you need a god to beat a god. That's why Jung famously advised the creators of AA to make their members submit to a higher power. Mortals can't stand up to the gods. Jung said that when we killed the gods by ceasing to believe in them, they became neuroses. But they always *were* metaphors—or a psychological framework to understand our souls."

"So what god do I use to beat Dionysus?"

"Perhaps we start with the god you already have. The god of your childhood. The other twice-born god with long flowing hair who is often associated with wine."

"Jesus?"

"Jung believed that Jesus was a radical evolution in human psychology. Before Jesus, all the gods would kill humans for almost no reason at all. The Greek gods played with humans like toys. Turning themselves into animals and raping women. Killing men. The God of the Old Testament tortured poor Job, asked Abraham to kill his own son, and wiped out much of humanity with floods and plagues. You were supposed to fear Yahweh, who demanded sacrifices. But Jesus is an all-powerful god who sacrifices *himself* for mortals. When he is struck, he turns the other cheek. He promotes love, tolerance, and charity. When he turns his blood into wine, it isn't to inspire divine madness, but to cleanse people of their sins and make them whole. He is a god who willingly relegates his ego to save others. That's a better god for you right now, here in early sobriety. Without the numbing agents of drugs and alcohol, as we start to deal with your childhood trauma, as we start to break down the old psychological defenses that your unconscious has been using as protection for almost fifty years, it will feel like you are being psychologically crucified. You are going to hurt like you've never hurt before. You are going to have to willingly submit to it. And the pain's going to get a lot worse before you are ultimately reborn anew."

"Why are you pushing Jesus? You're not even a practicing Christian," I said, because Zeus wasn't.

"I'm not asking you to be a practicing member of any religion. I'm encouraging you to find a mind frame to help you survive what is coming. It's about using symbolism as medicine. You are a professional storyteller. This shouldn't be a hard concept for you. You really need to start thinking symbolically. You need the right lifesaving narrative. *Now.*"

I sort of got what he was saying, but mostly I just appreciated that he wanted to re-father me. After listening to all the complaining you've done about your father over the years, Dad, I bet some part of you can relate.

"Okay, Zeus, I'll be your baby Dionysus," I said to my analyst and then laughed. "I'll live in your thigh."

"Kick and punch my hamstring, if you must. Teethe on my femur," he said, allowing a playful smile to bloom across his face. "I'll tolerate it until you mature."

5.

Last night I had a panic attack that immediately sucked me down into a shame spiral. After doing so much work on myself via four and a half years of analysis, after putting in almost seven years of sobriety, after trying so hard to get my mental health under control, the experience was humbling.

It's the winter of 2025. I'm fifty-one years old. I'm living around the corner from Mom and you. And the simplest thing can still bring me to my knees.

Here's what happened:

Alicia and I attended the Beaufort International Film Festival. In the afternoon, we saw a lovely documentary on the Italian American cookbook writer Marcella Hazan, after which we went home. I wrote a little in this memoir. Did some tax prep. Went for a run. Then Alicia and I ate a stew that she had prepared in her new Crock-Pot. As I sat at the dinner table gazing at my wife and consuming the delicious food she had made for us, I felt so happy. Our border terrier, Kingsly, was sitting like a good boy in the dog bed under the breakfast nook counter, not even whining for food. (Desi had died years before.) Alicia and I were in a really good place. We both love living in the Lowcountry. We had four days' worth of film festival tickets, and all the movies were being screened less than a ten-minute drive from our home. Life was good.

After dinner, it was time for another screening. I showered and dressed. Then I drove our beater Jeep over the old swing bridge that connects Lady's Island with downtown Beaufort. We parked in the college lot. It was lightly raining, and I was glad to be wearing my favorite slouchy beanie. It's black with thin gray stripes and fits my head perfectly. I feel photogenic whenever I wear this particular hat. It somehow sharpens the angles of my cheekbones, and the gray stripes make my beard look less white than it really is. It's a Pistil hat. I think mine is officially called an Ace Slouch Beanie. But this particular black-with-gray-stripes design is no longer for sale on the Pistil website or anywhere else. I know because I have looked for it many times so that I might have a spare. Alicia gave me the hat in question several years ago for Christmas. It might just be my favorite gift that she has ever given me in the thirty-one and a half years we've been exchanging presents. Noting my approval, she's gifted me several other Pistil beanie hats, but I seldom wear any of them, because I love the original one so much.

Dad, you might remember that, as a young child, I struggled with change, and I was notoriously picky about what I would wear. I went through a phase where I refused to wear more than two colors at a time. One Easter Sunday when Mom put plaid pants on me, I said the multiple crisscrossing colors made me feel like I was going crazy. I said it literally hurt to wear them. You said, "You're wearing whatever your mother puts on your body." When I couldn't take the pain anymore, I ran out into the backyard and repetitively slid on my knees across our small patch of grass, collecting as many grass stains as I could. I knew there was no way you'd take me to church wearing grass-stained pants. When you saw what I had done, the astonished, wide-eyed look on your face was hard to interpret. I thought for sure you would backhand me to the ground. But instead, a funny little grin appeared on your face for just a second. It made me feel like you understood why I had done what I had. Like you too felt as though you might go insane if you were forced to wear the wrong color or pattern or fabric. And I could tell some part of you at least admired my moxie. But then the smile vanished, and you screamed, "Young man, you better run up to your room and change before you feel my hand on your behind! And apologize to your mother! *Now!*"

When Alicia and I reentered the film festival here in present-day Beaufort, someone asked for our zip code, which we had already given them earlier in the day. Then a thin man with white hair asked if we had purchased tickets. Ours were digital, and on Alicia's phone. We asked if he needed to see them. He said he trusted us, but he also didn't trust us. It was hard to read his tone. Was he joking? Was he really asking to see our tickets? He didn't have a scanner or anything like that in his hands. I began to wonder whether he really was working for the festival or was just an old guy practicing some sort of stand-up routine. We forced laughs and tried to enter the screening room, which is when he said—in a more serious voice—"You had better just let me see your tickets." Alicia held up her phone and showed him her digital ticket, which is when he pointed to me and said to my wife, "Do you have one for him, or am I going in with you?" which was just strange and maybe even creepy. The whole exchange made me feel anxious. Alicia showed him my digital ticket, which he inspected like he thought we might have forged it. I was tempted to take a twenty out of my wallet and just give it to him. But he finally relented. Alicia and I entered the screening room and sat down at the end of a row. I stuffed my favorite hat into the left pocket of my old black Patagonia puffer coat and settled in for another round of cinema.

Alicia and I were probably the youngest people in attendance, and we were completely anonymous. No one knew who I was, which was fantastic. I just wanted to see the films and then leave. But I was also receiving work emails from my producer at the time, who said Ryan Gosling liked a screenplay I had written but was unfortunately passing. Then one of my producers asked if I thought Jeremy Allen White was too young for the role. They had just wrapped a movie with Mr. White and thought maybe we could get him to read. It was kind of delightful to be quietly fielding such emails, sitting anonymously at a local film festival. Like countless Hollywood projects, the movie I was currently working on would probably never get made. But I was in the game, and I was about to watch a film with my wife, and—as I said before—life was good.

We were shown a short film first. It was about a demented old man who is being transported out of a low-budget memory care facility in the middle of the night. In a van, two nefarious-looking young men drive him around for a bit. They knock on the doors of several houses, but no one answers. Ultimately, they leave the old, demented man sitting in a wheelchair in front of a shady-looking home in the middle of nowhere. The entire audience gasped as the van drove away, and then the credits rolled. I think the film was supposed to raise awareness about elder abuse. And I swore to myself that nothing like that would ever happen to you, Dad. *Over my dead body.* I kept saying that in my mind. *Over my dead body.* Which is when I realized the short film had really disturbed me.

When the feature film began, I could immediately tell we were in trouble from a writing perspective. This might sail over your head, Dad, but there were multiple frame narrations that overlapped and bled together in confusing ways, as well as some dialogue that could have used some serious punching up. I could feel Alicia shifting beside me as the writing problems mounted. But there was also lots to admire about the film. It was a clever idea, overall. The costumes were impressive. I ended up kind of at least appreciating the audacity of the multiple frame narrations. It also had a bit of fading star power.

When the film ended, it was after Alicia's bedtime, so she whispered, "Okay if we skip the Q&A and just go home?"

I nodded and then we sleepy Gen-Xers were quietly exiting the screening room full of night-owl boomers.

Just as soon as we were in the hallway, I reached into my pocket for my cherished hat, but it wasn't there. I felt my stomach drop.

"Was I wearing my favorite hat when we entered the building?" I asked Alicia, even though I knew I had been.

"I don't know," she said in a way that let me know she'd clocked the rising anxiety in my voice. "Maybe you left it in the Jeep?"

When we exited the building, the cold, light rain let me know there was no way in hell I had walked outside earlier with my bald head uncovered.

"They don't make that hat anymore," I said to Alicia. "I can't get another one online. I've checked a million times. I've even searched eBay for a used one."

"It's probably in the Jeep," she said.

But it wasn't.

I started to have a full-on panic attack. Even as it was happening, I realized my reaction was absurd. The hat probably cost forty dollars. I had worn it for a good six or seven years. So I had already gotten our money's worth out of it. And it was just a hat. *Things get lost*, I told myself.

Then I was back in the dark film-festival screening room. As the credits continued to play, I was on my hands and knees with my iPhone flashlight lit. I searched and searched, but my hat was gone. I had felt it in my pocket several times during the film, whenever I had reached in for another cough drop. But now it was nowhere to be found. I began to sense people staring at me. When my self-consciousness built to a breaking point, I gave up the search and retraced the steps I had taken when I first left the auditorium. I even went into the men's room to see if I had somehow dropped my hat in there before the films began. When I didn't find it, I started to have paranoid thoughts about being pickpocketed. I had a vision of someone seeing me dropping my hat in the hallway and then stealing it once I was gone. *It's just an old hat. No one would want it*, I told myself. But the paranoid fantasies persisted.

"I asked the people at the help desk if anyone had turned in a hat," Alicia said. "No luck. Maybe you left it at home?"

I knew I hadn't, but we drove home anyway. Alicia and I talked about the film and how we might have edited the script, but I was mostly mourning the loss of my hat, which felt like a tremendous blow. By the way my stomach was churning and my blood was pounding in my temples, you'd think one of my fingers had been severed from my hand. It was ludicrous. And I knew it. But some dark part inside kept saying, *It was the best gift my wife ever gave me. It was my favorite hat. I felt comfortable in it. And I* never *feel comfortable. This is a big loss. And I must have done something shameful to bring this upon myself. This happened because I'm not a good person. Jeremy Allen White is going to star in my movie? Who am I kidding? I can't even keep track of my favorite hat. I'm a failure. I'm a moron. And now—whenever it's cold out, for the rest of my life—I'm going to look asinine because I'll be wearing a new hat that doesn't complement my best features at all.*

"I'm really freaking out about my hat," I said to Alicia.

"If it's hysterical, it's historical," she said.

Then I was flashing on the time when she and I were first married and living outside of Philadelphia. Her mom and dad were in town. Alicia and I thought it might be fun to get both sets of parents together. You, Mom, Barb, Peague, Alicia, and me—we all went to a Cuban restaurant in Philly that Alicia and I liked a lot. It was on Second Street. But just as soon as we sat down, Alicia and I realized our mistake. You and Mom frowned at the menu. Back then, you didn't eat anything other than what your father would have referred to as "American food." You didn't seem to appreciate the lively Havanaesque atmosphere either. And you were not saying much to my in-laws. Mom tried her best to keep the conversation going, but your silence and displeasure were palpable. When your food arrived, you looked at it like you wanted to murder the chef. Then you grunted and withdrew even further. It was a long and awkward dinner that ultimately ruined the restaurant for me. It had been one of Alicia's and my favorite spots in the city, but I don't think we ever went there again afterward.

The second part of that evening was a viewing of a touring Cirque du Soleil performance. There was a huge old-timey tent. Maybe it was down by the South Philly stadiums. Our tickets had the six of us sitting high on bleachers, which we had been told were actually the good seats, because those offered the best views of the high-flying action. I love Cirque du Soleil, Dad. I find it mesmerizing. It never fails to transport me to a different, more surreal, dream world. Alicia loves it too. And, in our youth, we figured there probably wouldn't be anyone in the whole world who wouldn't want to sit through a Cirque du Soleil performance. If someone didn't appreciate the music and costumes and artistry and story, he had to at least appreciate the death-defying athleticism.

Right?

Turns out, Dad, that you are the person who wouldn't want to sit through a Cirque du Soleil performance. As amazing feats were paraded before our eyes, you squirmed in your seat with your arms crossed and a frown plastered on your face that was more depressing than the Grim Reaper's scythe blade. Everyone around us could feel your displeasure. The whole time, I just kept saying in my mind, *Please, let this be over soon. Please.*

An hour or so into the show, you started feeling your pants pockets. Then you loudly said, "I've dropped my wallet. I need to find my wallet." There were performers risking their lives on high wires, so someone shushed you. You turned toward them and said, "My wallet.

I think it's fallen under the bleachers." An usher quickly approached and said that distractions in the stands weren't just rude to the other paying customers but actually dangerous to the performers. "But my wallet," you said to him. "It's fallen down there. *I need to get it.*"

The distance between our bleacher seats and the ground was maybe forty feet. If I thought I could have made it without breaking a leg, I would have dropped down there myself, if only to escape the mortification, because I knew this was only just the beginning.

The usher clocked the manic look in your eye, and then he started whispering into a walkie-talkie, explaining what was going on.

"All my credit cards are in my wallet! I'm going down there!" you yelled.

"Sir," the usher said. "You are putting the performers at risk. Someone is retrieving your wallet right now. Everything is okay."

"I want my wallet!" you yelled.

"Sir, you need to be calm."

"Mike," Mom said. "It's okay. You need to be quiet."

People were turning around and staring. Barb and Peague were pretending not to notice what was happening. Alicia was rubbing my back. And I was flipping back and forth between being furious with you for embarrassing me in front of my in-laws and feeling like I was going to jump up, grab the usher by the throat, and scream into his face, "Can't you fucking see my father needs his wallet!"

The usher put his walkie-talkie to his ear for a second, and then he said to you, "Great news, sir. We have retrieved your wallet. Just enjoy the show, and we'll give it to you at the end."

"No. I want my wallet *now*. All of my money and credit cards and my driver's license are in there," you said. "How do I know you won't steal anything? *This is bullshit!*"

The usher got on his walkie-talkie again, then he said to you, "Can you at least wait until this act is finished?"

"Yes," Mom said as she rubbed your back and tried to get you to calm down.

I screamed in my head, *Just give him his fucking wallet! Please! You have no idea how bad this can get!*

"They have my wallet," you said to your wife. "I need my wallet."

And the scene above instantly became one of the many anxious times forever frozen in my memory like psychological fossils. Whenever I examined it later, you seemed so young as you demanded to have your wallet returned, like some part of you was still only seven years old. I would wonder how you were able to be successful in the banking world. And if you were a savant like Dustin Hoffman's character in *Rain Man*. I'd feel so sorry for you. But I'd also feel this deep sense of having lived through something perverse. Like I knew it shouldn't be so hard for you to be at least civil to my in-laws. And I knew that dropping your wallet—especially when someone was retrieving it for you—shouldn't make you lose your mind.

Ten minutes later, during a lull in the Cirque du Soleil show, a man ran up the bleachers and handed the usher what you had lost. You jumped up out of your seat and then stuck your palm out, demanding that your billfold be returned. The usher put it into your hand. You did not say thank you or offer him a tip. Instead, you sat down and furiously went through your wallet's contents. As you rifled through everything, I was sure you would drop money or a credit card or something, and then the whole hellish drama would start all over again. But Mom monitored the situation carefully and got you to put your billfold away. Then you sat next to me like a psychological volcano spewing out toxic lava. And I felt like one of those eternally-frozen-in-rock Pompeii people. The stiff look of horror on my face was a testament to the fact that I got absolutely no joy out of watching something that had never once before failed to fill me with awe and wonder and delight.

* * *

Another time, Alicia and I were following you, Mom, and Megan as we drove home from Micah's college graduation, which was in Lynchburg, Virginia. Your tire blew out on a back road. When we all pulled over and you got out of the car, you started pacing and yelling, "I don't know what we're going to do now. Why did this happen to me? I can't take this. *I just can't!*"

"Dad," I said, "we're going to change the tire. It's okay."

"I don't even know if I *have* a spare!" you screamed.

"Well," I said. "Let's see. Can you pop your trunk?"

"Matthew, you don't know what you're doing!"

"Yes, I do, Dad," I said. "I've changed a tire before."

"Bullshit!"

"I have. Pop the trunk."

Mom popped the trunk. I took out the luggage and found a spare and a jack. I put the jack under the car and lined it up with the frame. Then I began loosening the lug nuts.

"You don't know what you're doing, Matthew! You're going to ruin my car!"

"Just trust me, Dad. Okay?"

"I *don't* trust you!"

"Mike," Mom said. "He's changing your tire."

"He has no idea what he's doing! And now we're stuck here! And I have to get to work tomorrow! How are we going to get home? Why does this happen to me?"

As you yelled and paced and ranted, my heart pounded.

I got all the lug nuts loose and then started cranking the jack.

"Matthew doesn't know what he's doing!" you yelled once more at Mom.

"He's changing the tire, Mike."

As you glared down at me, verbalizing what little faith you had in your eldest son's ability to do something that pretty much everyone in the entire world can do, I worked with the speed of someone who had a gun to his head and could hear the gunman counting backward.

I thought that you'd be thankful when I got you back on the road, but when I finished putting the flat tire in your trunk and reloading all the luggage, you said, "What happens if we get another flat? Now we don't have a spare tire! I have to go to work tomorrow!"

Mom got you back in your car. I got into mine. When we all started driving again, Alicia held my hand as she and I continued to follow you down the road.

"He didn't even say thank you," Alicia said.

"I know."

"I'm sorry that happened to you."

"I did the worst part to myself."

"What do you mean?"

"I really thought he'd see that I saved the day. Like he'd maybe even be proud. But I'm Charlie Brown. Dad is Lucy. And he always pulls the football away."

"Stop trying to kick a field goal."

"I wish I could."

"Why can't you?"

"You'll never understand."

"Why?"

"Because you're not your father's eldest son."

"That sounds vaguely sexist to me."

"Sorry. But it's just different for sons and fathers. It's different for men."

Alicia pulled her hand away from mine, and then we drove on in dreadful silence.

* * *

On the night I lost my favorite hat at the Beaufort Film Festival, I lay in bed feeling like I was going to throw up. I kept telling myself it was insane to get so upset about an old—albeit beloved—piece of clothing.

You're not a child and it wasn't a security blanket, I told myself.

Then—through the darkness—I whispered, "Alicia, are you awake?"

"Yep."

"When I lost my hat tonight," I said. "Did it remind you of that one time my dad—"

"Lost his wallet at Cirque du Soleil?"

I swallowed hard.

"You were nowhere near as bad. *Obviously*," she continued. "I didn't want to bring it up earlier because I didn't want to freak you out."

"I feel sick to my stomach."

"About losing your hat? Or about acting like your dad?"

"I don't know."

"You're not your dad."

"But I am. At least a little."

"No, you're not."

"Because of all the work I'm doing in analysis?"

"Because I would have never married your dad, and I married you."

"Maybe I lost my hat so I'd have more sympathy for my father. Maybe I'm supposed to write about this in the memoir."

"You're *definitely* supposed to write about it in the memoir. But I have to go to sleep, okay?"

"I love you."

"You're not your father."

"I love you."

"I love you too."

As Alicia drifted off to sleep, I thought about how hard it must have been for you, Dad, that night at Cirque du Soleil. I know your career wasn't going as well back then as you would have liked. My father-in-law was the head of an infectious-disease ward at a big-city hospital. And you've never been great in social settings. But I wanted you to be the type of dad who mixed with in-laws and appreciated Cuban food and enjoyed artsy French Canadian acrobatics. And you had at least accepted the invitation—albeit with pressure from Mom, no doubt—and had maybe even done your best to be what most would call a normal human being. But you couldn't fake it. The same goes for that time I changed your tire. Your constant inability to be what I needed made me hate you. And maybe that wasn't fair. Because I would have sure felt mistreated if someone had tried to shame me for the fear and self-loathing I felt when I lost my favorite hat, as stupid as I knew my reaction was.

When I reached in my coat pocket and my beloved hat wasn't there, I instantly felt possessed. Maybe a little by sentimentality. Maybe a lot more by some sort of obsessive-compulsive tic I still have regarding my clothing. Maybe because I unconsciously believe that everything good in my life will one day be taken away, and consequently, I am always looking for symbolic proof of this dysfunctional life thesis. Maybe by all of the above.

But as I lay in bed feeling sick to my stomach, I understood that I was not above your mental illness, whatever it might be. Even after all the work I've done in analysis, I still find myself in these very you-like situations. And—as I just wanted sympathy for the intense way I felt about a fucking hat—I realized you had needed sympathy when you freaked out about the lost wallet and the blown tire. In the first case, I wanted you to help me impress my in-laws. In the second case, I wanted you to see me as your hero. In both cases, I was failing to see you as you really were. I failed to empathize with your pain, and then I blamed you for not empathizing with mine. There is still a part of me that wants to say you are the father and I am the son, so it was your job to do the empathizing. You were supposed to give, and I was supposed to receive. But you can't give what you don't have. I now see that I need to look in the mirror and examine the ways in which I am frail and weak and even ill. I need to accept those off-putting parts of me, if only so I can begin to accept the off-putting parts of others. I need to discard the needy-son mentality and put on the giving-father mentality. It's a long overdue maturation process that I'm attempting to ramp up with the writing of this memoir.

So, Dad, I'm sorry for wanting you to be something you weren't. I'm sorry for judging you so harshly back when I was a younger man. And I understand how it feels to have irrational and paranoid thoughts. It's frightening. It's painful. It's alienating. It can make you feel like you are dying. It can make you feel like the entire world is against you.

As I lay there in bed that night, mourning the loss of my hat, I told myself that despite my wife insisting otherwise, I *am* my father, and it's my job to redeem us both. After I was done with that prayer, I fell into a deep sleep.

The next morning, I got up and made myself purchase three new Pistil hats on the internet. They were not the same as the old one, but I told myself that change could be good, and I was going to embrace it with a more mature-father mindset. Then I got to work writing this chapter.

Around noon, I quickly ate some oatmeal and then shaved and showered.

On the way back to the film festival, I said to Alicia, "You know, I really think I needed to lose my favorite hat so that I could write what I did this morning. Like parting with my favorite piece of clothing was a sacrifice demanded by the writing gods. And I think the chapter

I'm writing about it was worth losing an old hat. I'm getting the better end of that trade. So I've made peace with losing the irreplaceable beanie that made me look and feel my best. The piece of clothing I will love most in this lifetime. Fare thee well, good hat. Thank you for your service."

"So you think the writing gods took your hat?" she asked.

"Metaphorically speaking? Yes. It needed to be sacrificed."

"Okay," she said and then laughed.

"You think I'm crazy?"

"I'm just glad you're in a good mood. It's Thursday afternoon and we're going to a film festival. It feels like we're playing hooky."

"I've officially said goodbye to my hat," I declared. "Now let's have fun today."

And when Alicia and I went back to the same seats we had sat in the night before, I immediately found my beloved hat tucked deep between the armrest and the seat cushion.

6.

Dad, we need to talk about my drinking problem.

Maybe you'd say I don't have a drinking problem now that I am almost seven years sober. But I will always have a drinking problem, no matter how many years of sobriety I rack up. And my problem is mostly the insatiable need I've often felt—and still occasionally feel—to disappear. That need existed long before alcohol ever passed through my lips. Alcohol just made the fantasy possible.

Besides the few years right before your dementia made itself known to us—back when you were having a nightly glass of wine—you were never really a drinker. You've told me that you used to drink a little beer in college. But when you became a banker, and had to entertain clients, you learned a handy trick: you would slip away from the barroom table under the guise of needing to use the bathroom and then have a private chat with the bartender, to whom you would hand a few bills. This was prepayment for serving you just soda water on ice whenever you'd order another vodka soda so that you could appear to be going one-for-one with your heavy-drinking bosses and clients. Since your anxiety was always through the roof, I've never really understood how you managed to resist the sweet instant relief that alcohol eternally offers to us anxiety sufferers.

Of course, your maternal grandfather was a bona fide drunk. Your mother had to clean up his puke every morning back when she was a teenager, after he had locked her mother away in a mental institution. When I once asked Grandmom why her mother had to be institutionalized, she said her mom used to take long walks and get lost in her thoughts. And she preferred making music to doing housework. Her father had been a violin maker. She played the violin and piano and was an excellent singer. This, of course, made the artist in me wonder if her great crime was having a creative temperament at a time when housewives were not permitted to be dreamers. I don't know the full story there. I only know that Grandmom hated the thought of anyone drinking alcohol. By the time I was born, Pop Pop didn't drink. And neither did Mom nor you.

While our family members kept no booze at home—except at Uncle Pete's place, of course—many of my classmates grew up with stocked liquor cabinets within easy reach. I was in the last year of elementary school when I found myself alone with such a friend in his house. Derrick Shield and I were watching TV when he asked, "Have you ever had peach schnapps?"

When I told him that I hadn't, he said it tasted like candy and that, sometimes, he snuck a little from his parents' liquor cabinet. Then he asked if I'd like a taste. When I said we'd get in trouble, he assured me he'd sipped a little peach schnapps many times before and his parents never noticed. Then he was pouring us two small glasses.

I'm pretty sure peach schnapps is a clear liquor, but I remember the liquid in my glass looking reddish orange. *Like a peach had been squeezed of its blood*, I weirdly think in my memory now.

"Give it a try," Derrick said. "It's not enough to get you drunk or anything."

As I accepted the glass, I knew I was doing something forbidden. That made it all the more irresistible. I had never once before even thought about drinking alcohol. But it was now the thing I most wanted to do in the world. I flashed on our gym teacher talking to us boys in health class about masturbation. "Maybe you are home on a Saturday night because you don't have a date," he said, and I thought, *We're in elementary school. Who goes on dates?* Then he told us what masturbation was and how to do it. I hadn't previously known. But after that particular health class, I couldn't stop thinking about it. And then, once I gave it a try—*wow*—I was beyond hooked. The feeling right before I took a sip of peach schnapps reminded me of the moment right before I first experimented with masturbation in the shower. It felt like I was about to jump off a cliff, and something deep inside of me was certain that I would sprout wings and fly before I hit the ground. When it came to jerking off, I absolutely did. It was like kissing the sun and living to tell the tale. I couldn't see straight after that first climax. I couldn't wait to do it again. Nothing had ever made me feel better. Nothing had so instantly taken away the anxiety and shame and fear. But when I took my first sip of alcohol, I could taste the poison right away. I knew I was consuming something that was not good for me. While my body had said "Hell, yes!" to jerking off, it immediately said "No, thank you" to alcohol. The liquid in my mouth was sweet and fruity, but it tasted like cough medicine and coated my teeth with a stickiness I intuitively rejected. When I swallowed, it burned a little—like the beginning of a sore throat.

"You have to get used to it," Derrick said. My elementary-school-aged friend swirled the liquid around in his glass like a seasoned connoisseur, before he drained it in one gulp. So I did the same. He carefully put the liquor bottle back in the cabinet, and then we put our dirty glasses in the kitchen sink.

I asked if we would start to feel drunk. My friend laughed and said not to worry. We'd only had a taste. We wouldn't be feeling much of anything at all. I wondered why anyone would drink peach schnapps. It didn't taste all that great, and it didn't seem to do anything to you either.

When Derrick's father came home, I started to feel extremely guilty. That guilt felt like a premonition when Mr. Shield entered the living room and said, "I know you two have been drinking my liquor.

Don't even bother lying. You want to know how I caught you?" He didn't wait for either of us to respond. "You left the glasses upside down in the sink. They reeked of alcohol when I lifted them. If you had washed and dried and put them back in the cabinet, you would have gotten away with it."

Derrick smiled, as if he had simply been caught farting. I went white as a ghost.

"I'm not so mad about you boys drinking," Mr. Shield said. "I did that when I was your age too. But you *stole* from me. You *stole* my liquor. Had you asked, I might have given you some. But you *stole.* I don't like when people steal from me."

His repetition of the word "stole" felt like getting my front teeth knocked out one by one. Since Derrick had offered it to me, I hadn't even considered that drinking from his dad's liquor cabinet was theft, but, of course, it was. Stealing was a sin. *Thou shalt not steal*, my church had told me many times. My heart was pounding. I couldn't breathe.

Derrick seemed unfazed, which astounded me.

His father looked at me and said, "Matt, I can't even tell your parents about this. I know your dad would murder you. He'd go crazy. Which is why I have to be so hard on you myself. You can't steal liquor from people. It's not right. And it's up to me to make sure you understand that. Because your father would overdo it. I can clearly see how bad you feel about this, so I've done my job."

Mr. Shield knew you went crazy sometimes. I was shocked by this discovery. I didn't think anyone else outside of our family had any clue whatsoever about how insane you could be behind closed doors. I had previously believed that I might have even been making your explosive moods up in my head. But I wasn't. Someone else had experienced your insanity and knew it was dangerous. This person was even altering his behavior in an effort to keep you from going nuts. He was doing what I did all the time. He was trying to control your rage by changing how he would have normally acted if you weren't in the mix. I wasn't alone. He was trying to protect me. From you. I was overwhelmed with gratitude. Yes, I was happy Mr. Shield wasn't going to rat me out, but I was even more grateful to know that someone outside of my family could see the way you were. It made me feel a lot less crazy myself. And much less alone.

Once Mr. Shield had left the room, I said to Derrick, "What's your dad going to do to you?"

"What do you mean?" he asked.

"As punishment," I said.

"That *was* the punishment. The talk."

"Nothing else is going to happen to you?"

"We didn't do anything that bad," Derrick said with an ease and confidence that felt godlike to me at the time. "We just had a sip of peach schnapps."

I left Derrick's house that day with stomach acid climbing up my throat. It wasn't from the booze. It was from the shame and guilt of having been caught stealing. Mr. Shield kept his promise and never told Mom and you that I had stolen liquor from his cabinet. But I *had* stolen. And I never could look him in the eyes ever again. Later—when Derrick and I graduated from the Oaklyn school system and went on over to Collingswood High School—Mr. Shield would sometimes drive us there. He would immediately tell me a joke whenever I got into his car. I think he could tell how tense I always was. Maybe he felt bad for having guilt-tripped me, back when he caught us drinking. He sometimes let me work in the store he owned during the holidays so I could earn extra money. But to this day, whenever I think about him, I hear him saying, "You stole from me," and I still feel like I'm going to vomit, which I realize is not normal.

In junior high, one of my classmates would often throw parties at her apartment after school. Her mother would happily purchase alcohol and cigarettes for eighth graders. Whatever anyone wanted. I'd go to her parties, but I'd never drink. Every once in a while, I'd take a puff of a cigarette. I was pretty sure it was illegal to buy booze and smokes for fourteen-year-olds. But we had a supplier, so we were all experimenting with adult things.

By the time I got to high school, pretty much everyone was drinking. Some were also experimenting with weed and acid—even cocaine. I was pretty prudish about these things. But I befriended a classmate named Earl.

The first time I went to Earl's house, his mother walked right up to me and said, "If you drink any of the beers in the fridge—even one—you do not drive. I'd rather have you drinking here than in some dangerous place. If you get even a little buzzed, you stay the night."

"Mom," Earl said. *"Stop."*

Then we went up to his room.

"Did you want a beer?" Earl asked me. "Because you can have one."

"I'm okay," I said.

"Yeah," he said. "It's like four in the afternoon."

But, as I started going to Earl's house more frequently, I realized that he and his brother often did have beers together. And his mom and stepdad didn't even blink when they did. Eventually, I got up the courage to have one with them. There was no pressure. No big cheer when I said I'd take a beer. It was like they were handing me a glass of water. We never even got close to drunk. In French class, I had learned that French teenagers often drank glasses of wine with their families, and I wondered if we were acting European at Earl's house. So I'd have a beer every once in a while at Earl's and privately marvel at how chill his family was about it.

From time to time, I'd go to a drinking party. I'd pay the five bucks or whatever to get in, but I'd never drink any of the liquor or beer and would almost always leave within a half hour of arriving. Whenever anyone would encourage me to ease up and have a drink, I'd tell them I was driving or had to get home soon.

For much of high school, I was in long-term relationships with girls who didn't party. We'd spend our weekend nights going to the movies or watching TV or talking alone somewhere or kissing.

But toward the end of high school, back in 1991, there was this period when I was single. I had been talking to this girl, Jacki, from Haddonfield, where I would eventually teach. Everyone in Collingswood hated Haddonfield. They were the rich kids who always beat us in sports and drove better cars than we did and lived in bigger houses and were headed to better colleges and even better lives. Our parents hated Haddonfield people even more than we did. All that made the Haddonfield girls irresistible. Forbidden fruit. A few of my friends were dating Haddonfield girls. And Earl had introduced me to Jacki. Jacki was a gifted athlete. She followed what had seemed to me to be an insane training regimen, which burned an astronomical amount of calories. I once watched her eat ten tacos in one sitting at the Oaklyn Taco Bell. And, yet, she had rock-hard abs. She also had a pretty face and mischievous eyes. When I got poison ivy, she herself wrote me a prescription from her doctor father's script pad, which was hands-down the most impressive thing I'd ever witnessed a girl my age do. She was confident. She was clever. And she seemed headed for a better life than I could imagine for myself back then. She also seemed to really like me, which I found astounding at the time.

Another friend, Kevin, was having an end-of-summer party at his house. Earl was going and said Jacki was asking if I'd be there. Through Earl, I let her know I would be.

I knew Kevin like the back of my hand. We'd done a lot of growing up together. I'd spent years hanging out in his house, which was just five or so blocks from mine. It was like having home-field advantage for the date. But I was nervous when I walked into the party. All my Oaklyn friends were there. They all knew Jacki was coming and that I liked her. So they teased me about it, joking that this particular Haddonfield girl wasn't going to slum it with an Oaklyner like me. But then Jacki was actually walking through the front door. She immediately ditched her girlfriends and walked right on over to me. Kevin introduced himself to Jacki and then said, "Matt Quick is a good man," as he handed each of us a Coors Light. Once he walked away, we cracked the beers open.

"Sit down," Jacki said.

I sat down on a chair. Then Jacki was on my lap with her arm around my neck.

Holy shit, I thought. *This is happening.*

She smiled at me.

"I'm glad you came tonight," I said.

"Of course," she said.

I thought, *If someone as attractive and smart and strong and well-familied as Jacki was actually choosing to spend her weekend night sitting on my lap, well then, I couldn't be all that bad.*

I noticed my windpipe didn't feel like it was being crushed. I didn't feel anxious. I felt happy. I was so attracted to Jacki. She was cute and insanely fit, for sure. But I think I was mostly attracted to her confidence. Her ability to identify something she wanted and to go after it. To drive to a town where she hadn't grown up—a town that many communities looked down on—walk into a party, and claim her spot on the lap of a guy like me. Just because she felt like it. Because she could do whatever she wanted. Because she was alive and young and knew that she was meant to enjoy her time on Earth.

I lifted the silver Coors Light can to my lips and swallowed a sip of its ice-cold contents.

Then Kevin was striding toward me, shaking his head in disgust.

“This is fucking bullshit, Quick,” he said.

“What?” I said.

“Your fucking mom’s nose is pressed up against the front window of my house, that’s what. You better make her go away. If she calls the cops, I’m gonna be really fucking pissed at you.”

Jacki laughed almost melodiously. She so easily found the comedy in the situation. And I immediately knew I couldn’t be with her. Because I was imprisoned, and I would never be free.

I stood up and ran to the front window. My mother shook her head at me and then strode away.

“Why was your mom looking in the window?” Jacki asked with an expression of delight on her face. It was like she and I had reached the end of our novel’s first chapter, and Jacki couldn’t wait for me to turn the page so we could see what happened in chapter two.

“I have to go,” I said.

“Real cool mom, Quick,” kids at the party said. “Are the cops coming? Do we need to run?”

“I don’t think she’ll call the cops,” I said.

“Are you positive?” Kevin asked.

I knew Mom only really cared about making sure I wasn’t at a drinking party. I knew that if I went home right away, my classmates would be spared more trouble.

“I gotta go,” I said again to Jacki.

She looked me in the eyes and put a hand on my arm as she laughed and said, “What’s the worst she can do if you stay?”

“You don’t understand. *I really have to go.*”

“Let me drive you.”

“It’s only a few blocks. I’m okay.”

“I’ll give you a ride. *I insist.* I haven’t had anything to drink at all. Your mom made sure of that.”

Then we were in Jacki's car. She was driving. And I was starting to feel like I was five years old. I was scared stiff of what would happen to me when I got home. I knew you, Dad, would go psycho. I knew there would be screaming. I was pretty sure there would be some over-the-top punishment.

When I pointed to our little green house and said, "That's me," Jacki pulled up to our front curb. I felt embarrassed on multiple levels. She lived in a big expensive home in Haddonfield. I'd been in it. And when she said, "This is your house?" I sort of instantly understood why you had been embarrassed of our Oaklyn home all these years. Jacki was only confirming that she had the right place. But I was ashamed anyway—of living in a small house in a neighborhood that wasn't as desirable as the one Jacki lived in, of having a mother who still spied on me even though I was less than two months shy of my eighteenth birthday, of the fact that I felt nauseous, and of my shaking voice.

"What do you think is going to happen when you go inside?" Jacki said.

"I don't know," I said.

"This is really serious, huh?" When I didn't say anything in response, she said, "*Wow.*"

"I really have to go."

"Well, maybe we can get together once you've served whatever sentence your parents give you."

I nodded, but I couldn't make eye contact before I got out of her car.

"In the few minutes we actually got to spend together tonight, I had fun. Certainly, a new experience for me," she said and then laughed in a way that made me believe her.

But then she pulled away, and I entered our house.

The second I stepped inside, Mom said, "I'm just walking through the neighborhood with my friends, and then they're saying, 'Look, there's your son with a girl on his lap and a beer in his hand.' And I said, 'Not *my* Matthew.' But then I looked in the window and—*sure enough*—there you were. *Drinking.* Who was that girl on your lap?"

"You're grounded," you roared at me. "For your entire senior year. You go to church and school. *That's it.* Nowhere else. You are now a prisoner."

"I just had a sip of a beer. *One sip*," I argued.

"Why don't we call your grandmother?" you said. "You can tell her you're drinking beer now. See how that goes over. She had to clean up her father's puke every morning. She watched your uncle Pete drink away his college opportunity and then end up in Vietnam. Go ahead and call your grandmother. Tell *her* you only had a sip. See how much she loves you when she finds out you're a *drunkard*."

"I'm not drunk."

"I'm really disappointed in you, Matthew," Mom said. "Go to your room."

I ran up the stairs and flopped down on my bed. As I stared up at the drop ceiling, I thought, *Just minutes ago, Jacki was sitting on my lap and smiling. And I was at a party. Enjoying myself, for once. I was doing it. I was being a normal person.*

Then I started imagining my classmates talking about what had happened. How my mother had appeared in the window and shamed the confident girl off my lap and the beer out of my hand. I couldn't tell what would hurt worse: losing Jacki or the inevitable teasing I was sure to take when I went to school on Monday.

I was the high school senior whose mother still followed him around like he was a toddler, telling him what he could and couldn't do. I was the high school senior who went home when his mother said so. I was the eighteen-year-old grounded for an entire year just because he'd taken a single sip of shitty low-alcohol beer.

When I dragged myself to school on Monday morning, I was shocked to discover that my classmates generally felt sorry for me.

There was teasing, but when I stared at the floor in total submission, my fellow Oaklyners switched gears and mostly said things like, "Man, what the fuck is up with your parents?"

For my entire senior year, I didn't have another single sip of alcohol.

But for whatever reason, I started to party regularly during my sophomore year at La Salle University. I'm not sure why I started hardcore drinking. I mean, everyone was drinking at college. But I had managed to resist it freshman year. I'll write about what happened to me at the start of college later in this memoir, and maybe that will shed some light on things for you, Dad.

But for whatever reason, my love affair with alcohol began in the fall of 1993. I met Alicia at a kegger the first week she was on campus. We started calling her "Two-Beer Bessette" because she'd get absolutely and hilariously smashed off just two cans. Soon, it would take a bit more for me. There were these liquor stores just off campus that customers couldn't even enter. I had to stand outside, where I'd stick money through a little circle cutout in the wall. A mysterious hand would pass bottles back through. I started experimenting with all sorts of cheap alcohol. Ripple wine. Forties of malt liquor. Plastic bottles of gin and vodka. I can't pinpoint exactly when I realized that alcohol turned down the volume on all the shame and anxiety I'd been carrying around since I was a little kid, but once I realized that booze made all the worst feelings disappear, I started drinking with more and more frequency.

On New Year's Eve, I went to a party near the Villanova campus with my three best friends, and we drank all night long. Beer. Shots of whiskey. It was a blur. I drunk-dialed Alicia from the house phone. She was at her parents' ski home in Vermont. The drinking erased any guilt I might have otherwise felt running up some stranger's phone bill. I laughed and told Alicia that I loved her and was having the best time I had ever had in my entire life.

One of my best friends and I decided we would go outside and chug a bottle of pink champagne at midnight. We were both already beyond drunk. But when 1993 turned into 1994, we stood in the freezing cold backyard, popped the cork, and started chugging, passing the bottle back and forth until it was all gone. I felt as though the stars above us were spinning. When I reached out for the fence so I could find my balance, I started stumbling across the lawn, because the fence was twelve feet away. The next thing I remember was throwing up in someone's hamper. I woke up the next day in a stranger's bedroom. My friend was asleep next to me. I started puking again and continued to do so all morning. I even threw up on my friend's front lawn while we were dropping him off at his home. From the front doorway, his mother watched me with a worried look on her face. I swore I would never drink again.

I got drunk the very next weekend.

During my junior year of college, I realized that I could control my level of drunkenness by forcing myself to vomit. If I got too drunk—whenever the world started to spin—I'd just go into the bathroom, stick a finger down my throat, and throw up in the toilet. Some people called this technique "puke and rally," meaning once you purged your stomach, you were ready for more alcohol. I liked to call it "pulling the trigger." I started doing that weekly. As disgusting as all of the above is, I really began to love drinking. It wasn't the social part of it. I didn't love going to parties. I just loved turning off all the anxiety and shame and guilt and fear. Whenever the invisible hand started squeezing my throat, all I had to do was drink until it went away. Alcohol never failed to vanquish all of my worst mental health symptoms. It was undefeated.

When I began student teaching in the second semester of my senior year at La Salle, I started having regular panic attacks. I mostly kept it together at the school where I had been assigned, but when I came home at night I would obsessively prepare for the next day, trying to anticipate any possible scenario that might come up during whatever lesson I was going to teach. In an effort to make absolutely sure that I wouldn't embarrass myself in front of my students, I began holding myself to impossible levels of perfection. My fellow student teachers would prep for a few hours after each school day had ended. I'd prep from four in the afternoon to eleven at night. I'd white-knuckle it through my days. And, looking back now, I'd even say I did a good job. My students seemed to like me. Some would write me long thank-you letters when I left. My cooperating teachers and professors gave me top marks. But every night, when I returned home from my day of student teaching, I would lesson plan for an insane seven hours, trying to memorize an absurd amount of information, writing out multiple pages of handwritten notes for each lesson. Then, at eleven p.m., I'd turn on the little TV set in my on-campus single room, climb into my bed, watch a rerun of *Cheers*, and drink straight gin until my brain shut off.

When I started working full-time as a teacher, the alcoholic in me found himself in good company. There was one grizzled teacher who took nips from a flask all day long. Another teacher's aide regularly came back from lunch smelling strongly of booze. There were plenty of older male teachers who loved taking me to the bar, where we'd never fail to put away more than a few. The town in which I did the majority of my teaching had a robust drinking culture. I'd see parents at the local pub. Sometimes they'd buy me a beer. They never seemed to care that I was imbibing in public, maybe because they were out drinking too. And so, drink I did.

But no matter how much I drank, the anxiety and shame and guilt and fear just kept coming back.

Then I became a writer. Writers are supposed to drink. I'd get drunk with my graduate school buddies. While enrolled in Goddard College's low-residency creative writing MFA program, I drank an ocean. I wrote four novels and dozens of shorter pieces in two years. But I drank just as hard. When we were on campus, my friends and I drained endless bottles. Every single night. And when I started publishing, there was booze at every event my publishers threw. At one conference, my publicist told one of her underlings to make sure I had a full drink in my hand at all times as I worked the room. As the young twentysomething kept handing me a fresh beer or scotch every fifteen minutes or so, I thought, *This is the job for me.* Because with alcohol in my veins, I actually could work a room quite effectively. My anxiety was often so high in crowds that five or six drinks would just barely drop me down to normal-human level. And then once the event was over—just as soon as I was alone again in my hotel room, and extreme anxiety had quit squeezing my adrenal glands like a milkmaid on speed—I would instantly be transformed from a charming and gracious author to a staggering, slurring, fall-down drunk.

The first publishing lunch I ever went on with an editor was more of a drinking session than it was a shared meal. And I thought, *Oh, man. Day drinking. This is the profession for me.* When I co-headlined a literary festival in the Philippines, there was a large bottle of Johnnie Walker Red on the nightstand of my hotel room in Manila. The card read, *Compliments of your publisher. To get you through the week.* When I did the literary festival in Edinburgh, Scotland, they served authors high-end scotch before we took the stage. In Rio, Brazil, I dropped my luggage off in my hotel room and immediately went out for drinks with my publicist for the week. When I went to my publishing house in London, everyone drank a celebratory glass of champagne with me.

The same thing happened when I went to my publishing house in Toronto, Canada. Drinking was what you did in publishing.

At the end of my drinking days, I was mixing in tablets of clonazepam with my regular alcohol consumption, which was superb at first. The first time I took clonazepam, I thought all my problems were over. I'd found my wonder drug. On clonazepam, I could do media interviews without the faintest trace of anxiety. But then I found I needed a little more to get the same results and then a little more and a little more. And, of course, I was completely ignoring the warnings on the labels that said not to drink alcohol while taking. I once woke up in a hotel room in the middle of the night gasping and feeling absolutely certain that my heart had stopped for a few seconds. Then there was the flight when I was traveling home from London and the flight attendant kept putting little bottles of scotch down on my tray. Each time, he'd weirdly say—in an evil-sounding British accent—"Checkmate." Even though I had used clonazepam all week to get through publishing dinners and readings and interviews, I had also drunk alcohol daily and just kept drinking more and more scotch on the plane. And then my heart was beating heart-attack fast. No one was sitting next to me. I pulled the blanket over my head and began praying I wouldn't die. I was certain I wasn't going to make it, but I was also too ashamed to yell, "Is there a doctor on the plane?" Then I realized I hadn't taken clonazepam that morning. I was going through withdrawal. The ensuing pounding headaches, nausea, sleepless night, paranoia, and suicidal ideation were debilitating enough to make me never want to take it again. And even as I continued to drink heavily, my withdrawal put me in a fierce people-repelling mood for the next week or so.

When we bought our home in the Outer Banks, the ten-foot-long full bar was a selling point. You've sat at our old bar, Dad. But you probably don't remember. There were endless cabinets for an army of bottles and pint glasses and shot glasses and highball glasses and tumblers and whatever else serious drinkers might need. And I kept an entire full-sized refrigerator loaded with high-alcohol microbrews. When you have a bar in your home, you tend to drink. And, oh boy, did I. Sometimes friends would come over and play poker and other games in my bar while we all drank. Sometimes we'd drink on my deck overlooking the Albemarle Sound. We'd go out to the bars and drink. With Alicia as my designated driver, I liked to stick my head out the window on the way home and let the warm ocean air and the night's stars blur by.

But I often drank by myself too, long after Alicia had gone to bed upstairs.

Our bar top was clear epoxy. In the epoxy were little frozen relics from the original owner of the house: pictures of shirtless young men holding surfboards or fishing poles; young sexy women in bikinis; casino chips; tickets to sporting events and concerts and comedy shows; pot leaves and the covers of reggae albums. We'd heard rumors about the man who had originally built and first lived in our house—the dude who had filled the bar top with images of his life. He allegedly got caught flipping too many beach properties during the housing market crash, and he lost everything, including the house that we were currently living in. I'd stay up late at night examining the contents of the bar top, which seemed to tell the story of the original owner's life. It was probably a good thirty square feet worth of images. Every time I looked, I'd notice something I hadn't quite taken in before. Judging by the images he preserved, he had once relished living the high life. But he only got to live it for a relatively short amount of time, before he lost it all. And, as I'd keep pouring myself more drinks all alone at my bar, I'd wonder if I would lose everything too. From talking to my neighbors, I learned it had happened fast for the original owner of my house. He was crushing it. Making money hand over fist. Then the housing-market bottom fell out. When we first moved into that Outer Banks house, I was making money hand over fist too. I had multiple book contracts and multiple movie deals and multiple screenwriting contracts. It all felt too good to be true. And gazing down at the pictures and images in the bar top every night when I drank alone, I wondered if they were cautionary hieroglyphs from a man who had already walked the road I was walking.

What goes up must come down, I'd think. And then I'd drink some more.

There wasn't one event that made me decide to get sober, Dad—there were many.

I started getting sober *before* the bottom of my career fell out, so to speak. My career took a nosedive *right after* I got sober, which made me think a lot about the worrying tales I'd heard about musicians and comedians and writers who had lost their creative sparks when they gave up drugs and alcohol. And I would soon learn why alcohol was such an important part of my creative process too.

The first time I really thought I needed to get sober, I was at the Wright Brothers Memorial with Alicia when a storm snuck up on us. We had been walking under the bluest of skies. And then—in an instant—everything went dark and lightning strikes were tearing that same sky in half. Lightning kills people every summer on the Outer Banks. The locals had long ago made sure we knew to take cover at the first signs of a storm, and Alicia and I thought we were in the worst place imaginable: a huge open field with a tall monument in the center, inviting a blitzkrieg of lightning to rain down all around it.

"*Run!*" Alicia yelled and then took off.

I sprinted for my life but only made it twenty or so yards before I started to feel like I'd have a heart attack if I continued. As lightning continued to fill the air with so much electricity you could actually taste it, I slowed down to a walk. And as I struggled to catch my breath, I thought, *If I don't die right now, I have to get myself in better shape. I'm only in my early forties. This is beyond pathetic.*

Then we went to Florida with two other couples. My buddy's wife took a lot of pictures and then—once we returned home—printed up memento albums for all of us. While sitting at the bar in my home with our friends, all of us flipping through the pictures, I pointed to a man in one of the shots and said, "Who's this guy?" Everyone laughed, thinking I was making a joke. The laughter confused me. I looked a little harder at the picture and realized it was me. But I had somehow gotten so fat, I did not recognize myself, which is when I realized alcohol had begun to alter my senses even when I wasn't drunk. I had become so dependent on booze that I had begun subconsciously disbelieving what I saw in the mirror every day—or maybe I just imagined myself looking so much better than I actually looked. Whatever it took to keep drinking every night.

Then my toes and ankles started to hurt. When I went to the doctor, he told me that my blood pressure was alarmingly high and I also had gout. I told him I couldn't have gout. That was something only old ladies got. My doctor patiently explained that gout was something that people who consumed too much sugar got. I said I hardly ever ate sugary things. I wasn't a dessert guy. I never went to Duck Donuts. Then he said there was sugar in alcoholic beverages.

"Oh," I said. "You're not going to ask me to give up drinking, are you?"

To my great relief, he recommended drinking in moderation without defining moderation. Then he gave me prescriptions to treat the gout and high blood pressure. But when I took his medicine, I felt depressed and tired and generally cranky. I went back complaining, and he began this experiment to see if any of the many drugs available would work for me. He would go on to prescribe me several different types of medicine before I said, "Enough." Each new pill had made me feel worse than the one before. None gave me any sort of relief, which kind of pissed me off. The doctor I was seeing was much younger than I was. A few times, in response to questions I'd ask him in his office, he had pulled out his phone and googled the answers, which didn't exactly inspire confidence. One didn't need a medical degree to understand that my problems were being caused by excessive alcohol intake, poor diet, and not enough exercise. So I decided to do my own experiment.

I started to radically cut back on the drinking—immediately going from several drinks every single day to one or two on the weekends. I had recently begun smoking a little weed, which I quit altogether. I decided to entirely eliminate sugar from my diet as well. And when I went to restaurants, I began to pay attention to what people were ordering, which I cross-checked with how they looked. With most middle-aged people, what they were publicly eating usually correlated in painfully obvious ways with how they appeared. People making unhealthy choices usually looked unhealthy. After decades of making unhealthy decisions about what I was putting in my body, I, of course, looked unhealthy. So I decided to see if putting healthy food into my body would change how I looked and felt.

I combined that with a running routine, incrementally upping the miles every week.

The results were immediate and quite frankly stunning. I lost sixty pounds in just a few months. People didn't recognize me anymore.

And when I went to a bar, I began to notice that women would glance over at me. I'd ask Alicia what was going on, and she'd say, "You really don't remember, do you?"

"Remember what?"

"What it's like to be attractive."

"Am I really *that* different looking?"

"You definitely let yourself go," Alicia said. "It's nice to have you back."

When I next went to the doctor, my blood pressure was perfect, and all my blood tests came back fantastic. He was shocked.

"Why don't you just tell everyone to eat healthy and exercise before giving them drugs?" I asked him.

He was a pretty fit guy himself. It looked like he regularly worked out, and I imagined he ate well too. He paused and then frowned, before he said, "Because no one listens when you recommend diet and exercise. You are the exception. I'm sure someone told you about diet and exercise long before you had your health scare. For many years, you didn't listen either."

I also knew that I had the time and resources to make the change. I had banked some cash. I was self-employed. I worked from home. I didn't have kids. I had a wife who made the healthy living switch with me; stocked our refrigerator with organic, unprocessed food; cooked nutritious meals for us; and encouraged me every step of the way. We could afford the higher costs of fresh fruits and vegetables and locally caught seafood and ethically raised poultry. In that way, we were extraordinarily privileged. We made the commitment and did the work, but our circumstances had afforded us the opportunity. Had I still been working seventy hours a week in public education and taking home a schoolteacher's paycheck, making such a radical shift would have been much harder.

Here's the rub, Dad.

While I had never in my life looked more physically fit on the outside, on the inside I was falling apart. More so than before. *Much more.* I could no longer say, *I'll feel better once I give up the booze and get back in shape*, because I had already done those things. I began to realize that all the eating and drinking and smoking and pill-popping had been serving an important psychological purpose. At first I don't think I could have said exactly what that was. But soon after I stopped numbing myself with drugs and alcohol—and as I started to eat for nutrition only, instead of using food as a way to comfort myself—I began to feel things I hadn't felt in a long time. Or maybe it's more accurate to say I started feeling these things more intensely and without any breaks. It was like someone had reached into my skull and turned up the volume on all of my worst thoughts and beliefs about myself. And, in response, something deep inside of me started screaming.

I tried to make the screaming stop by going for long runs. I tried to exhaust myself so thoroughly that I would no longer be able to feel anything, nor would I be able to think. I'd chase a runner's high.

Every.

Single.

Day.

For hours.

The strange part was that everyone enthusiastically cheered on my new addiction as being healthy. Whenever I saw anyone, they'd immediately tell me I looked great, which, of course, meant that I had looked like shit for so long. But I drank up their praise. And I told myself that I just had to keep running, keep eating well, keep holding myself to this new standard, and eventually the screaming inside of me would go away.

But the screaming didn't go away. Even when I made the ultimate sacrifice: giving up my weekend drinks and saying goodbye to alcohol forever. I thought surely God would take away the screaming once I sacrificed my favorite thing in the world forever and ever, amen. But complete sobriety had the exact opposite effect. The volume on the screaming inside of me just kept getting louder and louder.

And then soon, all I was doing was running. I'd go to Nags Head Woods and disappear into the trails. I wasn't writing. I dropped most of my friends. Without drinking alcohol and eating unhealthy food at the many local restaurants, I wasn't even sure what I *could* do with most of the people I'd previously been hanging around. I'd go for walks with Alicia. We went to the movies and watched TV. We'd swim in the ocean. We'd sunbathe and play Kubb on the beach. I had one or two supportive friends whom I'd meet for lunch every now and then. Sometimes my buddies would go running with me, or we'd take long walks in the woods and talk, but mostly, I'd run my miles alone and wait for the screaming inside of me to stop.

And Uncle Pete kept haunting me.

You never remember this, Dad, but your older brother died somewhat unexpectedly in 2014. He left a voice message on my phone just hours before he exited this world.

Pete and I had always talked about writing an account of his Vietnam experience. He would tell me all sorts of stories about his time in the army, saying the tales were for what he liked to call my "little book." But, for many years, he claimed to be in a legal battle with "the fuckin' VA." I never quite understood exactly why he was suing "the fuckin' VA." I think maybe they were denying that his brain tumor was agent orange–related. Regardless, he always said he couldn't let me write our "little book" until his lawsuit was resolved. He imagined the government might somehow turn our project into a legal defense weapon. I never understood how that could happen, but Pete was adamant about waiting until the lawsuit was finished.

After Pete's second brain surgery, he spent a lot of time recovering in the hospital and then at a rehabilitation place. And he'd call me on the phone. I'd lie in my hammock behind our house, gaze out at the Albemarle Sound, hold the phone a few inches away from my ear, and listen for hours to him ranting from his hospital bed. He was so resentful. He was wildly paranoid. He was often on the verge of lunacy. And he was furious with you, maybe because you never visited him while he was recovering.

"I don't care how much money your father makes," Pete would say to me. "He'll never be *half* the man I am. Fuck your father! *Fuck Michael!*"

But the last voice message Pete ever left me was happy—triumphant even.

My voicemail recorded him saying, "Wanted you to be the first to know, girly man. I finally did it. I beat the fuckin' VA. They caved. Gave me what I wanted. Now we can write that little book of yours. I'm coming down to OBX to get some of that good weather you've been getting. You can take out your little tape recorder. And we'll sit on your deck looking at the water while I tell you everything. I'm coming."

He died the next morning, before I had a chance to call him back.

I listened to that voice message a million times.

Each play, I heard him say, "Now we can write that little book of yours," and I'd think about how he had repeatedly called from the hospital and basically downloaded his entire life into my mind. Because he was expected to make a full recovery, I hadn't recorded any of our conversations. Now that Pete was dead, there was no way I could pen the type of nonfiction book he had imagined we'd write together. But I began to feel overwhelmingly called to process all the Vietnam War baggage with which he had entrusted me.

In anticipation of someday writing the book he had wanted me to write, I actually *had* written down many of the phrases he used. And I had jotted down some of his anecdotes about his time in Vietnam. All the larger-than-life, government-fearing, traumatized, insane stories he told about himself and others. I missed Pete. *A lot.* The thing I missed the most about him was his voice. Hearing it always felt like simultaneously being punched in the face and yet also being lovingly hugged somehow. It was like he was always saying "Fuck you" and "I love you" at the same time. There was something honest about it. Almost charming. Pete had been a consistent presence in my life. He always called. He always checked in. He always wanted to know what was going on with his eldest nephew. I loved him for that.

If you can capture what you loved about Pete in a novel, I told myself, *it would be genius.*

So I started writing *The Reason You're Alive.*

Once I had the voice right, the book wrote itself. I felt like Pete was in the room with me yelling the story into my ear. It felt like I was just typing. When I finished, I was pretty sure it was the best thing I had ever written. We sold the movie rights at auction. I was hired to write the screenplay. An A-list director was brought on to direct. My publisher agreed to publish it, albeit for significantly less money than my previous two books. And it garnered some pretty good reviews. It was the first time I did a book tour without drinking. I talked a lot about Pete at my events. I led with love. People really seemed to connect with the book. People seemed to really like the new healthier me too.

But as I was getting physically healthier, my career started falling apart.

The Reason You're Alive is perhaps my best reviewed book, but it is my least read.

When Trump won in 2016, people in Hollywood became less interested in making a film about a tell-it-like-it-is, Republican, gun-owning Vietnam vet reconnecting with his liberal art-dealer son. Our director dropped out. Miramax—which was the company developing the project—was sold. The producer I was working with was let go. And the new studio head had no interest in the project whatsoever, which effectively killed—what felt like at the time—my last legit shot at making another Hollywood film.

That's when the writer's block really kicked in. I was sober. I was eating healthy. I was exercising like a madman. I had dropped a ton of weight. I had passionately written what I believed with all my heart was my best novel yet. And my career was in shambles.

It was hard not to suspect that my getting sober had produced unintended consequences. And without my nightly escape into drugs and alcohol, I had to manage all of the fear and guilt and shame and paranoia without any relief in sight.

So I just kept running and running and running, chasing the runner's high. But I started to build up a tolerance for running. I needed to run longer and longer distances to numb out, and there were only so many knee-and-ankle-crushing miles that my middle-aged body could weather in a single week.

I'd lie in bed thinking about the original owner of the waterfront home I was living in. I'd think about how he had lost everything in the blink of an eye. And I was certain that I was going to lose everything too. The winds had shifted. I didn't know what to do. I'd shake my fist at God and say, "Why did you give me so much when I was drunk and arrogant? Why am I now failing as a sober, more humble man? What should I do? How do I get rid of all these catastrophic feelings now that I'm no longer drinking and smoking and taking pills?"

God had, of course, given me an ace wife and the money and time I needed to kick my substance abuse. He had also given me the space and freedom to dry out and start dealing with all of the many feelings and emotions that alcohol had punted down the road for decades. And He'd put me in an astonishing location to do all that in as well. But I was still too narcissistic and resentful to appreciate any of the many gifts I had been given. So I continued to suffer.

I now think I needed to suffer. That the suffering was actually a gift from God. I needed to get well acquainted with just how ugly I had allowed myself to become—just how vain and proud I could be. I needed to realize that everything good in my life was only there because God had allowed it to be there. It was not my glory that had made these things so.

Drunk, I easily pretended that I had *earned* all the good things in my life.

Sober, I knew that I hadn't.

Yes, I'd made sacrifices, taken risks, and had worked insanely hard. But there were plenty of people who did such things and did not receive the good fortune I had.

Sobriety was beginning to flay my defensive outer skins of pride, narcissism, and greed. The flaying was painful business, and my untrained hands were hacking away without anesthesia.

The only escape I had was running. If I wasn't running, I was paranoid. If I wasn't running, I was internally screaming. The sick parts of me would have done anything to make the pain stop.

If I drink alcohol and gorge on food, the healthy part of me said, *I will die.*

Sobriety is killing me anyway! some demonic voice deep inside of me would yell back.

I woke up every single night at three a.m. with my heart pounding and my palms sweating. I was convinced that my career was over. That I had blown every single one of my many miraculous opportunities. That I would not get another. That I had failed to provide for my wife long-term. That I didn't have enough money to get both of us comfortably through the rest of our lives. And I was pretty sure I wouldn't be able to remain sober if I had to do anything other than run a brain-anesthetizing number of miles every day. It felt like I was eternally sprinting on this gilded treadmill. And, if I ever dared to step off, I might literally die. But I didn't want to be on the treadmill anymore.

Then I began to wonder if dying might be all right. I started thinking about dying all the time. The relief I'd feel. But I didn't tell anyone. I suffered in solitude. Oh, how I suffered.

In many ways, those were the scariest and loneliest years of my life. And yet, it took another twenty-four months for me to find the necessary humility and bravery to ask Zeus for help.

7.

Last night—for my wife's forty-ninth birthday—you, Mom, Alicia, and I went out to dinner at Dockside here on Lady's Island. You mostly smiled through the meal and said the food was good and that you were hoping we'd get dessert. I took a picture of Mom and you. In it, the river's framed by the windows behind your backs. You have on the white Nike baseball hat I gave you for your last birthday, which makes you look younger and more handsome than you usually appear. And Mom looks great like always. The sun is setting behind your heads. It's the magic hour. And the pic now stored on my phone makes you both look as if you are living your best golden years.

The TVs over the bar were showing clips of last weekend's football games. You kept asking if what you were seeing was live and if our Philadelphia Eagles were playing. Whenever I said the TVs were only showing highlights from the previous weekend and that the Eagles weren't playing again for another four days, you'd say, "Okay, that's right. Did the Eagles win last weekend?" We'd watched the game together, of course. And you've been watching a replay of the entire game every day since, each time fully believing it's being played live, moaning and cheering with un-fakeable authenticity, repeatedly saying, "I'm not sold on this quarterback," and "This coach needs to be fired." Despite your dim assessment of Jalen Hurts and Nick Sirianni, Philly beat Washington for first place in the division. I told you all of this again and again, every single time your eyes noticed the football on the restaurant's many screens. And each time, in response, you'd say with boyish hope, "So the Eagles are still in the playoffs?" Whenever you asked if the Eagles were in the playoffs, I'd explain that they were in first place, but it was still November, so the playoffs remained several weeks away. And you'd say, "That's right," as if you were only testing to see if I knew the correct answers.

You smiled when Alicia opened the birthday presents Mom got her, and you smiled when the server brought out two pieces of key lime pie, one with a lit candle.

"Aren't we going to sing?" you asked.

And Alicia said, "*No.*"

Which made you say, "Okay, I love key lime pie."

And then you ate with gusto, like you always do whenever dessert is placed in front of you.

It was a great evening. One of the nicest meals out I've ever had with you. Not because of the food or the atmosphere, but because you seemed relaxed and at ease. And you were cordial to Alicia. Sweet even. Present. You've been increasingly pleasant to my wife since you got dementia. More accessible. Sometimes you even warmly yell her name when she enters your house. When I come solo, you often say, "Where is Alicia? Isn't she coming over? Is she okay?" with what feels like genuine concern. Just a few years ago, I would have never dreamed this possible.

You used to be nasty to my wife. You didn't welcome her into the family when she first came to our Oaklyn house, back when she was just seventeen. She was afraid of you from the moment I had first said, "Dad, this is Alicia," and you just looked away without saying a word.

"Your father hates me," Alicia said to me afterward.

And I said, "He kind of hates everyone. He definitely hates me."

I didn't initially tell Alicia that you had once routinely called one of my former junior high school girlfriends "Thunder Thighs" and had used her real name to refer to the blow-up Shamu whale that we used to take to the beach. I didn't tell Alicia how your teasing had scarred me, even though my ex-girlfriend—who didn't have an ounce of fat on her body, by the way—never knew you said these vile things. Your shots hadn't been delivered for her humiliation. They were meant to humiliate me. The worst you ever called Alicia was "bohemian," because she would travel with a small backpack instead of a large suitcase and had a wild head of curls. I knew that was progress for you—even when you originally failed to make eye contact with the love of my life, let alone say hello or use her name.

For the next few trips around the sun, you acted like Alicia wasn't going to stick around, like she was temporary, just a stranger passing through our lives for a brief period of time. That went on for three and a half years, even as I started making summer trips to Massachusetts and began getting to know Alicia's family, and she came to the Outer Banks with us.

In late 1996 I told you that Mom and I were going to Jewelers' Row in Philly to shop for an engagement ring. You looked away and said nothing. Not *congratulations*. Not *how exciting*. I could feel the tension in your body, but I didn't know what it meant. *Did you disapprove of Alicia? Did you think I was making a mistake?* I got the sense that you really just didn't want me to be happy, because I was in love and Alicia was good for me. She was the best thing that had happened to me by far. And she came from a family that was better off than we were, which I thought the banker in you would appreciate. She grew up with an in-ground swimming pool in her backyard, she had traveled a lot, knew French, was teaching me how to ski, had introduced me to hiking mountains, and had the loveliest face I'd ever seen. I was mentally a mess back then, and I knew Alicia was going to be a game-changing life partner. I was not going to do better. So your silence confused me. I wondered if you didn't want me to know love. I also wondered what you would think if you could watch the movie of our life. Would you root for the Michael Quick character on the screen who refuses to say anything at all when his first-born son says he's going to propose to his girlfriend? Because that was a pretty big father-son scene.

I asked for my future father-in-law's blessing in a hotel room. He had flown Alicia and me to Atlanta, Georgia, so we could attend her cousin's wedding. I paced the hallway for a good twenty minutes, trying to get up the courage, composing a speech in my head that might possibly convince Dr. Bessette to let the lowly me marry his daughter. At the time, I was just a half year out of college and living in your house, Dad. And—with my secondary education slash English degree—I was making eight dollars an hour working with mostly nonverbal teenagers diagnosed with severe autism and Down syndrome. I thought, *Why would this successful and well-respected man bless me when my own father had said nothing?* To my fragile ego, knocking on the hotel door and asking Dr. Bessette for his daughter's hand in marriage seemed like a suicide mission. But I knocked anyway.

When Dr. Bessette answered, I asked if I could come in and have a brief chat. Next, I sat down at a little table and just sort of rambled. I said I knew I hadn't accomplished much in life, but I loved Alicia; and I was a hard worker; and I loved working with young people; and I hoped to be a writer one day; and Alicia and I were so happy together. I said, "I promise I'll take care of your daughter, sir."

Dr. Bessette—whom I would end up calling by his family nickname, Peague—smiled and said, "I know you will."

The words stunned me, Dad, because I couldn't imagine you saying them. But I seized the moment and said, "May I have your permission to marry your daughter?"

In his thick New England accent, Peague said, "Sure."

I worried that he was only being sarcastic, so I said, "I'm going to find a way to make more money. I'll eventually get a tenure-track teaching position. It's just that I love working with the kids at Bancroft and I'm learning so much. But I'm also looking for a real job. With health insurance and a pension. And I'll definitely get one and—"

"*I know*," Peague said with a little grin on his face. "Welcome to the family."

"Don't tell Alicia I asked for your permission," I said. "She thinks asking for the father's permission is sexist, and I want my proposal to surprise her."

Peague laughed and then said, "Sure," again.

Mom helped me with the cost of the engagement rings, which was her and my little secret until now. Rings plural, because Alicia said she wouldn't wear one unless I did too. She thought it sexist for the woman to be marked as off the market when the man was not also marked. So I, too, wore an engagement ring, albeit with no diamond—just a white gold band. Alicia, of course, wouldn't take our last name either, Dad, which bummed me out just as much as it probably irked you.

On February 21, 1997, I picked Alicia up at La Salle University, under the guise that I was taking her to visit your parents in Lititz, Pennsylvania. But she knew something was up when we drove south instead of west. Eight hours later, I took her to the beach I loved best in the world. Milepost 21. Nags Head, North Carolina. Outer Banks. Right where Uncle Pete had built his vacation home, "The Quick Getaway." I spread a blanket out under the stars, popped the most expensive bottle of French wine I could afford at the time, poured two glasses, and then proposed. Because the winter air was freezing cold, we quickly kissed and hugged and chugged our wine. In the hotel room I had rented, I'm sure we made celebratory love, although I actually don't remember that part. I only remember being on the beach and my heart pounding as I asked the question and then—for some unknown reason—immediately confessing that I had her father's blessing. Alicia said, "Yes." Then our bodies were shivering together as one under the stars.

You said nothing to me before the actual wedding in Massachusetts. No words of advice. No *I'm proud of you.* No *congratulations.* On the drive up to the wedding, you said you were sick and lay down in the back seat while Mom drove. I drove up separately with friends, but Mom somehow managed to bag me smoking a cigarette at a North Jersey rest stop. When she frowned and shook her head at me, I nearly threw up. You continued to be sick at the hotel. At the rehearsal dinner, you were moody and aloof, like always. But at the wedding reception, we had a good band, and you actually danced. In my memory now, I see you grooving out there on the dance floor with Megan. Pop Pop talked the band into backing Grandmom and him, as they sang "Makin' Whoopee." Alicia's and my college friends went nuts when your parents took the stage. It was fantastic. Pete and Jon were there. Everyone else from the families was there too. And even though you didn't say a word to me all night, I caught you smiling a few times, which made me think that maybe some part of you was happy for me. I took that as a win. You never said anything at all to me about the fantastic party my in-laws threw. You never thanked them either.

Years later, my father-in-law's colleague, Dr. Bishop, pulled me aside at his own daughter's wedding on Cape Cod. And with so much joy in his heart, he told me, "On the day you and Alicia got married, I thought to myself, *These two kids are the role models for love.* I'd never seen two young people happier." There were other men out there who could so clearly see what my own father could not. Or maybe it was just that they could voice it with life-affirming joy in their hearts. They could give because they had.

Back then, you weren't as successful as you'd come to be much later in life. You'd only just moved out of the small house you were embarrassed of—my childhood home—to the bigger house in the much-more-prestigious neighborhood of Haddonfield. I didn't fully understand why any of that mattered at the time, but I get it now. With me just out of college, Megan still in, and Micah entering soon—plus a bigger mortgage and higher property taxes—you didn't have the money to help pay for a wedding. You were barely surviving mental-health-wise. You worked at the bank, giving all you had to its success. And you just didn't have much left over to offer beyond that.

But while you had been withholding at best and were psychologically savage at worst to Alicia for decades, at the Dockside birthday dinner, you were actually nice. Sweet, even. You said "happy birthday" to Alicia for the first time in the thirty-one years you'd known her.

My analyst says it could be the newly added antianxiety medication, and maybe so. But your finally treating Alicia with the love and respect she deserves makes it so much easier for me to love you the way you need to be loved these days.

So thanks for that, Dad.

Regardless of your antianxiety meds' efficacy, I'm giving you credit.

8.

Today I'm flashing on this one magical afternoon just after Mom and you gave me permission to write this memoir.

We were sitting in your living room, here on Lady's Island. After placing a running tape recorder between us—and checking to make sure its two little black eyes were spinning—I said, "Dad, what do you want my readers to know about our relationship? What do you want me to tell them about you and your first-born son? What would *you* tell them?"

Without hesitation, you said you wanted my readers to know that you were a named executive at a publicly traded bank. You wanted them to know that you used to help people. That you would give loans to good companies that had bad debt. "Everyone deserves a second chance," you said multiple times throughout your monologue, and with conviction. You said you would restructure the bad debt with new better loans. And once the companies were back on their feet, they would pay off the old bad loans. You said you had saved a lot of companies from bankruptcy. You said you had saved the jobs of many people. Hundreds, maybe even thousands, of people got to keep their jobs because of this process you facilitated. You said life was about helping others, and you had spent your whole career doing just that. You said you battled with Moody's and Standard & Poor's when they thought your bank's plan was not viable. You said you had proved them wrong two years in a row, and on the third year, they said, "Mike, you beat us. We admit that you know more about the local market than we do." You claimed that was the best day of your life. Then your bank was sold for a lot of money, and you got a payout that would take care of Mom and you for the rest of your lives. You said that your boss had lost the board, so you had to sell. You would have liked to have avoided the noncompete clause and to have stayed in banking for a few more years, but they wouldn't let you. Just weeks after the deal was done, your boss got cancer and died twelve or so months afterward.

I noted how when you retired, you almost immediately got dementia, only we didn't know it for years to come.

"But what about you and me, Dad?" I asked. "What is the story of *us*?"

That's when you grabbed your chest and said, "I don't think I can do this, Matthew. My brain doesn't work so well anymore. I feel like I'm having a heart attack. I can't answer all of your questions. *I just can't!*"

I immediately turned off the tape recorder and began rubbing your back and telling you to breathe, which you did, sucking in long swigs of air through your mouth and nose.

Then you asked, "Can we go out back and look at the tall tree?"

So I fixed us two bowls of pretzels and grabbed some seltzers out of the fridge. We sat down on your screened-in back porch, under the haint blue ceiling. We munched and sipped and then you said, "Do you see how tall that tree is out there in the distance?"

You had shown me this tree ten billion times before, so—without even looking—I said, "It's *really* tall."

"I can't believe how tall it is," you said.

"Dad, do you remember our walk earlier? You saw that gigantic yellow spider. And you were so impressed with how big it was. And then I asked what your favorite insect is. Do you remember what you said?"

You blinked at me, totally not remembering.

"You said you didn't like any. So I said, 'What about a lightning bug?' And you said, 'Nope.' So I said, 'What about a ladybug?' And you said, 'Oh, whenever I see a ladybug, I pick it up and put it on a leaf so it can get something to eat.' And when you looked at me to see if it was a good answer, I kissed you right on the forehead. *Do you remember that?*"

"You kissed me on the forehead? *Really?*"

"I do it all the time, Dad."

"I don't know about that."

"It's true," I said.

"Oh, wow. Do you see the clouds above the tree? Right over there. That one looks like a lightning bolt! *See it?*"

I tried to follow your outstretched fingers with my eyes, but all I saw above the trees was a puff of white that didn't look like anything at all.

"Do you see the lightning bolt?" you asked with so much hope in your voice. "*Right there.*"

"I do," I lied.

Then—in a much more pensive voice—you asked, "What's that old song about clouds?"

I thought about it, running through all your favorite folk and rock acts from the sixties and seventies, and then said, "'Both Sides Now' by Joni Mitchell? Do you want to listen to it?"

"Maybe," you said.

So I pulled it up on my iPhone and hit play.

Joni strummed her guitar slowly and then began singing about different cloud shapes; and friends turning on you; and ups and downs; and saying I love you proudly. You became still and you got this faraway look in your eyes. Then your lips and tongue began to move almost imperceptibly. When I listened hard, I began to hear the whispers emerging from your mouth. You were trying to sing along, and I believe some deep part of you actually *was*, but you couldn't quite do it in real time. Instead of singing, it began to look as though you were praying. And I noticed that your eyes were welling up. Then I couldn't move if you paid me a billion dollars. I could barely breathe. I just sat there frozen, watching you channel Joni Mitchell, seeing the song purify you in some holy way.

When it was over, I had to look away so you wouldn't see the tears in my eyes. The moment might have been the most human you have ever seemed to me, and I was deeply grateful for it. It felt like I had been in the presence of God, that I had witnessed a miracle.

The next week, they cut down the tall tree you loved so much to build a new house. Mom and I worried that you would be devastated. But you never seemed to notice.

Life's illusions, Joni Mitchell tells us.

9.

Dad, do you remember the first time you came to my Outer Banks home on the Albemarle Sound—the one I bought with my Hollywood money?

This would have been September 2014. Mom and you had rented a beach house in Duck for the week. You brought your mother down. Grandmom was in her nineties. She had lost a son earlier in the year—the son who had first introduced our family to the Outer Banks. Pete.

I cleaned and cleaned before you all arrived. Maybe I was a little too proud of my big new house on the water. I owned a nicer home than anything you had or would ever live in. I had hoped you would do the math and see that my decision to become a writer wasn't so idiotic after all. I had fantasized about your eyes growing huge as you walked up the steps into the grand cathedral-like open space that was the main living area. That when you saw the forty or so feet of windows all lit up with brilliant sunlight and breathtaking water views, you'd be dazzled enough to put your arm around my shoulders, give me a little squeeze, and say, "I had my doubts, Matthew. But you proved me wrong. You sure have done well for yourself."

Mom and Grandmom played their parts. They cooed and cooed when they took in the house and all that water beyond it. But you threw yourself down onto our leather couch, crossed your arms as tightly as you possibly could across your chest, and frowned.

"Are you feeling okay, Dad?" I asked.

You refused to respond.

I think Mom could tell how much this wounded me, because she made a big show of saying, "This house is just *gorgeous*."

"Really something, Matthew," Grandmom said to me. "Your grandfather would have loved this water view."

I could feel your fury rising with each new compliment the women in your life offered me.

Alicia and I gave Mom and Grandmom a tour of all three levels while you stared daggers into my empty fireplace.

Out on our deck, your tiny mother reached up and grabbed both of my cheeks with her little wizened hands. As I stared down into the marvelous maze of wrinkles that was her face at the end, her eyes twinkled behind her glasses, and her facial expression beamed as she said, "You've really done the family proud." Then she kissed me right on the lips before she let go and turned her attention to the huge orange ball falling down through the sky toward the mainland beyond the sound.

"We have to get back to the rental place!" you yelled out from the couch. "I don't want Wally left alone for too long!"

"He's really going to pretend to be worried about the dog?" I said to Mom.

She didn't even try to spin things for you. She just put her arm around me and echoed her earlier sentiments, saying, "This property is absolutely stunning."

Then you were sliding the screen door open and sticking your head out into the early evening air. "Doreen, the dog is home alone. We have to go."

"Mike," Mom said. "Come join us. It's wonderful out here."

"I'll meet you in the car."

You stomped across the hardwood flooring, down the stairs, and out my front door.

"Why does he hate me so much?" I asked Mom.

"He's just tired," she said.

I watched Grandmom standing by the railing. She was staring peacefully at the sunset. She was so calm, she almost seemed holy. And I thought, *What the hell happened to my father when he was a child?*

Once you were all gone, I said to Alicia, "Why do you think my dad acted like an asshole tonight?"

"He *always* acts like an asshole," she said. "The real question is: Why did you think he'd act any differently?"

"I thought now that I *finally* had something impressive to show for all the hard work I've been doing over the last decade, he might . . ."

"He might what?" Alicia asked.

"I don't know," I said. *"Love me?"*

"Your father is a fucking monster," she said. "He's never going to stop abusing you. *Never.*"

Even after that stupendously vile Dad performance, we began inviting Mom and you to have Thanksgivings with us in our new home. We did this a few years in a row. Mom and you would bring your Scottish terrier, Wally, and we'd all take walks on the beach with our Scottish terrier, Desi. We'd order an entire precooked Thanksgiving meal from a little gourmet shop in Duck. On Thanksgiving mornings, you and I would drive north in my much-newer-at-the-time Jeep to pick everything up. And I'd think about how weird it was to spend an hour-long round trip with you, just to procure food. I'd imagine we were like the fathers and sons of old who returned from hunting parties with the day's meat, only we'd provide Alicia and Mom with an entire feast already cooked. And then we'd all eat at the dining room table. Alicia and I would give Mom and you the water view. Next, we'd watch football downstairs on the puffy leather couches by the bar. And I'd slowly get buzzed on beer and whiskey, while you nursed a single glass of white wine over the course of several hours.

I wouldn't say these Thanksgivings were ever huge successes, but as long as I kept drinking through them, Mom, you, and I tended to get by. They were always hard on Alicia, though.

The last time you came for Thanksgiving, Alicia had asked me not to invite you, but I had anyway. Before you had even arrived, I felt guilty about forcing my wife to endure your rudeness through yet another holiday. I don't remember you doing anything worse than you usually did back then. But one morning, I was woken up by a question.

"When is your father leaving?" Alicia asked in a way that let me know the correct answer was "soon."

As I tried to blink away my hangover, I said, "What did he do this time?"

"When I said good morning to your dad in the kitchen, he—once again—completely ignored me," she said. "It was like I was invisible and he was deaf. So I said good morning much louder, but he *still* ignored me. It's just fucking rude. I know he's your dad, but what the fuck?"

"I'll say something to him," I said.

"No. Don't. We have to get through the end of the visit. Maybe I just needed to vent at you."

But I could tell my wife had had enough. It was *our* house. So you, Dad, were going to respect Alicia in it.

I exited our bedroom, crossed through the great room, and then found you looking out the window in the sunroom. You had your cell phone to your ear. I instantly knew you were talking to a banking associate because your voice was pleasant. It was your hey-I'm-a-normal-guy-just-like-you voice, which you never used with me back then. Since you were facing the sound, your back was turned toward me.

"You wouldn't believe how beautiful my son's house is. It's *huge*. I'm looking at the water right now. Million-dollar view. We're having a *fantastic* time here," you said.

I had the urge to start running and tackle you through the glass windows, to power-drive you down into the earth that was a full story below us. My wife, Alicia, has never once been disrespectful to you, and you had intentionally ignored her, humiliating her in her own kitchen. But for some douchebag who had worked for your precious bank, you played Mr. Congenial? And while you had never once told me you liked my house, you bragged about it to a business associate?

"That's right. My son did write *The Silver Linings Playbook*," you said to your friend. "He bought this house with his movie money. I'll send you pictures. You should really see this place."

Fuck you! I screamed in my head, and then I was storming back into our bedroom.

"What did you say to your dad?" Alicia asked.

"Nothing," I said. "But he's never coming here for Thanksgiving ever again."

And it felt like I was being ripped in two. My choices were: Have my father around for the holidays and condone him disrespecting my wife. Or stick up for my wife and never watch another Thanksgiving football game with my dad again. If I tried to speak with you about your behavior, I was pretty sure you would scream at me until I lost my mind and started acting just as crazy as you. And I didn't want to do that either. Any choice I made, I lost. Alicia had kept her mouth shut and put up with your strange ways for decades, but I just couldn't justify her having to feel uncomfortable in her own house during the holidays. Not anymore.

The next summer, with a vomitous knot in my stomach, I called Mom to tell her that I didn't think we were going to be able to host Thanksgiving.

"Oh no," she said. "We *love* having Thanksgiving on the Outer Banks. Did you want to have Thanksgiving here in Pennsylvania?"

"I think Alicia and I are going to have Thanksgiving alone this year."

"Because of your father?"

"I don't really want to talk about this, Mom."

"Matthew, your father loves you."

At the sound of the word "love," I exploded, saying, "Then why is he so rude to Alicia?"

"She intimidates him."

"*Alicia?* She's the least intimidating person on the planet. Everyone gets along with her. *Everyone*."

"I don't know what to tell you."

"Why is Dad the way he is?"

"I told you. *I don't know*."

"Why do you let him get away with it?"

"What do you want me to do? *Divorce him?*"

"It would be nice if he simply said hello to my wife when she says good morning to him in her own house."

"He says good morning to Alicia."

"No, he doesn't. He blatantly ignores her when she speaks to him."

"Maybe he doesn't hear her. Alicia does often speak quietly."

"No one else in the entire world ignores my wife when she says hello. *Only Dad*."

"Your father is peculiar."

"He's obnoxious."

"I can't give you another father, Matthew. This is the only one you have."

"Well, that might be true, but OBX Thanksgivings are over. *Forever*. It's not fair to my wife."

"You want to know the worst part?"

"Enlighten me."

"Each time we leave your wonderful house, every single time we cross that bridge back to the mainland," Mom said, "your father says, 'I had the best time at Matthew and Alicia's.'"

"Mom, there's absolutely no way Dad says that. I would bet my eyes that he didn't say that even one time, let alone always."

"Every single time he leaves your beautiful house."

"Then why is he so weird to Alicia?"

"Your father is a weird guy. *I don't know why.*"

"Well, we're not hosting Thanksgiving."

"And you're not coming here either."

"No, we are not."

"To punish your father."

"Someone has to."

"Well, that's very sad. Because your father really does love you. He might not know how to show it. But he does. I swear to you. Your father loves you."

"He should act like it then."

"He won't always be around, you know. He's not going to live forever."

"On that guilt trip, I say goodbye."

"Matthew, don't you dare hang up on—"

After I hung up the phone, I went down to my bar, poured myself a big glass of the best scotch I had, and then proceeded to get absolutely shit-faced.

10.

Zeus and I were a half year into our analytic relationship when we had our most important conversation about you, Dad.

Although Zeus had said nothing about the black T-shirt I wore to every session, he had wasted no time educating me about my wounded masculinity. He'd assigned multiple Jungian books every week. I first made my way through most of Robert A. Johnson's work, starting with *The Fisher King & The Handless Maiden*. Then we spent a lot of time talking about Parsifal, whose widowed mother tries to keep him out of the world of men. But when the young, sheltered man meets knights for the first time, something ignites in him, and he intuitively knows that he must walk in his dead father's footsteps. When he says goodbye to his mother, she dies of a broken heart. His journey, of course, leads Parsifal to eventually meet the wounded, suffering father in the form of the Fisher King. Johnson suggests that because Parsifal is still wearing the shirt his mother made for him, he is unable to end the wounded king's suffering. As Johnson points out, Parsifal—having failed to take away the Fisher King's pain—must spend the first half of his life doing all the things that knights are tasked to do. It's not until he arrives world-weary at midlife—having long ago taken off the well-worn shirt his mother made for him—that he is given a second chance to ameliorate the Fisher King's misery. Parsifal is now able to end the father's pain, which allows the wounded king to die peacefully.

"What does Parsifal's tale bring up for you?" Zeus asked me via Zoom on a Friday night in early 2021.

"You think I'm midlife Parsifal," I said. "And you think I must end my dad's suffering?"

"You can't cure his dementia."

"But you think I should ease his psychological pain. Like Ray Kinsella in *Field of Dreams*."

"Interesting."

"My father fucked me up when I was a kid. Now I'm supposed to save him as a reward for all the pain and misery he put me through. *Really?*"

"Maybe you are supposed to save yourself. And by rescuing yourself, you will become useful to others—including your father."

"I don't think you understand," I said. "My father was *appalling*. He never once came through for me. He never hugged me when I was a kid. He never even smiled at me. He downloaded all of his worst thoughts and feelings into me. There was violence too. Every big milestone, every single one of my accomplishments—he shit on them all. When I told him that I'd sold my first novel and even had a movie deal, he said, 'You know you have to pay taxes on that money.' Direct quote. Then he said *he* was going to write and publish a book one day. He didn't even congratulate me."

"Sounds like your father is wounded. He's in pain."

"He was an asshole to me."

"Maybe we should take a moment to honor the ways in which your dad actually did come through for you. What are his accomplishments as a father?"

"Are you serious? He didn't do *anything* for me."

"Nothing?"

"Zilch."

"So when you were a baby, you went out and earned the money you needed for food, clothing, and shelter? You paid for your own diapers and bottles?"

"Of course not. But *everyone's* father gives them the bare necessities."

"Not true. Many men have impregnated women and then abandoned them. Plenty of sons have grown up with no fathers at all. Your dad stuck it out. He's still sticking it out."

"Yeah, but he shouldn't get credit for just sticking it out."

"Why?"

"Because that's what fathers are *supposed* to do."

"What are sons supposed to do?"

"Oh, my father was the shittiest son ever."

"Tell me about it."

"He hates his father. Constantly bitches about how his dad didn't love him, didn't support him. My dad is the king of resentment."

"Do you know anyone else who constantly bitches about how his father never loved him? Do you know anyone else who feels resentful toward his father?"

"Okay. So I'm a hypocrite. Noted."

"It was easy for you to love your grandfather because he was good to you, right?"

"Of course."

"Was your grandfather good to your dad?"

"Well," I said, "not according to my father."

"What do you think is the truth?"

"I think Pop Pop was messed up from World War II. And he probably had PTSD."

"That must have been hard for your father. Growing up with a dad suffering from PTSD. And before most people even understood what post-traumatic stress disorder was."

"I know all about PTSD."

"What are you implying?"

"I never knew when my father was going to start screaming or grab me or throw me."

"Are you suggesting your father had PTSD from his childhood?"

"Maybe *I* have PTSD from *my* childhood."

"So you are exactly like your dad."

"What?" I said. "No. I'm *nothing* like him. I chose not to have kids so I wouldn't do to a son what my father did to me. I didn't pass it on."

"Pass what on?"

"I don't know. Misanthropy? Misery? Being an asshole?"

"And yet you're still suffering. And your father is still suffering. You're the same—at least in that way."

I looked away from the laptop screen and stared hard at the wall.

"Why did you love your grandfather so much?" Zeus asked.

"Because he always lit up when he saw me. He'd sing out my name like it was two musical notes. He hugged me."

"He loved you."

"Yeah, he did."

"What would happen if you lit up whenever you saw your dad? What would happen if you sang your father's name like a song? What would happen if you hugged him?"

"He should be doing all that for me."

"But you're not the young inexperienced Parsifal anymore. You're the world-weary middle-aged Parsifal. The shirt your mother made for you disintegrated long ago. You've done all the things knights do in the world. You've saved the fair maiden. You've slayed the dragons. You've proved yourself chivalrous. And yet, you still are in so much pain. And your father, he continues to suffer. What will you do about that?"

"Why is it *my* job to take away my father's suffering? Why shouldn't it be *his* job to take away *my* suffering?"

"Because you're not a little boy anymore."

I swallowed hard here, Dad.

"Now," Zeus said, "what has your father done for you?"

"I don't know. I guess he provided food and shelter and clothing, like you said."

"Pretty important stuff, don't you think? For most of human history a man would be treated like a king just for pulling off that little miracle. Because what would you and your mother have done without those things?"

"I see that, I guess."

"What else?"

"He paid for most of my college education."

"Also pretty extraordinary, considering what college costs."

"But everyone's parents do that."

"Everyone's?"

"Sometimes he gives me money at Christmas."

"That's nice."

"I'd rather have love."

"Some people express love through gift giving."

"I don't know that I believe in all that love language bullshit."

"You think love languages are bullshit?"

"I don't know. But my father mostly provided money. That pretty much covers it. Seriously. I've said everything I can think of. I don't think my father has done anything else for me."

"What about giving you life? Lending his seed so that you might come into this world and experience all that it has to offer."

"Sometimes I wish he hadn't brought me into this world."

"That's because you are sick. And we are trying to get you well. There is a big part of you that wants to be well. I feel it. There is a big part of you that wants to love and be loved. It's all over the pages of your novels."

"You read my novels?"

"That surprises you?"

"Yeah. It actually does."

"I told you during the first session. I love you."

"I really don't like when you say that."

"That is glaringly apparent."

"Then why do you keep saying it?"

"Because you need to hear it."

I looked away again here, holding back tears. We Quick men don't have too much practice with "I love you."

"Listen to me," Zeus said. "If you hate your father, you will always hate yourself. Your father is in you. And your father's father is in you. And all of his many fathers—all the way to the beginning of time—all of them are in you. In your DNA. But, also, *in you.* There is an army of men inside of you. And they all want to cheer for you. Because when you get to experience love in the world, they get to experience love once again *through you.* And when you accomplish something, they get to accomplish something *through you.* You are their redemption. You are their great hope. You are what keeps them alive."

"So when I fuck my wife, do they get to fuck my wife?" I said, like an asshole.

"*Yes,*" Zeus said.

"Well, that's not creepy, is it?"

"It isn't literal. *It's a metaphor.* And you really have to work on your ability to think symbolically."

"Why?"

"Because literal thinking is making you sicker than you have to be."

"So how do I harness the power of this so-called army of fathers who live inside of me?"

"You can start by doing an active imagination this week, because we are almost out of time. Find a quiet spot, close your eyes, drop down, and ask the unconscious to show you what you need to see. Ask the fathers in you for help. Speak to them. Write it all down and we'll talk about it next session."

I left that video call thinking everything my analyst had said was total bullshit. I had no intention of doing the assigned active imagination. To be honest, a big part of me wanted to continue being resentful and to see you suffer more, even if it meant I had to continue suffering too. I didn't believe that you and I were even remotely the same, despite half of my DNA being yours. I really thought I could afford to hate 50 percent of myself for the rest of my life. I didn't see much value in redeeming the father. I wasn't Parsifal and you weren't the Fisher King. That was just a bygone fairy tale.

Or was it?

That week, I thought a lot about Terry Gilliam's film *The Fisher King*, starring Robin Williams and Jeff Bridges. I'm pretty sure I saw it in the theater back in 1991. I'd definitely watched it multiple times since. I, of course, understood that it was a modern-day take on the Grail myth, but—while I had loved the film—I hadn't ever before bothered to do any deep digging into the source material. And I began to realize that there was a world of myth and symbols and metaphors woven through our everyday surroundings, hiding in plain sight. How many people who had seen Gilliam's *The Fisher King* had bothered to ever read Parsifal's tale? What other bits of ancient wisdom were out there hiding in pop culture? Why had these particular stories survived? Why did they continue to resurface in modern times? Why did so few people take notice?

The night before my next session with Zeus, I took a bath. I don't usually take baths. But in our Outer Banks house, we had a deep soaking tub with jets in it so that you could get a little massage. Alicia used this tub almost every day. She was always trying to get me to use it too, saying it would relax me. So—under the ruse of needing relaxation—I ran the hot water, lit the candles that Alicia kept around the tub, poured in some Epsom salt, turned off the lights, and then lowered myself into the water. This might have been the first time I had ever used the soaking tub in the seven years we had owned it. When the water line rose high enough to cover all the little jet holes, I hit the button that made the water massage my body. I don't know why I was surprised to find that it was relaxing—Alicia had previously extolled the benefits of a good soak a billion times—but I was amazed anyway.

As the heat transferred from the water to my flesh and then sank into my muscles below, I thought about how nice it would be to see Pop Pop and Uncle Pete again, if only in my imagination. Then I was closing my eyes and trying to sink down into the unconscious like Zeus had taught me so that I could do the assigned active imagination. As I concentrated on my breath and my heartbeat, I began to see the color red. Then I was talking to the color red, asking it to put me in contact with the fathers who lived within me, who were in my DNA. "Please," I said to my unconscious and maybe even *the* unconscious, "I need to speak with my many grandfathers. I seek the Grail. I wish to end my father's suffering and my own."

And then I was descending through clouds, moving down into an ancient seafaring world that looked like some mysterious amalgam of Germanic and Celtic and other cultures I couldn't guess. Gathered by the shoreline was an army of men—just like Zeus had promised—only they were unarmed. A few held their faces in their hands. Some nervously raked their fingers through their long beards. Many were staring up into the heavens. Others were staring at their boots. It was like they were all in limbo. As I prepared for my landing on the beach in front of them, not a single one paid me the slightest bit of attention whatsoever. But—left and right—there were men as far as the eye could see. When my feet hit the sand, the sea was at my back. I was between the great army and the water.

"Hey! I'm Matthew!" I yelled, feeling rather foolish. "You live in me! You are in my DNA!"

None of them looked up. A few yawned. One lifted a leg and let out a thunderous fart.

"I'm looking for my grandfather," I continued. "Harry Quick. He died in 2012. *Please.* I need to speak with Pop Pop. And, if possible, my Uncle Pete who died in 2014. My father is sick. *I am sick.* I need your help. *I beg of you.*"

A few men in the army began to murmur to each other. I realized that they were speaking languages that I didn't know, passing some message down the line, left and right. I wondered how long ago these men had walked the Earth. Could it be that a few were from the time of Christ? Were others from even earlier centuries?

Like the tail of a giant snake, the right side of the army began to wiggle. I didn't know what was happening at first. Then I understood that men were stepping aside so that something could pass through. Somebody was fighting his way toward me.

It took a long time for this man to traverse the tail of the great army. When he emerged from the horde in front of me, I saw that it was not one man but two.

"Pop Pop!" I cried out. *"And Uncle Pete!"*

I ran toward them and threw my arms around their heads, pulling them in close so that I could feel the whiskers of their cheeks against my own.

"You remembered us," Pop Pop said, as I released them from my hug. "You didn't forget your family."

"Told you," Pete said to Pop Pop. "Pretty boy's down for the mission."

"How could I ever forget either of you?" I said.

"It's been a while," Pop Pop said.

"Your father never comes to see us," Pete said.

"Uncle Pete," I said, "how are you inside of me? You aren't my biological father."

"We share DNA, genius. And did I not look out for your dumb fuckin' ass while I was alive?"

"My analyst says I need to get this army of fathers to help me," I said.

"Your analyst?" Pop Pop said, making a funny face.

"Dad and I are sick," I said. "We need help."

"If you're sick, we're sick," Pete said. Then he held his arms out toward the great army. "Fuckin' all of us."

"Can you talk to these men for me?" I asked.

"Doesn't work like that," Pop Pop said, shaking his head.

"How does it work?" I asked.

"You're the goddamn general," Pete said. "You have to command."

"How?"

"Just give them something worthy to do," Pop Pop said. "That's what all men need. Give them that, and I think the rest will follow naturally."

"What's a worthy task?" I asked.

But the great army of men had begun to reabsorb them.

"Wait!" I yelled. *"I need you!"*

"Give us a worthy task!" Pop Pop yelled back, right before he completely disappeared back into the giant snake of forefathers.

"Hello!" I yelled. "Can anyone help me?"

The army stood slouched and unhearing.

"I'm in so much pain!" I screamed.

Not a single member of the army turned his head toward me.

"My father's dying! We're running out of time! And we must do something! *Your sons need saving!*"

All of the men in the great army turned and faced me. Then I was somehow making eye contact with thousands of men all at once. I saw hunger in their eyes. I saw hope. I saw pain. I saw understanding. But most of all, I saw a monumental need to be useful. To be given a target. To be deployed in service of something worthy.

"I don't know exactly what needs to be done, but I'm pretty sure I have to make peace with my father before he dies. And I suspect that I need to heal myself so that I might be useful to others again. I'm done with drinking. I'm taking care of our body now. I'm working on my mental health. And I think there might be other hurting men out there who also need help. Men like my father. Men who have been abused. And even men who have done the abusing. So many men need help. And I think that down the road—if we fight with wisdom and integrity and passion—*we* might be the force that helps them. I believe that with your help, we can radically ease the suffering of many men. And if we do that, we will improve the lives of even more women and children. People like my mother and wife and sister and nieces and nephews. *Does that not sound like a worthy task to you?*"

In my active imagination, after having spent almost all of what little I had left in the tank, I saw the entire army's shiny eyes scanning me, searching for a reason to disbelieve, and I worried that they might.

So I told them, "I don't want to feel suicidal anymore. I want to live. I want to make the lives of others better. My analyst says I have to forgive and love my father so that I can forgive and love myself. That his DNA is our DNA. That we are all the same. Can you help me redeem my father? Can you help me redeem myself? Can you help me finally leave behind boyhood and become an adult? Will you initiate me into manhood? Please fathers. *Please help me.* So that I might be able to help others."

For a long moment, the army just stared at me.

Then someone far away yelled, "Ah-*tennnnnnnnnnnn*-chun!"

All of the men straightened up their spines and became stiff as boards.

"Turn!"

The entire army pivoted and faced the horizon to my left.

"Forwaaaaaaaaaaard *march*!"

All of the men began moving in unison. Their steps made the ground shake. It felt like an earthquake. Endless fathers passed before my eyes. Then I saw Pop Pop and Pete marching. As they passed, your father and brother turned their heads and gave me stiff salutes.

And when I opened my eyes again, the tub jets were off and the bath water was cold. In the flicker of candlelight, I reoriented myself back into this world. I swallowed and felt a lump in my throat. I started missing Pop Pop and Pete again so much, but then I said, "They're inside of me. In the giant army of fathers," which made me feel 100 percent backed by a mighty force and ready for whatever might come.

It was an unfamiliar, good feeling. To be backed. To be supported. And I thought, *I wish I could give this to my father too. I wish I could give it to my brother. I wish I could give it to all of my male friends. To men everywhere.*

I got out of the water. I dried off, dressed, and made my way into the bedroom, where Alicia was under the covers reading a book. Desi the Scottie was snuggling with her.

"You were in the tub for a really long time," Alicia said. "What were you doing?"

Somehow I knew that what I had seen was not to be shared—not yet, anyway.

"Just thinking," I said.

"S and T," Alicia said.

"What?"

"Soaking and thinking."

"Something like that."

And then, quick as it had come—once I was squarely back in the physical world—the feeling of ten thousand fathers moving with purpose through me like an awe-inspiring giant snake of soldiers was gone.

11.

On a warm October day in 2024, I tried to drive over the historic bridge that connects Lady's Island with downtown Beaufort, but the middle section was swung open so that a tall ship could pass through. As I sat stuck on the wrong side of the river, I texted Uncle Jon, telling him the situation.

He texted back saying he could see that the bridge was open from where he was standing and would wait for me down by the river.

At the back of a long line of stopped vehicles—as I impatiently waited for a ship that I couldn't see to pass through the middle of the bridge I needed to cross—I thought about how, for much of your life, you hated your younger brother, Jon. If hate is too strong of a word, Dad, I feel confident at least saying you were perennially angry with him. I never really understood why. Uncle Jon always seemed pretty innocuous to me. He'd hang in the background of our family gatherings. He'd sit half hidden behind the spindles of the staircase while everyone opened presents on Christmas morning at your parents' house. He cheered on the unwrapping of every single gift. Uncle Jon always smiled whenever anyone looked at him. And his laugh sounded like a series of high-pitched grunts that a ticklish Muppet might emit. I found everything about Uncle Jon to be exceedingly benign. When I got older, I sometimes ran into him on the PATCO trains to Philly, or I'd see him standing on a city sidewalk. Every once in a while, I'd accidentally catch him smoking a cigarette, which he would immediately ditch down a street drain or behind a bench. Then we'd both pretend that he didn't smell like tobacco smoke. "*Matthew!*" he'd exclaim. "How are you?"

You were convinced that your younger brother was in cahoots with your older brother, Peter. And Jon did do a lot of computer-related work for Pete, helping him—as a trader of stocks—make the transition from pencil and paper to keyboard and screen, back before everyone was on the internet. Jon used to go to Nags Head with Pete too and help him with his rental properties. I'd never heard Jon say a single bad word about you, but with all the paranoid propaganda you yelled into my ears over the years, I kind of bought that he actually was on team Uncle Pete, which I assumed meant that he probably also hated your guts but just did so behind my back.

For a time in my mid-thirties, Alicia and I started hanging out with Jon's middle daughter, Sarah. When Sarah and I began trading stories about the family, a different picture emerged—one of miscommunication and misunderstandings. We didn't really know what to do with any of that, but it made us sad.

After Pop Pop and Pete died, Jon and you had to look after your mother. She was living in a retirement home and was almost out of money. I'm not entirely sure what went down, but I believe Jon and you had different ideas about who should be in control of what. You had a lot more money than your younger brother had, so you could easily give Grandmom things that he couldn't. He had been tasked with keeping track of her finances, which were not in great shape, so he had her on a budget. And, in this way, I suspect Jon and you—and your wives—were working at cross-purposes.

I used to call it The Battle for Grandmom.

When your mother died, you and Jon apparently had a few productive talks, and some healing began. You golfed together once or twice. I think you exchanged birthday and Christmas gifts for the first time in years. There were also semi-regular, albeit brief, phone calls.

But it wasn't until the extent of your dementia was made known that Jon decided to really let bygones be bygones and began making what I consider a truly heroic effort to bury the hatchet forever. He started driving to South Carolina from New Jersey once every season, just to sit with you and take you to play golf and have a few meals. To be honest, Dad, you are still stiff with Jon. And you never say all that much to him. I often have to prompt you to give him a hug when he leaves. When I take pictures of you two, I have to remind you to smile, which is strange because you now talk about loving him all the time when he isn't here. When we take walks together, you often say, "I miss my brother Jon. Should we call him later?" But when we do call him, you say little. Some might argue that you are just not a talkative man, but you routinely talk at me for two hours straight on our walks together.

The tall ship passed and the bridge put itself back together again. Then I was cruising into downtown Beaufort. After I parked, I jogged the two blocks to Bay Street, where I found Jon sitting at one of the iron tables in front of Hearth, the wood-fired pizza place that your grandchildren love so much.

"Sorry I'm late," I said. "You never know when the bridge will be out. Part of the charm of this place."

Uncle Jon waved off my apology as he stood.

I noticed that he smelled of cigarettes, even though he'd still never light up in front of me. I wouldn't mind if he did. But for some reason, I'd just never previously said so.

We went to Superior Coffee. Inside, I was surprised to hear Uncle Jon speak to the young cashier like she would actually be interested in the minutiae of his and my lives, which reminded me so much of Pop Pop.

"Well, how are you today?" he greeted her. "I hope you'll make us drinks and take care of us. I came all the way from New Jersey to speak with my nephew, Matthew, here."

The young woman behind the cash register smiled politely but seemed too shy to respond, so Uncle Jon and I just read the menu boards. I ordered some sort of fruit smoothie, and he got an iced tea. There were no other customers, so our drinks came in record time. Then we were sitting at one of the tables out back and looking at the river, as a cool breeze blew through our shorts and T-shirts.

"You know," I said, "I might write this scene into the memoir."

Uncle Jon smiled and then said, "You can write whatever you want in your memoir. If anything I say helps, then good. Put it in."

"I really admire your making such an effort with my father. You've kind of been a role model for me, as I work on forgiving Dad myself."

"I always liked how close you were with my parents, Matthew. You were good to them and they loved you. And it's good that you are here now helping your mother."

"Why do you think you and my father were at odds for so many years?"

"What was that? I can't hear so well sometimes."

"WHY DO YOU THINK YOU AND MY FATHER WERE AT ODDS FOR SO MANY YEARS?"

"Oh," Jon said. "You know at some point, I kind of just tuned everything out. It was like I was seated at the top of a stadium and the rest of the family was on the football field below. And everyone but me was playing a game of football. Sometimes I would look down at the field and say, 'That was an interesting play,' but then I would turn my head away from the action and not pay too much attention. I didn't want to play in the family football game. After a while, I didn't really want to watch it either."

"Why not?"

"You know, I can't really remember much about the past. I think I've blocked it all out."

"Was your childhood *that* bad?"

"I can't really tell you."

"That makes me think it was horrific."

"Maybe."

"Is it that you just don't want to talk about it?"

"I'd tell you if I remembered."

"Do you remember living on Lawnside Alley? My father talks about how hard it was for him to move away from that street."

"I don't really remember much about it. I was younger than your dad. But I liked living on Park Ave. In the winter, there would be these spots in the park that would flood and then freeze. We would ice skate."

"What was my father like as a child?"

"Again, I don't know. He was three years older than me. I really don't remember so much from those times."

"You were up at the top of the football stadium not paying attention?"

"That was later. When I was an adult."

"Then why don't you remember?"

"It was a different time."

"Your father was hard on you?"

"Yeah, probably."

"I heard that you had ear infections as a kid, and your parents maybe didn't get you proper medical attention."

"Again, that was so long ago."

"Did you have a happy childhood?"

"I think my parents did the best they could."

"But your dad taught you how to play golf, right?"

"He did."

"Because you didn't want to play football?"

"I like golf. It's a good game."

"Was it considered less cool to be a golfer than a football player? Football seemed to be a big part of my father's high school identity."

"I just was a golfer."

"Did you like playing golf with Pop Pop?"

"I've always liked golf."

That was pretty much all I got out of Uncle Jon when it came to his childhood, which made me think growing up the son of your World War II–veteran dad was even worse than I had previously imagined. Someone who came of age in a happy, loving home would not have had the need to block out so many memories. You too, Dad, have always been selectively vague about your childhood.

I asked Uncle Jon a lot about his career. Turns out he was in charge of the computer system of a bank. He liked working with his teammates and smiled ear to ear when talking about them. He liked traveling to other states to train new teams. He loved problem-solving. He often worked long hours and brought his work home with him. I got the sense that he had worked every bit as hard as you did, but in a less-lucrative, behind-the-scenes sector of banking. He seemed proud of the good work he had done, but I never got the impression that his work defined him, like your work defines your sense of yourself—still to this very day. He seemed free of all that somehow.

Whenever he talked about his daughters and grandchildren, that's when I loved Uncle Jon most. He is unabashedly in love with his kids. He smiled and laughed when he told stories about babysitting the grandchildren and their dogs. And he lit up brighter than his phone screen when he showed me pictures. He worried about the future of the country, not for himself but for his grandkids. And his concern and affection for those children felt more genuine than anything else we were experiencing that day. Something came alive in him when he talked about his offspring. He wasn't like most old people who want to brag and show off. Uncle Jon's genuine love for his daughters and grandkids brought tears to my eyes. I wanted to drink it up all day long.

"So how is the memoir writing going?" he asked me, which was nice. You, Dad, have almost never asked me about my work.

I told him the writing was going slowly—because it was at the time—and that part of me was terrified of publishing such intimate material, especially what we'll get to at the end of this memoir.

"I really enjoy reading your Substack posts," he said.

I thanked him for his support because he had been a paying subscriber, back when I was still selling subscriptions.

Then he said, "I think everyone has a God-given talent. And everyone's job in life is to find out what that talent is and then do that thing. Your talent is clearly writing, and you're doing it. That's good." Then he went on to list what he thought his three daughters' God-given talents were—with enough pride and love to make me feel a little jealous—before he circled back and said, "Matthew, you need to keep writing. And what you are doing for your parents, it's special."

"I'm mostly doing it for me," I said. "To heal my father issues."

"Okay. But it's good for your mom and dad too," Jon said. *"Very good."*

I looked to our left and saw a flock of nuns in full black-and-white habits. They all had on oversized gold crucifixes. They were skipping and singing and acting a little drunk as they headed our way. When a few caped and masked superheroes linked arms with the nuns and then began kissing them, I remembered it was Halloween.

"Do you think metaphorically sitting at the top of the stadium while the family played football down below was a form of dissociation?" I asked Uncle Jon. "Did you do that to block out the pain? Do you think growing up in your parents' house was so bad that you had to go somewhere else in your mind? Because my dad was pretty hard on me when I was young. He often got a little crazy. I think I dissociated. *A lot.* And I'm only beginning to realize that my father might have been unconsciously re-creating the exact same horror show that you and Dad and Pete had experienced."

"Maybe," Uncle Jon said. "I go to church now. I do service. I collect unsold food from restaurants for people in need. I do what I can to help. I don't think about the past, and I've tried hard to make peace with your father."

"You driving down here so often really is impressive," I said.

"We're family."

"Do you remember your parents calling my dad Michelle?"

"I don't know."

"You didn't like being called Po' Jon, did you?"

"No. I did not."

"Why do you think your parents called you that?"

"I was at the top of the stadium," he said. "I really wasn't paying much attention to what was happening on the field."

"It's nice to sit with you," I said.

"It's beautiful here in Beaufort," he said. "I hope my girls get to see it someday soon. It would be good to get the families together."

"Like old times."

He nodded.

When we finished our drinks, we walked a little along the waterfront, past the many bench swings and the marina full of docked sailboats.

Then Uncle Jon said he wanted to get some rest before he came to my house later for Alicia's home-cooked fish tacos and a pie we bought from the store. Since it was October 31, we were celebrating Mom's birthday.

It was strange to think that in the first decade after Pop Pop died,

I'd hardly seen Uncle Jon at all. Before you were diagnosed with dementia, I had never previously had afternoon tea with Uncle Jon even once. We'd never before in our entire lives had a conversation that lasted for more than five minutes. But there I was in downtown Beaufort giving him a big hug, after chatting with him for more than an hour. It kind of felt like a miracle. And I realized that he and I had been missing out—for more than fifty years—on the goodness of the uncle-nephew relationship. So I swore I would do my best to keep in touch with Uncle Jon from then on. And we've been writing letters to each other ever since. I tell him all about our adventures together here in Beaufort. He writes about his daughters and his beloved grandchildren. He lets me know that he is looking forward to the vacations he plans with Aunt Alice. He tells me about interesting weather patterns that are headed his way and ours. But I think the most important thing is that he keeps writing. He keeps visiting. He keeps showing up in the ways that he can.

As he makes his efforts to love you as much as possible before your brain is totally gone, I can feel the overwhelming decency in it. And it restores my faith in men. Because you often were not great to Jon, Dad. For many years, you hardly spoke to him at all. You did not take an interest in his children. You were often furious with him because you thought he was siding with Pete. You created dark narratives about him for your entire life. You did not appreciate all that he tried to do for Grandmom at the end of her life.

You used to call him Po' Jon too. All the time.

And yet he drives the twenty-some hours round trip to see you. He shows up. He takes you golfing. He reads your son's work. He loves you in the best ways he knows how. Lately, he's been ending his letters to me with these words: "You are loved, Matthew."

So I try to learn from my good uncle's example. He's no longer sitting at the top of the metaphorical football stadium. After a half century, he finally walked down all those steps, climbed over the railing that separates the fans from the players, and put himself in the game. He's on the field with us now. After all these years. That's really a hell of a thing, Dad.

Some might even call it love.

12.

After months and months of donning black, I decided to wear a mint-colored T-shirt to analysis, thinking Zeus would surely notice the drastic change and comment on it, which I thought would *finally* lead us into a frank and in-depth discussion about my occasional thoughts of suicide.

As I sat at my desk waiting for my analyst to start the session, the pointy ends of my shit-eating grin were practically piercing my earlobes. But when Zeus's face appeared on my laptop screen, my wardrobe change didn't make his eyes grow wide, or his mouth hang open, or his head do a double take. Instead, he said—with what sounded like disappointment—"I've read your piece about the shelf-falling incident."

In the childhood bedroom that I shared with Micah in our old Oaklyn house, back in the eighties and early nineties, there was a wooden shelf hung four or five feet over the headboard of my twin bed. Over the years, I'd loaded it up with all sorts of things: a dozen or so hardback novels, framed pictures of girlfriends, a Dominique Wilkins Starting Lineup action figure, various small trinkets. But the most dangerous thing up there—looking back now—was a cast-iron, coin-operated dispenser with a glass fishbowl full of different colored gumballs. When I was maybe seventeen, the shelf collapsed in the middle of the night, and its contents rained down on my head. I had been sound asleep, and then it felt like someone was punching the side of my face over and over. I had no idea what was happening, and for a few seconds, I couldn't move or breathe. When it was over,

I tried to speak, but I couldn't. I was frozen. A second or two later, I started screaming and I couldn't stop. Our two-story house was less than fourteen hundred square feet, and Micah's and my bedroom shared a wall with yours, so you heard me loud and clear. While I was still shrieking, you ran into our room and flicked on the lights. You looked annoyed, which made me feel ashamed. I wanted to stop screaming, but I just couldn't. When you saw the fallen plank of wood and its former contents littered around my mattress, you shook your head and matter-of-factly said, "It was only the shelf." I realized that I was no longer in any danger, but I *still* couldn't quiet my terror. "You're fine. Stop yelling," you said, and then went back to bed. That's when I saw the gumball machine. It had landed on my pillow where my head should have been. I must have rolled over in the middle of the night. I stopped screaming and picked up the dispenser. It was weighty. I felt its cold metal base in my hands and thought, *This could have killed me.*

When I first told Zeus that story, I said, "I remember my father coming into my room, but then I don't remember anyone else checking to see if I was okay. And Dad mostly seemed mad about being woken up, probably because he had to go to work in the morning. I could have been maimed or worse, and no one seemed to care, which maybe made me care a little less too." That instantly gave Zeus a big, old Jungian-analyst hard-on. He was sure that I had subconsciously blocked out details about the shelf-crashing incident and that delving deeper into this particular memory would put me back in touch with the very childhood traumas that I had spent so many years drinking away. He saw this particular memory as the first crouton of a psychological breadcrumb trail.

After reminding me that memory is notoriously unreliable, Zeus had me interview Mom, you, Megan, and Micah about that night. Megan—who would have been fourteen or fifteen at the time—said she vaguely remembered it but couldn't say anything more. Mom said, "I ran into your bedroom right behind your father. You weren't hurt. We all just went back to bed." When I asked my brother what he remembered, Micah claimed he had checked on and comforted me. He would have been nine or ten at the time. He said he put one hand on my left shoulder and his other on my right forearm, and as I was screaming, he kept telling me that I was okay. I have no memory of my little brother even waking up, which would have been insane, as he was only sleeping six feet away from me in the other twin bed, and I had been yelling loud enough to wake up the entire town of Oaklyn. You said you didn't remember the night at all, which wasn't surprising.

I had told all of the above to Zeus in the previous session, which made him more excited than anything I had said before. "I really, *really* think you need to go deeper into this memory," Zeus had said. "As an INFJ on the Myers-Briggs, you will instinctively want to use your feeling function rather than the sensate function. But rather than tell me how you *feel* about all that happened that night and assigning value to it, I want you to use your five senses to *describe* everything in as much detail as possible. Put yourself back in the middle of that memory. What are the walls, floor, and ceiling of your childhood bedroom made out of? Describe your bedsheets. Had they been washed recently? Were they stiff with dried sweat? How does the room smell? What can you see? What can you taste? Describe the sound of your wailing in great detail. Meticulously describe all of the objects that fell. How exactly did the crash sound? Was it one crash or a series of crashes? Which objects hurt more when they hit your head? Document as much sensory information as you can. Describe every detail you can remember with as many words as possible. Use thousands. Exhaust yourself. Unload. *Purge.*"

"That's not how I write," I had said.

"This isn't for publication."

"Yeah, but I write how I write," I had noted and was surprised by my defensiveness, but I couldn't bring myself to dial it down. Next, I heard myself saying, "If you start messing with my writing process, you're going to fuck up my career."

"Only, you *aren't* writing. You've been blocked for years. And you yourself have been telling me that your career is already 'fucked up.' Isn't that why you entered into analysis in the first place?"

"I don't see where this sensory stuff is going, how this is helpful."

"Trust me."

After that previous session, I ultimately swallowed my pride and did the assignment—albeit half-heartedly.

"So," I said to Zeus in the session to which I wore the mint-colored T-shirt, "how did I do with the sensory details?"

Zeus frowned and said, "You only wrote a few paragraphs."

"How many were you hoping for?"

"I think you should write pages on that night. Fill an entire notebook if you can. You have to reintegrate—"

"I'm not fucking doing any more of this bullshit. Okay? Forget it. I write how I write. I can't write any other way."

"I really think that—"

"What books have *you* published? What makes *you* the authority on writing?"

"Matthew—"

"I'm paying *you*, okay? You're supposed to be doing what I need you to do. Not the other way around."

Just as soon as the words were out of my mouth, I regretted saying them.

Zeus lowered his chin here, leaned forward, stared deep into my eyes, and said, "I find that last comment . . . *distasteful*."

The ensuing silence was so loud, my ears started ringing.

Even as the words were coming out of my mouth, I was ashamed of the spear-like sentences I'd been hurling at Zeus. The word "distasteful" cut through me like a chainsaw. *I found myself distasteful.* That was the entire problem—why I was here with Zeus in the first place.

"I'm not a prostitute," he said to me. "I'm your analyst. I have many years of experience. You pay me to help you, which I am trying very hard to do."

"I'm sorry," I said, but the words somehow sounded more like *fuck you.*

My fists were clenched off-screen. My knee was going up and down. I was gritting my teeth so hard it felt like they all might explode into clouds of dust at any moment. I was furious, but I didn't know *at whom*. Was I mad at Zeus? Was I mad at myself?

"Why don't we try orally discussing what your senses picked up the night the bookshelf fell? Would that be—"

"I don't want to do that."

"Why?"

"I just don't."

"Maybe you don't *feel* ready to go there, but—"

"My shelf fell down. That's all that happened. End of story."

"It's symbolic. And there's a reason why it's so charged for you."

"I'm done analyzing the shelf incident."

"I think that's a mistake."

When I didn't say anything in response, Zeus observed me for a long moment. Then he said, "Okay, have it your way. But at some point, you're going to have to write in depth about your trauma—things much worse than that shelf falling on you in the middle of the night. Essential parts of your soul were torn off in your childhood. You need to sew them back on. *Eventually.* You're not ready now. Okay. I can be a patient man. But my sense is that you would rather not continue to be in pain for the rest of your life. Doing the healing work hurts too. I wish it weren't so, but it is. Matthew, you *will* have to endure new temporary pain to get rid of the horrors you've been carrying around for decades."

I said, "Okay. Moving on. What's next?"

We stared at each other for a moment.

When Zeus started talking again, the only thing I could hear was my own bitter internal monologue, saying, *What kind of mental health professional doesn't pay attention to clothing? Why doesn't he care about my mint-colored T-shirt? I've worn black to every single previous session. Even the least observant shrink in the world would have commented on it. What the fuck?*

And then I started wondering if Jungian analysis was all it was cracked up to be.

13.

Dad, the first time I allowed myself to believe that you might actually be a feeling, caring, human being with a soul, I was forty-five years old and just a few months sober.

Alicia and I were visiting you and Mom at your town house in Ambler, Pennsylvania. This was the fall of 2018. You were retired, so I was no longer competing with the banking industry for your attention.

You and I were ambling through Ambler, which was nothing new. We'd been taking long walks together for many years. Other than riding subway cars home from Philadelphia Eagles games, strolling was pretty much the only thing you and I ever did together. Our walks were usually just me listening to you rant about all of the problems in your life. But on this one, you were different. *Suspiciously different.* You were happy.

"Dad," I said. "You're in a good mood. *I love it.*"

"Well, I like living in Ambler. They have this great historic theater."

"I know," I said. "I did a book event there once. You saw me speak onstage, right where the screen usually hangs. We've seen a few films there together. *Remember?*"

"Okay," you said. "But there's this movie playing that you and Alicia need to see. It's called *The Writer*. And it's very good. We should go see it together."

"But you saw it already," I said, as we turned onto the main street, where the Ambler Theater looms like a cathedral that time forgot.

"Your mother and I saw it," you said. "And—right when the movie ended—I told her, 'I'm going to take Matthew and Alicia to see this. Because it's about a writer.'"

"And we're writers," I said.

"You're going to love this one," you said. "I'm telling you. It's very good. Your kind of movie. And Alicia's kind too."

"What kind is that, Dad?"

"The good kind. Smart films. You know. The kind you like."

"Okay," I said.

"Can I take you to see it tonight?" you asked. "I'll pay for the tickets. Your mother and I are members of the theater, so I think we get a discount. I can use that to get you and Alicia in for half price too. But you won't have to pay a penny, because it will be my treat."

"Sounds good," I said.

As we continued our walk, you kept going on and on about how terrific the film was and how much we would enjoy it. I didn't mind, mostly because I had never before seen you this enthusiastic about sharing something with me. A very young part of me was delighted. Previously, you had often been grumpy about giving. There was this one Christmas where you signed "The Paycheck" instead of your name on the tags you attached to the few gifts you gave Mom, which were the only ones you bought, as Mom did all the shopping for us kids. But here you were now wanting to gift Alicia and me a fun trip to the movies. And you seemed overjoyed about it.

When we were close to your town house, you stopped walking, pointed up at the sky, and said, "Wow. *Look at that.*"

I tilted my head back, but I didn't see anything, so I said, "What do you see, Dad?"

"That cloud looks like *a lion.*"

Your voice had changed.

You sounded like a little boy.

The cloud you were pointing at looked nothing like a lion. It looked more like dried mayonnaise smeared across a diner countertop.

"It's *amazing*," you declared.

I laughed. I had never seen you like this. I wondered if you were on some sort of new medication. I thought about it and decided that I had never once before witnessed you experiencing bliss before. I'd seen you clap when the Eagles won a football game. I'd heard you cheer at the movies when Steven Seagal kicked some bad guy in the nuts. But when you were just talking with your eldest son, you had never previously seemed jolly. Not even once. I honestly didn't know how to respond.

"Do you see it?" you asked. "The lion?"

"Yes," I lied. Then I boldly put my arm around your shoulders.

My heart was pounding. I half expected you to hit me. I was waiting for you to start screaming. We were definitely in new territory here, Dad.

But when I squeezed a sideways man-hug out of you, you didn't flinch or punch my ribs or shove me away or tell me not to touch you—and that's when some intuitive part of me started to wonder if there was something seriously wrong with you. You had never acted this way before.

We went to the Ambler Theater later that night, where I discovered that the film is called *The Wife*, not *The Writer*. It's based on a novel written by Meg Wolitzer.

"Dad," I said, "I actually know the woman who wrote this story."

"It's a good movie," you kept saying. "I'm telling you."

"I hung out with Meg for an entire week in the Philippines," I said. "We headlined a literary festival together in Manila."

"You are going to love this one," you kept saying.

You insisted on buying Alicia and me tea and chocolate at the concession stand, which made my wife raise her eyebrows at me.

When you were busy paying the bill, she whispered to me, "Who is this stranger buying us gourmet movie snacks?"

I shrugged and made a funny face.

Then we shared a laugh, before you walked up to us and said, "You're *really* going to love this movie. I can't wait for you to see it."

You were acting like this was the best day of your life. Alicia and I were baffled, but we were enjoying every second of it.

As we all began to watch the film, I was reminded that it's about a *fraudulent* writer, whose wife is actually writing the novels that have made him a literary star. A dark part of me began to uncomfortably wonder if you were making a subtle accusation by taking me to see a movie about a man whose literary success is a sham. *Was tonight some sort of fatherly Trojan horse?* I did my best to push that question down into the dark unconscious place where I store all the things that are too painful to deal with in real time.

But when the film ended and the lights came up, I couldn't resist asking why you wanted me to see this particular film.

"Because it's about a writer," you said. "It's called *The Writer*."

"I think it's called *The Wife*."

"No," you said. "It's called *The Writer*."

Alicia and I traded a glance.

As we walked out of the theater and into the lobby, you asked my wife what she had thought of "*The Writer*." I could tell Alicia was also a little curious about why you had brought us to see this particular film, but with sparkling diplomacy, she said she had enjoyed "*The Writer*" quite a bit and then thanked you for taking us.

"You're welcome," you said. "I knew you two would like it. *I just knew it*."

Alicia and I made eye contact again here, mostly because you had spent the majority of the previous twenty-five years completely ignoring her. The inquiry about "*The Writer*" might have been the first question you had ever asked her. You had spent entire meals without even once turning your face toward her. I don't think she had even ever previously heard you say her name.

Could it be that retirement was bringing out the best in Dad? I wondered.

I had only known Pop Pop in his retirement. You'd always told me that your father had been a total bastard when he was working as a banker—never a bastard at work, but at home when the doors were closed. But then he quit banking and mellowed out. By the time I was born, Pop Pop was ready to love his grandkids. He was ready to do some atoning. And, as we made our way out of the theater, I was hoping that you were ready to do some atoning too.

As we emerged onto the street from under the marquee, you turned toward my wife and said, "Alicia, what did you think about the movie *The Writer*?"

She looked at me, unsure of what to say.

"Dad," I said, "she just told you what she thought. Like five seconds ago."

"She did?" you said. "Well, you liked it, right, Alicia? *The Writer*. It was a really good film."

"I did," she said. "Thank you for taking us to see it."

We took two steps and then you said, "Alicia, what did you think about the film we just saw? *The Writer*?"

Alicia and I both felt the rip in the fabric of our lives, but I think we were just so drunk off you acting like a person with whom we might share some common interest and pass time together—sans yelling and passive-aggressive sulking. Subconscious-movie-selection messages aside, it was one of the best nights I ever spent with you, Dad, and I think I just wanted to enjoy the moment, even though I was pretty sure some new thing was seriously off with you.

So I squeezed your shoulder and said, "She loved it, Dad. So did I."

You smiled triumphantly and then said, "I knew you would."

* * *

At the end of our visit, just before I got into our packed car with Alicia and Desi, you looked at me with tears in your eyes, and said, "I love you." That was the first time I had ever heard you say those three words. Hearing you say "I love you" felt like sticking my finger into an electrical socket. The shock hurt. But some strange part of me wanted to do it again and again. Could it be that after waiting four and a half decades, I would get the fatherly love and affection I had so desperately craved? *I'm not worthy of fatherly love*, some dark voice whispered in my skull. And then, immediately, I knew without a doubt that something was seriously wrong with you. But I was too overcome with emotions to do anything other than give you a big hug and say, "I love you too, Dad."

Mom caught my eye and cocked her head in a way that seemed to say, *See? I've been telling you for* decades *that your father loves you. What more proof do you need?*

When I got into my car and put my hands on the steering wheel, a tear rolled down my cheek. So I quickly put the car in gear and drove away. You and Mom waved and waved in my rearview mirror. Then—when I turned right—you were gone.

"You okay?" Alicia said, as she took my right hand in her left.

"My dad's never said he loved me before," I said.

"I know."

"What do you think it means?"

"I don't know."

"Do you think he meant it?"

"I do."

"But?"

"Something's off with him."

"Something's always been off with him."

"True."

"But?"

"But nothing," she said.

When I entered into analysis a few years later, Zeus and I talked a lot about how you, Dad, started saying you loved me only a few months after I quit drinking forever. I'm sure I started acting differently after getting sober. When Mom was cleaning out the old Haddonfield house, she found the half-filled bottles of whiskey I had hidden under the bed in the attic where I slept whenever I visited you. I made sure I always had a way to quickly numb out and disappear whenever I was within range of your worst weaponry. If I wasn't drinking while around you, I was thinking about the relief I would feel when I lifted one of those bottles to my lips.

Maybe just like you were noticing the beauty of clouds for the first time, I was also noticing your humanity for the first time, on this side of sobriety. *How much of our failed relationship was my fault?* I explored that question with my analyst. Obviously, when I was a child, none of what happened between us was my fault. But when you told me you loved me for the first time in Ambler, Pennsylvania, I hadn't been a child for the better part of thirty years. And yet, I had been clinging tightly to my childish mentality like a drowning man clings to driftwood. For decades, I had been adrift in alcohol's ocean. Maybe I was now washed up on dry land, baking in the sand, at water's edge, in the fetal position, but with my arms and legs still wrapped around the piece of psychological driftwood that had kept me afloat and saved my life. Maybe I could let go of resentment. Maybe this lone wolf could get up and start walking back toward people. Maybe I could even love them.

* * *

Over the next few years, whenever Alicia and I would visit, you'd take us out for dinner and then a movie at the Ambler Theater. And you and I would also take our long walks. Every time, it was some version of what happened above. And I started—for the first time in my life—enjoying my time with you. I began to look forward to seeing Mom and you.

Then in March 2020, right as the Covid lockdowns were starting, I received a call from a financial advisor we both used at the time. Alicia and I were visiting Megan and her girls, back when they were living in Baltimore. I was in our hotel room when the call came in. I was worried that the new strange pandemic had somehow affected our investment portfolio. When I answered the phone, the serious tone of Carlo's voice only added to my suspicion.

"Look," Carlo said. "I probably shouldn't be saying what I'm about to say to you. There are ethical and legal rules we have to follow, and your father hasn't given me permission to speak with you about his and my relationship. But I've been through what you are about to be going through. So I'm calling as a fellow human being here, not your financial advisor. Okay?"

I had no idea what he was about to tell me.

"Your father," Carlo said. "He's been calling me nonstop. And he keeps sending me emails too. The information he's sharing doesn't make sense. Especially coming from a man with your dad's financial experience. He's asking me to do things that would be calamitous for your parents' portfolio. And he's repeating himself. *A lot.* He's sent me the same exact email five times today."

"Okay," I said. "What do you need me to do?"

"My mother had dementia. This is how it starts. I'm not a doctor, but I know what this looks like. And you need to get ahead of it," Carlo said to me. "You have to get your mom to see that your dad really can't have access to the accounts anymore. I know your father is a well-respected businessman, so I imagine the conversation will be difficult."

"Okay," I said, still not fully believing what I was hearing, but ready to do what I was being told to do, like a dutiful son.

Then I flashed back on all the weird things you had said to us over the past few years.

There was that time on the beach in Duck, North Carolina, when someone you used to know unexpectedly approached our circle of beach chairs. You jumped up and began introducing everyone in the family to your newly arrived old acquaintance. But when you got around to Micah's wife, Kelly—who had been a part of our family for many years at this point—you couldn't come up with her name. We laughed it off. Maybe we said something about vacation brain or old age.

But then the next day, when you and I were sitting on the beach, you said, "What day of the week is it?"

"You really don't know?" I asked.

"I can never remember the days of the week anymore," you said.

"It's Tuesday, Dad. All day," I said, and then didn't think anything else about it.

There was also that time when we were visiting you in Ambler and you couldn't find your glasses. You freaked out and started ranting and raving, which was honestly nothing new. You drove back to your country club and searched the locker room.

When you returned, you accused some mystery man of stealing your glasses, roaring, "That person must have taken them!"

"What person?" I asked. "Who are you talking about?"

"The person!" you screamed back.

I think you eventually found your glasses in your bedroom.

Mom said, "This happens at least once a week now."

She told us about the time at a wedding—maybe a year previous—when you told your assigned table a twenty-minute story about going to New Zealand, which was received quite well, until you tried to repeat the same exact story five minutes later. Even though you never drank all that much, Mom initially thought you had possibly taken too many sips of wine. But she had since taken you to the doctor, who treated you for depression and gave you hearing aids and was taking a wait-and-see approach. We had all whispered *dementia* to each other, but mostly, the general consensus among us had previously been something like: *Men often change in retirement. Maybe Dad is changing. Yeah, it could be dementia, but nothing bad has happened yet. We're having the situation monitored by a doctor, so we can kind of pretend that it's not as bad as it seems.*

For my entire life, you were always so unlike other people, Dad. And you had spent so much time *not* saying "I love you" that when you started saying the magical words, I think I just stopped really noticing anything else. You were saying that you loved me. *You loved me.* And that was all that mattered back then.

But maybe the above is just my perspective. Other family members now claim that they knew you had dementia earlier and were advocating for a more proactive approach, but we didn't take that next big step until after the conversation I had with Carlo. Maybe that was coincidental and Carlo's warning had no influence whatsoever on the rest of the family members, but it certainly lit a fire under my ass.

When I got off the phone with Carlo, I called Mom and told her that you had repeatedly sent ill-advised emails to our financial advisors and that Carlo thought you definitely had dementia. Mom said Carlo wasn't a doctor, we didn't know anything for sure, and the actual real doctor—with whom she was friendly—was monitoring the situation. I raised my voice to her and said, "We need to take this *seriously*. We can't have Dad directing the money guys to do crazy things. You have to get involved. This is real."

I was pacing in the bathroom of our hotel room with the door shut, trying to shield my resting wife from the madness.

"We have no idea what's going on with this new disease," I said.

"Do you mean this new strange disease everyone is getting or whatever is happening with your father?"

"Both," I said. "Mom, I have to step up and be the man of the family now. You have to listen to me. I can protect you. We can get through this together. But we have to start working as a team."

"We haven't even gotten your father tested yet," Mom said. "He goes next month."

"Well, he's sending crazy emails to the money guys," I said. "And that ain't good. You have to give me formal permission to interact with your financial advisors on your behalf. Dad can't help you through all this anymore."

"Matthew, Carlo shouldn't have even called you. I'm angry that he did. I can take care of myself just fine and—"

"Mom," I said, "you have to let me help you. This *is* happening. We have to deal with it."

"I *am* dealing with it, Matthew," she said. "Every single day of my life."

"Then why is Carlo calling me about Dad?"

"He should have called *me*."

"Why do you think he called your son instead?"

"You don't understand what it's like to see your husband slowly lose his mind. Do you really think I don't know what's going on with him?"

"We have to team up, Mom. You're not going to be able to do this alone."

"If you want to help, *then help*."

"That's what I'm doing right now."

"Okay!"

"Okay then!"

Shortly after that, Mom took you, Dad, to see another doctor. When you struggled to count backward by seven and couldn't recall the three words you had been told to remember at the beginning of the conversation, you were referred to a specialist. You were given a three-hour-long cognitive test. When you were asked to draw clock hands on a blank circle so that it would read three-thirty, you couldn't do it. When Mom told me that, I realized that your dementia had already robbed you of much more than I had previously imagined. Then I understood just how much time mattered for us, Dad, because—long before I really started paying close attention—you had already been disappearing, and with shocking speed. As I struggled to digest that bit of mind-boggling news, everything in our father-son world changed.

14.

You, Mom, border terrier Kingsly, and I were driving back from Hunting Island State Park—here in Beaufort in the early fall of 2024—when Mom said, "Let's check out the place Micah and Kelly rented for Thanksgiving."

"We're not going to Philadelphia for Thanksgiving?" you said, even though you never go to the Philly area anymore and likely never will again.

"Everyone's coming to us, Dad," I said, from behind the steering wheel of the beater Jeep.

"Your sister is coming?"

"Yep."

"But not . . ."

"Aaron is off the team," I said, because he and Megan were in the middle of a divorce.

"That's right," you said. "Is he doing the right thing with the money?"

"I think so?" I said, but I didn't really know the full extent of what was going on. It was complicated, like all divorces are.

Aaron had made us a feast the previous Thanksgiving. He and Megan had rented a waterfront condo on Harbor Island. We'd walked on the beach with the dogs and the kids. No one fought. The food was fantastic. And the conversation was even better. If Micah's family had been there, it would have been perfect. I had even sent Aaron a fridge magnet afterward. It was a picture of him and me taken on Thanksgiving 2023. We're smiling together on the beach where the river meets the ocean. Under our faces, I had typed the words "Bros-in-Law." While Aaron had been secretly making plans to leave our family, none of us had any inkling. In retrospect, I've come to believe that the holiday feast was his way of saying goodbye.

Then—back in the early fall of 2024—in my beater Jeep, Mom was plugging an address into her phone so that it could lead us to the place where all five of our original family members would be having Thanksgiving that year.

We turned off the Sea Island Parkway and onto a road that time forgot. There was a small church. We passed overgrown lots, each dotted with a single trailer home. Gigantic live oaks reached out and hugged each other fifteen or so feet above the road, which was mostly shaded.

"Why aren't we having Thanksgiving at our house?" you asked.

I waited to see if Mom would field the question, which she didn't. I didn't want to be the one to say that you often couldn't handle the constant commotion that your four young and lively grandchildren produce. Apparently, she didn't either.

I said, "Micah wanted to make sure we had a water view for Thanksgiving."

"He rented a house on the water?" you asked.

"He did. It's going to be nice. I don't know when all five of us last had a Thanksgiving together."

"It's been years," Mom said. "Maybe decades."

"Remember when you guys used to have Thanksgiving with Alicia and me on the Outer Banks?" I tried.

"We used to love that," she said in a way that once again made me feel guilty for having prematurely ended that tradition.

The unspoken truth was this: Everyone thought Thanksgiving 2024 might be the last time you could be mentally present in a meaningful way. No one thought you'd be dead before Turkey Day 2025. We just didn't know how far your dementia would progress in the course of another year, because it had really been on the move since last Thanksgiving.

The place Micah and Kelly had rented was indeed on the water, with gorgeous marsh and river views. It had a large screened-in porch on the back with ample seating. It looked like the perfect place to have Thanksgiving. It wasn't anything like the palatial home in *The Big Chill*, but I thought of that movie, maybe because we were all gathering near Beaufort to mourn the loss of a loved one too. And that loved one—which, of course, was you, Dad—would be the main character of Thanksgiving.

"Pull into the driveway, Matthew," Mom said. "Let's get out and explore."

"The new renters will be coming today," I said. "We had better not."

"You're no fun," she said, as I did a K-turn and left.

Just two months later our entire family was on the wide, pristine beaches of Hunting Island State Park; and Mom was flying kites with the kids; and Micah and I were playing an epic soccer match with the kids; and Alicia and Megan were searching for shark teeth with the kids; and you even joined in when we played two-hand touch football with the kids; and we all walked the dogs for miles along the water's edge; and Kelly figured out the iPhone camera timer, put her machine on the jetty, and then the entire family smiled for a family portrait; and I marveled at how much fun I was having.

Then I flashed on this vivid memory of being under Uncle Pete's raised-up-on-stilts Nags Head house: The Quick Getaway. I'm fifteen or maybe sixteen. I have a towel around my waist, and I'm about to hop into the outdoor shower. The sun has bronzed my skin. The long swoosh of hair that hangs down over my left eye has been bleached even blonder. My body is lean and maybe at its peak. My stomach is flat, but I hate taking my shirt off. Sometimes, back then, you would grab the skin around my belly and say, "If you can pinch an inch, you're a fatso."

Earlier that day on Nags Head beach, you had used your favorite vacation nickname for me: "Sundial." Whenever I got out of the water and my bathing suit was clinging to my groin, you'd say, "What time is it, Sundial?" And I'd immediately feel obscenely naked, because you were drawing attention to the bulge protruding from the crotch of my bathing suit. Looking back now, I'm not sure why you were so easily able to shame me for having what you clearly thought of as an abnormally big bulge. I was completely flaccid whenever you said this. You were not shaming me for having an erection. You were making fun of the shape of my penis when it was not engorged with blood. But you always said the nickname Sundial in a way that instantly robbed me of what little big-dick energy I might have had back then. When I would immediately pull the wet fabric of my bathing suit away from my genitals and then wrap a towel around my midsection, clearly admitting shame, you would always double down, saying, "If anyone needs to know what time it is, just look at the sand under Mr. Sundial." Then you would laugh in a way that made everyone uncomfortable. No one—and I do mean *no one*—was laughing with you. Everyone in our family would just look away or change the subject. And I would always have this feeling of being knifed in my gut as I said to myself, *Dad, laughing at my dick in public is not normal, right? It's perverted, right? Just how fucked up is this?* I kind of thought the answer was "very," as in, it is very fucked up and very perverted. But no one else ever said anything about it. Not Mom. Not Micah and Megan. Not Grandmom and Pop Pop. Not Pete. Not my friend who sometimes came with us to Nags Head. Not the friends I made on the beach. No one. People would pretend they hadn't heard you call me Sundial, which is how I learned just how perverse your name-calling was. It was too shameful to even acknowledge.

My teenage guy friends had called me more fucked-up things than Sundial, but whenever they did, the comment came with a playful punch to the shoulder, a smile on the face of the insult giver, and a glint in his eye that said, *You're my boy, Quick, and this is how I say I love you.* But when you called me Sundial, there was no playful punch to the arm, the grin on your face looked twisted, and the look in your eye said something like, *Don't you dare feel even halfway decent about your body, boy, because you're going to damn well carry my shame for me.* I couldn't have put that into words when I was a teenager, but I intuitively understood what was going on. And when it came to carrying your shame, Dad, my answer was always, "Yes, sir."

You definitely called me Sundial on the day I made my way to the outdoor shower under Uncle Pete's house. I liked taking an outdoor shower. It was a nice place to introvert. After a day at the beach, everyone else was enjoying the air-conditioning inside. I wanted to be alone. I wanted to wash the salt off my body. I wanted to recover from the lingering effects of being—once again—humiliated by my father.

I had my hand on the rusted handle of the plywood outdoor shower door—so close to solitude—when I heard, "Matthew, I need a word with you."

I took a deep breath, let go of the handle, and then turned around to face you.

"Do you have any idea how hard I work to support this family?" you said.

I began the arduous task of pushing all of my feelings and beliefs and thoughts deep down into the place where you couldn't get to them. Everything inside of me began to feel dead. Then I presented the shell of myself to you.

"No, you don't understand, Matthew. I work myself to death just to make sure you have food and a place to live and nice clothes and a two-week beach vacation every year. Your uncle charges me money for this place. It's not free. And all I ask in return is that you respect me. I don't even make you get a summer job. Your life is easy. You have it so good. But can you give me the respect I deserve? No."

"Dad, how did I disrespect you?"

"Oh, everything you do is disrespectful."

"Can you give me an example?"

"Matthew, your whole life is an example."

"Dad—"

"I don't want to hear it. I just want you to know that I only get one vacation every year. Just two weeks. Sometimes I don't even get that. And every single year. *Every single time.* You ruin it for me. And I need you to know that you ruined my vacation again this year. So thanks for that, son."

As you turned and walked away, I said, "How did I ruin it for you, Dad? What did I do?"

"You know what you did, Matthew. You know," you said and then walked up the wooden steps that led to the first floor of Pete's little beach home.

I stood there for a long time blinking away tears and shaking my head at the insanity of what had just happened. I kept thinking, *Either my father is insane, or I am, because I have no idea what the fuck he is talking about. And* he's *the one who's always ruining* everyone's *fucking vacation.*

I wanted to scream. I wanted to run up the stairs, grab you by the tuft of hair on the back of your head, and then smash your face into the dining room table until it was a bloody mess.

But instead, I entered the outdoor shower, took off my towel, and then stood under the water for a half hour trying to stop shaking.

* * *

On the beach in Hunting Island State Park, South Carolina, as your four grandchildren ran through ankle-deep seawater with your wife and daughter and daughters-in-law—and your second son, Micah, walked his new gigantic puppy ahead of us—I put my arm around your shoulders and said, "Isn't it nice to have the whole family together again?"

You nodded and said, "Beaufort is so much better than the Outer Banks."

"It sure is, Dad," I said. "It sure is."

On Thanksgiving Day we all drove to the place Micah and Kelly had rented on the water. Kelly was busy preparing a feast. Micah was a generous host, making sure everyone immediately had food and drink. The four grandchildren began playing card games and hiding in rooms and running around with great joy. They were all still ten years old and under, so they would sometimes hop on my lap or give me a hug and kiss for no reason at all. They did the same to everyone else too. And I marveled at what a healing gift these four children were, because it was like starting over again. It was so easy to love Megan's and Micah's kids because they had no memory of our tricky collective family past, and we all did love them the best we could—even you did, Dad. There were times when your grandkids would generate a little too much noise, and the old yelling Dad would make a brief appearance, snarling, "It's too loud! Keep it down!" The children would freeze and blink at each other, not sure how to respond. But then they would take the play into another room and all would be well again.

Isla had made a little card for each family member's place setting, and when we sat down to dinner, she requested that we each read what the card said. Everyone was given accolades. (Although there might have been something about being "the best farter" written on my card.) But as I watched you tolerate this feast of kindness, I thought maybe we were really improving, at least generationally. Someone had brought a stuffed animal that doubled as a hat. It was, of course, a turkey. We all took turns inserting our heads into the hole where the stuffing would go if it was a real turkey and said what we were grateful for that year. It was really sweet. Kind of even normal.

After dinner, while the kids played, we adults gathered in various groupings out on the screened-in porch and on the couches in front of the NFL games, and I was surprised that talking mostly won out over watching football. It was a terrific day. Warm enough to sit outside with a fleece on or under a blanket. And the water behind the place was wide and full of life and lit up by the day's sun.

Since I get to see you all the time here in Beaufort, I tried to let Micah and Megan mostly have you. And it was nice to see them soaking you up one-on-one during different parts of the day.

We all lingered into the evening, and because Mom seldom gets to see her grandchildren, she kept you out past your usual bedtime. By the end of Thanksgiving, you were sitting on the couch with your arms crossed and your eyes looking vacant. Sometimes you wouldn't answer when someone spoke to you, but no one took offense.

When it was time to go, I kissed and hugged everyone goodbye. And as I thanked Micah for making this healing Thanksgiving Day happen, he wouldn't make eye contact with me, but just kept saying things like, "We're family," and, "My boys love their uncle Matthew and aunt Alicia." As I thanked Megan for bringing her girls and prioritizing all of us having a relationship with them, she said, "Of course, I want them to have a relationship with you and Micah and Mom and Dad." She and I compared notes on your decline, and we joked a little about how rocky the holidays had always been. But, then she, too, was driving away with her girls in the back of her RAV4.

Once Alicia had Kingsly strapped into the back-seat safety car harness, we got into her RAV4 and I began driving us home.

"That was really nice," I said.

"Then why do you say it in such a sad way?" my wife asked.

"I don't know," I said. Then I added, "It's like we're just pretending that eating together as a family is normal, when we original five family members haven't had Thanksgiving together for decades."

"Today might have been the last time too," she said.

"Why do you say that?"

"Your dad's not getting better. And he's the draw right now."

"It all feels way more charged, way more important than we were acknowledging today."

"I think you all acknowledged the importance just by showing up."

"Then why doesn't it feel like enough?"

"I ask myself that same exact question every single time I go home to Massachusetts."

"It's never going to stop hurting, is it?"

As Alicia reached over and took my hand in hers, I thought about writing all of the above into the memoir. Turns out it would take me four months to get up the courage. As I sit here typing on my laptop, I wonder if being shamed and humiliated as a child was the price of admission for living the writing life in the way that I do. Most of my writing heroes have trauma histories. Almost all of my writing friends privately nurse wounds that are remarkably similar to my own. My desperate need to fill the Dad-shaped hole in me—that's the power source that's fueled every line of writing I have ever produced.

In a strange way, I've learned to be grateful for the abuse, just like I am grateful for your dementia, Dad.

Zeus says there is a cost for everything. And that it must be paid. There is no getting around that. And, on Thanksgiving night 2024, as

I drove through the star-and-moonlit Lowcountry marshes that flank the Sea Island Parkway, I told myself this: Enduring heartache—even when surrounded by the people I love most in the world—was the cost of writing this memoir.

I sure as hell was paying it.

15.

This next story takes place in your old town house in Ambler, before Mom and you decided to permanently move to Beaufort. Alicia and I had driven up from the Outer Banks to spend time with you. We were all sipping tea and lounging around your living room on a Tuesday morning when I said, "I'm going to Zoom with my analyst on the third floor. We have a session scheduled. Can you give me some privacy for an hour?"

You and Mom both immediately agreed to stay put on the first floor, which was refreshing. When I was a child, privacy didn't exist in our small house. Neither did boundaries. Mom routinely used to go through my belongings, and she often quietly picked up one of the three phones in our house to eavesdrop on my calls with girlfriends. And there was no way you, Dad, would have allowed me to speak with a mental health professional back then either, let alone tolerated me doing so in your house. So it felt like we were all making progress.

"Tell your guy," Mom said, "that I see a big change in you."

"How so?" I asked.

"You're less angry. And just . . . *nicer*."

"What do you mean?"

"There was a time when I worried you'd never come visit your father and me ever again."

I wanted to say, *And why do you think that was?* But I didn't.

"Don't you think Matthew is nicer these days?" Mom asked my wife.

"Yep," Alicia said, nodding.

Your wife and my wife in agreement—another first.

"What do you think, Dad?" I asked. "Am I nicer these days?"

"It's nice that you came to visit us," you said without looking up from the day's *Philadelphia Inquirer*. "I won't bother you up there."

I said, "Thanks, everyone. *I think*," and then began climbing the steep, narrow, wooden staircase.

In the third-floor guest suite, I changed into my black T-shirt. Next, I put some pillows on the floor, sat my butt down in my makeshift nest, flipped open my laptop, set it on an antique chair, opened Zoom, and waited.

Zeus is not a punctual man, to say the least. He routinely starts sessions ten to fifteen minutes late and sometimes later. And I never know when a session will end either. His laissez-faire attitude toward timekeeping initially infuriated me, being a very schedule-conscious rule follower myself. But as he was also quite generous with his time, often extending our sessions well past fifty minutes—without charging me a penny extra—I made my peace with never knowing when sessions would actually begin or end. Sometimes, I imagined he was deliberately disregarding the clock just to teach me to be less anal.

So when twenty minutes passed without Zeus appearing on my computer screen, I didn't think much of it.

When thirty minutes passed, I smiled and said, "He's testing me. Seeing if I can tolerate an egregious amount of lateness."

But when forty minutes passed, my stomach started to gurgle and churn. Something was wrong.

I started having an internal argument with myself. *Has Zeus been hit by a car? Did he have a heart attack? Did one of his other clients go psychotic and kill him, like in* The Sixth Sense*? Has an asteroid crashed into his house?*

Have I failed analysis? Was he dropping me as a client?

No, that's not it. He'd never.

Has his spouse poisoned him? Was he the victim of a home invasion? Has he been attacked by a pack of rabid dogs?

He isn't still mad about the shelf-falling writing assignment? Is he trying to punish me? Had he been waiting for me to forget all about our shelf-falling-writing-assignment fight, savoring the planning phase of his revenge, allowing the dish to go cold before he served it? Was he intentionally fucking with my head?

No, he'd never do that. Not Zeus.

Then why has he blown off today's session without emailing or calling?

He wouldn't intentionally try *to hurt me.*

Then he must be dead. Or is being held hostage.

Text him.

No.

Why not?

What if he replies?

Then I'll know he's okay.

But if he's okay, it means that he doesn't care about me. People who care about me don't break important commitments.

So either something unspeakable has befallen Zeus and I'll probably never hear from him ever again. Or. *He's fine and has chosen not to let me know he'd be missing the session, in which case he is a sadistic motherfucker and trusting him was the worst mistake I've made in my entire life.*

It's clearly an either-or thing.

No possibilities exist in between those two extremes?

Don't be obtuse.

To Zeus, I texted, Hope everything is okay. I'm a bit worried. Waited an hour for you. Please let me know what's going on when you have a minute. Then I hit send and held my breath.

He's abandoning me.

Give him a second to respond.

But Zeus didn't respond.

I began to pace a U around the bed as I waited for the screen of my iPhone to light up with a text from Zeus.

Alicia entered and asked how my session had gone.

"Zeus blew me off."

"Really?"

"I texted him and got no response."

"I'm sure everything's fine."

"Can you maybe just give me the room? I think I need a second."

"I'll walk the dog."

She disappeared, and then another twenty minutes passed before my iPhone began buzzing. It was an incoming call from Zeus. I stared at the illuminated screen for several seconds.

Answer it.

I'm not sure I want to know what happened.

Remember what Zeus always says: Reality is medicinal.

"Matthew," Zeus said, when I answered the call. "I am so, so sorry. I set my alarm for p.m. instead of a.m. and, well, I overslept. I guess I needed the extra rest."

Then he did something that felt unforgivable: He let out a big belly laugh.

I became enraged. "I was worried."

"Let's talk right now."

"I thought you were dead. Or that you were dropping me," I said, noting the intensity of my words.

Don't let him know that he got to you. Don't let him know that you care, a very young voice inside of me commanded, but I no longer had any control.

"What the fuck," I added.

"Everything is okay," Zeus said. "I'm fine. You're fine. We're here."

"I'm dealing with a lot of shit right now. Being in my parents' home is complicated. You'd think my analyst would get that."

"I do."

"I needed you to be here this morning," I said. "And you *weren't*."

"How old do you feel right now?" When I didn't answer, he repeated the question.

"I really don't want to play your mind games."

"It's like you're the last kid waiting after baseball practice. The lights have gone out, no one is around, it's raining. You're scared. You feel abandoned. And your dad isn't showing up."

"My dad was the baseball coach so that never happened to me."

"But he abandoned you in other ways and my not being at this morning's session clearly triggered—"

"You aren't supposed to fail me like he did. You're supposed to be there when I need you."

All of a sudden, my body was shaking.

"Matthew," Zeus said in a stern voice, "I *will* fail you. That is one hundred percent guaranteed. And I will die one day too. I'm human. I am not a god. Neither is your father. And neither are you."

I swallowed hard.

He continued, saying, "The work is learning how to tolerate our own humanity so we can tolerate the humanity of others. I understand that your father didn't always meet your childhood needs—psychologically, emotionally, spiritually. I think you and I are doing good work here. I think we are slowly healing your father wounds. But I am going to make mistakes. You are going to make mistakes. All of which you can tolerate, because you're not a little boy anymore. Being in your parents' house—even though it's not the house in which you grew up—being under their roof again takes you back to a younger time. A lot of that is unconscious. Feeling abandoned by me also takes you back to childhood. That's okay. We will go there and see what lessons there are to be learned. But you are presently a middle-aged man. You can take care of yourself. You've been doing it for decades. And I *haven't* abandoned you. So step into your two hairy legs and be with me right here and now."

"Did you intentionally *oversleep* just to teach me this lesson?"

"I wish I was that much of a mastermind, but I was just tired and didn't set my alarm clock correctly. I'm not perfect. You don't have to be either. We can both give each other the gift of tolerating each other's humanity. I think having more respect for how God works would benefit you. Our two souls are coming together and making a third thing. As you and I keep mingling, all sorts of alchemy will occur. I'm not creating this. You're not creating this. Unconscious forces inside both of us are creating our experience. We need to maintain a reverence for that."

"I really thought you were dead."

"How did that make you feel?"

"Stupid."

"Why stupid?"

"Because I'm trusting you, and I don't trust anyone."

"You don't trust anyone because you can't endure their fallibility. You can't endure their fallibility because you had to hold yourself to such high standards of perfectionism just to survive your childhood. It was a fantasy—that you could be perfect enough to earn the love of your father. But there is no amount of perfection that can earn you the right to be loved. You were born worthy of love. There is no amount of perfection that will make others worthy of being loved. They were born worthy of love. But since your father didn't know how to love you when you were young, your sense of what love is was perverted. We are slowly fixing that."

"What if I had missed a session without calling you beforehand? You would have surely charged me for it."

"Do you want me to give you a free session as compensation for your time? I'm happy to."

"No."

"You just wanted to point out my hypocrisy?"

"I just really needed you to fucking *be here* this morning."

"I know. I'm here now."

"Can you promise that you'll never miss another session?"

"I will most definitely miss another session at some point. I am human."

"There are surely other analysts who never miss sessions without notifying clients first."

"And yet, you are here with me. Why do you think that is?"

"You're going to say it's because I need to be with you."

"You found me. I didn't solicit you."

I took a deep breath and then said, "Listen, I'm sorry if I was an asshole about this."

"You weren't an asshole. You were just being your traumatized self. Working through it, staying in analysis even when it's hard, committing to this relationship even when it's not perfect—that's the work."

"Okay."

"So you're not breaking up with me for setting my alarm clock incorrectly?" Zeus asked.

"I'll be there Friday night."

"We'll see if I show up," he said and then laughed.

A part of me wanted to scream, *That's not fucking funny!* but I somehow found myself chuckling a little too.

16.

You started seeing ads for the *Captain America: Brave New World* movie back when we were still watching Eagles football together, before the 2025 playoffs ended. "I wanna see that," you'd say each time you saw the trailer. I don't know why you have always loved Captain America. You insist you've never read the comic books. I think you might just be patriotic. But it's an ongoing mystery.

I didn't have much interest in seeing the film and thought that—because you have dementia—you would forget about it, just like you forget about almost everything.

On the last Thursday in February, Alicia and I picked Mom and you up for a movie night. You got into the back seat of Alicia's RAV4 and proclaimed, "We're finally going to see *Captain America*."

"No, Dad, we actually aren't," I said.

"We're not going to the movies?" you asked.

"We *are* going to the movies," I said.

"To see *Captain America*?" you said.

"Nope."

"Then what are we seeing?"

"*Paddington in Peru*," Alicia sang out.

You laughed and then said, "You're kidding."

"Nope," I said.

"But that's a movie for children," you said. "We are not children."

"Let's be children tonight, Dad," I said.

It takes forty minutes to drive from Lady's Island to the Bluffton movie theater, so I put on the Fleetwood Mac mix I made for you, which got you humming quietly in the back seat, while Mom got all of her pent-up extroverting out by telling us news about friends and family.

When we entered the movie theater, you pointed to all of the gigantic ads for *Captain America* and—with great enthusiasm—said, "See. *Captain America* is playing here. And we're watching it tonight."

We got popcorn and drinks and then sat down in the heated reclining seats, where you said, "Okay, I'm ready to watch *Captain America.*"

"Mike," Mom said, "we're here to see *Paddington in Peru.* Alicia and Matthew wanted to see it. We're just tagging along."

"But *Captain America* is going to play on this screen right now," you said, which is when Mom gave me a *guess-we'll-see-how-this-goes* look.

All through *Paddington in Peru*—as Olivia Colman proceeded to steal every scene she was in—I kept expecting you to jump up out of your seat and demand to see *Captain America*, but, instead, you chuckled along with the family-friendly jokes. There is one part in the third act where Antonio Banderas gets hit in the groin with a flying book, and—as he doubled over in pain—you laughed audibly, which let me know you were really enjoying yourself. You have always loved physical comedy.

When the film ended and the rest of us stood up, you said, "Where are you guys going?"

"Dad," I said, "the movie is over."

"But *Captain America* is coming on. That was just the preview, right? We have to watch the movie now."

We'd been sitting there for more than two hours, but somehow you believed you had only watched a single preview.

"We'll see *Captain America* later, Dad, I promise. It's a movie for men. And Mom and Alicia are here. We have to come back without them," I tried.

"Okay," you said and then stood up.

But when you once again saw all the *Captain America* advertisements in the lobby, you said, "Why can't we see *Captain America* tonight?" just as we were crossing paths with a large, Southern gentleman.

"Y'all didn't take Dad to see *Captain America*? What'd y'all see instead?"

"*Paddington in Peru*," we told him.

"Guess y'all wanted the warm and fuzzies tonight, huh?"

"Yep," I said.

"You really ought to take your father to see *Captain America* next time," he said, as he disappeared into the theater behind us.

"*See?*" you said.

So I promised I'd buy tickets for Sunday afternoon, when Mom and Alicia would be at the classical music series of live performances that they have been attending here in Beaufort.

Three days later we were back at the theater, and you were in heaven. You cheered as Captain America beat up the bad guys; and flew through the sky with his mechanical wings; and dealt with rogue, hypnotized-by-the-villain jet pilots attacking their own aircraft carriers; and intercepted missiles. All this before Captain America even takes on Harrison Ford's Red Hulk. I wouldn't say I loved the film, Dad, but I loved watching you watch it, because you were like a seven-year-old boy. The wonder on your face and in your eyes was priceless.

"Did you like the movie?" I asked when it was over.

"It was *Captain America*. Of course I liked it."

When we got home, Mom told me that you had to go for blood work in the morning, couldn't eat breakfast, and had to produce a urine sample. She was nervous about all of that. She said she never knew how you were going to be about these things.

"Well," I said, "he was great with me today."

"You want to take him to his medical appointment?" she said.

"I gotta work, Mom. The memoir is flying out of me. I'm in a groove. And that happens less and less the older I get, especially on this side of sobriety."

Mom kissed me good night. I kissed you good night. And then I was in my own bed trying to get a decent night's rest so that I could write in the morning.

I woke at six a.m. to a thread of texts from Mom. She had been up all night sick and didn't know what she was going to do about the blood tests you needed. She said she couldn't take you and getting them rescheduled would be a nightmare. Then she asked me to come over and help. There were green vomit emojis sprinkled throughout her words.

Even though I am here in Beaufort to help Mom help you, my first response was *Uggghhh*. I wanted to write. I'd been writing better than I'd written in years. I didn't want to mess up my flow. I pretentiously—and anachronistically—thought, *Ernest Hemingway would have gotten his words before he even checked his text messages.* But I texted Mom back, saying I'd take you to your appointment.

When I arrived at your house, Mom was lying on the couch with a big red bucket on the floor next to her.

"Where's Dad?"

"In the bedroom."

I knew you getting ready without Mom's help was no good, so I speed-walked through the house.

I found you pacing with no shirt on. Your pants and belt were undone. You had on socks, but no shoes. There were different tops spread out on the bed.

"I can't do this!" you yelled.

"I got you, Dad. Let's get you dressed."

"Your mother put the pee cup right next to my bed, but I didn't see it. And I peed in the toilet. And now I can't pee again. *It's ruined.*"

"Dad, let's just get you dressed," I said, as I pulled a blue V-neck T-shirt out of your drawer. "Here, put this on."

"Are you sure it's right?"

"One hundred percent."

You put it on.

"Okay, Dad. Let's get you in this black zip-up hoodie. Just like the one I have on. We can look cool together."

You began to put on the hoodie, so I searched the floor for your sneakers. When I looked up again, you were taking the hoodie off.

"Dad, what's wrong with that hoodie?"

"I didn't pee in the cup!"

"It's okay."

"No, it's not! My brain isn't working!"

"Dad, we just have to put on the hoodie. We have to look cool together."

I helped you put on the hoodie once more, and then we got your sneakers on.

When you stood up again, you started taking off your pants.

"Dad, those pants are good. Super cool."

"I have to tuck my shirt in," you explained.

"Okay."

"I didn't pee in the cup, you know."

"You can pee in it when we get there."

"What if I can't?"

"No one will care. It will be just fine."

"I need a jacket. I'm cold."

"Okay, let's go to the coat closet."

I gave you your favorite black jacket, which you inspected and then decided you did not want to wear. So I held up your blue jacket, at which you wrinkled your nose.

"How about a vest?" I asked. "But we really have to go, because we're late."

You grabbed one vest, but then handed it back to me, saying, "This is no good."

"What about your green Eagles vest?"

"Okay," you said.

When you put your arms through both holes, I was so grateful that I almost kissed you.

Then we were walking past Mom on the couch. She said, "I emailed you the paperwork."

"Are you going to be okay?" I asked.

"Just get his labs done, please. And thank you."

In the Jeep—as we pulled away from your front curb—you screamed, "I don't have my pee cup!"

I actually jumped and then reflexively slammed on the brakes.

When I calmly pointed to the empty pee cup in the dashboard cubbyhole, you said, "Oh."

"I got you, Dad. Have I ever let you down? Did I not take you to see *Captain America* yesterday, just like I said I would?"

"That was a movie. This is real."

"Okay, Dad, but we are fine. It's sunny out. We're together. Everything is aces."

"My brain isn't working right. I can't remember to do things. I didn't pee in the cup."

"But you will, Dad. I have faith in your bladder. Let's listen to Fleetwood Mac."

I put on the old trusty Fleetwood Mac mix, praying the whole time it would calm you the fuck down.

Their song "Dreams" came on and I waited.

When you said, "I love Stevie Nicks," I breathed a sigh of relief.

You were good for the ride through Lady's Island, but when we crossed the bridge to Port Royal, traffic was backed up and you started to freak out again.

"Do you know where we're going?" you asked.

"Yep."

"Why are all these cars here? We're going to be late. I don't like this."

"What would happen if we *were* late, Dad? What would happen if I threw the pee cup out the window? What would happen if we didn't get labs done at all?" When I turned to gauge your expression, you looked beyond panicked. So I said, "Nothing. That's what. Like Captain America, we are Ameri-*cans*, Dad. We have freedom. We *can* do what we want."

"But we'll get in trouble."

"With whom?"

"Mom will be mad at us."

"How would she even know? It's only you and me here."

"The doctors would yell at us. They'd tell her."

"No, they wouldn't. They wouldn't care at all if we didn't show up today. They'd charge us money, but they wouldn't yell at us. They wouldn't even call Mom."

"But we have to get my labs done."

"We don't *have* to do anything, but we *can* get your labs done, if you think it's a good idea. Otherwise, let's grab some breakfast."

"I think we should get the labs done."

"Why?"

"Just to make sure I'm healthy."

"Okay. We *can* do that if you want. But only if you think it's a good idea."

"Look," you said. "Those azalea bushes are blooming."

A rush of purple passed by the passenger-side window.

"They're beautiful," I said.

"Thank goodness you're here, Matthew. I don't know what I would do without you."

When I heard those words, I had to fight hard to keep the tears from coming, because I could tell you meant it.

The Labcorp waiting room was packed beyond capacity. Many people were standing as they waited. You took the last seat in the room, and I stood next to you. Every thirty seconds, you poked my thigh, and—when I bent down—you'd whisper, "Did you check me in?" and I'd say, "Yep, Dad. I got you. Nothing to worry about." We did that exchange at least twenty times.

I marveled at the strange and lovely waiting-room play we were all in. It was rich theater. There were folks from all walks of life there. People in expensive designer clothes and people in blue-collar work uniforms. One woman wore a huge knee brace. Another woman was on crutches. We had most of the races covered. There was a man who had Native American symbols stitched into his clothing. There was a young woman in a cheerleading jacket. There was a dark-skinned man with an amazing, eight-inch, gray beard that gave me serious beard envy. Everyone in the room was monitoring the situation, and whenever someone obviously needed a seat more than others, at least three people offered up their chairs. It gave me a lot of faith in my fellow humans. You offered your seat to several women, but I think they could tell you had dementia, because they all smiled at me as they politely declined.

The woman who drew your blood was young and friendly. She said she went to an oyster festival over the weekend but didn't eat any because she's allergic to shellfish. She laughed easily and I liked her a whole bunch. You did too.

When she finished with the blood, she asked for the urine sample. You averted your eyes and hung your head.

She looked at me.

"We were hoping that could be done now," I said.

"No problem, Mr. Quick," she said to you, Dad. "You can just fill up your cup in the bathroom."

"I don't know if I can," you admitted.

"Well, you can try," she encouraged.

Then I was in the bathroom with you. The top of your pants was pulled down around your thighs. You had your penis in one hand and the cup in the other.

"I can't do it," you said.

I turned on the sink faucet, hoping the sound of water flowing would do the trick.

We waited for a good thirty seconds.

I could sense you flexing all of the muscles in your midsection.

And then I heard the triumphant sound of you peeing.

"I don't know if I can fill it, Matthew."

"You don't need to fill it, Dad. You just need to pee as much as you can without overflowing."

But then your pee stopped altogether.

"I'm a little dry," you said.

I was afraid to look, but when I did, you had filled it almost three-quarters.

"You crushed it, Dad."

"I did?"

"You have more than enough in there. Excellent work."

As you quickly screwed the cap on, you said, "I thought I had messed it up and I didn't."

"Dad, you have won the morning."

"Does that mean I get an oatmeal raisin cookie?"

"I think it does. *I really think it does.*"

We turned in your urine sample and then drove into downtown Beaufort. On the ride, you asked, "Is Mom okay?"

"She's just a little sick," I said.

"Is she going to die?"

"No. She just needs to sleep."

"Is Mom okay?"

And then we repeated those lines for the next ten minutes.

I got you a peach tea and an oatmeal raisin cookie at Superior Coffee. We said hello to Alicia and a writing friend of hers. They were coincidentally seated and chatting right outside of the coffee shop.

As we walked away, you said, "Why doesn't Alicia want to be with us?"

"She's having woman talk with her friend, Dad, and we're having man talk."

You nodded in understanding.

On the bench swing by the river—as you ate your gigantic cookie and sipped your tea, and we watched the swing bridge open to let a sailboat through—you got a little philosophical. You said that Mom was a pleaser and a perfectionist, but there is no perfection in the world. You said all you can do is keep trying. But nothing stays the same and everything changes. Then you said you had mixed emotions about your support group. You said you always fended for yourself, did for yourself—but now you needed support, because of your dementia. Then you said the world isn't perfect, but Mom doesn't know how to break her perfectionism. You seemed really sad on her behalf.

When you finished eating and drinking, we walked around The Old Point.

I pointed to an ancient live oak that was massive and otherworldly. Each of its many thick limbs were bearded with Spanish moss. "Look how the morning sunlight illuminates it all," I said. "Isn't it gorgeous?"

"I like that," you said. "But I worry we wear out Mom. She gets tired. Because we're all here in Beaufort. Maybe we're too much for her? Maybe we made her sick?"

"Let's send her a picture of how much fun we're having," I said and then took a selfie of us, telling you to smile big, which you did.

When I sent it, Mom immediately texted me back, writing: Your father is always happiest when he is with you.

As we walked past all the old mansions, you kept exclaiming, "*Wow.* I've never walked down this street," even though you have walked down all of these streets many times.

Just as we were leaving The Old Point, you said, "I like this moment, but—"

"Dad," I said, cutting you off. I wasn't really sure why I felt so compelled to offer what I was about to voice. My well-meaning Dad interventions have been historically quelled by your maniacal screaming. My batting average here is abysmal. Regardless, I said, "You have to take the buts out of your life, Dad. I like this moment too. *Period.* We're having a nice walk through a gorgeous place on a lovely Monday morning. Let it be nice. No buts."

For a second, I thought I might have gotten through to you. That I had actually made history by saving the day.

Then you said, "Sometimes I feel like your mother is going to walk out on me. She wants to do something good with the rest of her life. And my brain is breaking apart. Marriages are difficult. There have been a lot of ups and downs with your mother and me. I think she might want to move on without me. Find a new man. But if she takes my half of the money, Matthew, I'm going to be so pissed."

"Mom's not going anywhere."

"I just don't think she's happy with me. She's constantly on the internet."

"Dad—"

"If she hates me so much, she should just divorce me. I'll give her half the money. Then I'll pack my clothes and disappear. Your mother needs people around her and I'm not the right man for that."

"You're the right man for me, Dad."

"You're my son, Matthew. *You don't count!*"

"What's that supposed to mean?"

"You *have* to be around me."

"No, I don't. I *choose* to be around you."

"Your mother and me are only two ships passing in the night. That's just the way it is."

"I think all the care Mom's giving you is a hell of a way for her to say that she loves you. It's a preposterous abundance of love. If only you had left off the 'but' earlier, Dad."

"What?"

"You said, 'I like this moment, *but*.' And after all the good times we had this morning, you could have just said, 'I like this moment.'"

"I don't know what you're talking about, Matthew. My brain doesn't work anymore. And I'm tired. *I'm so tired.*"

I took a deep breath and surrendered to the moment.

Then I said, "Dad, do you want a chicken sandwich for lunch?"

"It's lunchtime?" you said with hope in your voice.

And then we were driving to the Lady's Island Harris Teeter, where you immediately selected a chicken Caesar wrap for lunch, before we had an argument about which premade salad you would have for dinner, because they all had hard-boiled eggs and cherry tomatoes on them and you hate both. "We'll pick them out," I kept saying, to which you kept replying, "Nope." We both said our lines a half-dozen times. I was worn down. I was supposed to be writing. I was starting to go crazy. I was thinking, *If this is what Mom has to deal with twenty-four seven, she's not going to be able to cope for much longer.* I was about to say, "Dad, just pick a fucking salad," when you lifted your eyebrows above your glasses and said, "Would you maybe eat my tomatoes and eggs, Matthew?"

"Absolutely," I said.

Which is when you pointed to the chicken-and-ham salad and said, "That one."

In the parking lot, you asked me why you didn't get a drink and—when I said you'd get a drink at home—you screamed, "I'm not going home if your mother is there! She never lets me have any money for my wallet!"

"Dad, you have money in your wallet. Pull it out of your pocket and see."

You laughed like I had said the most ridiculous thing in the world. Then you took your wallet out, opened it up, and were shocked to see it was filled with twenty-dollar bills.

"Did you put this money in here, Matthew?"

"Mom did," I said, "but I can give you some *more* money if you want it."

"Your mother is stealing my money. *I know it.*"

"Dad," I said. "Can we just be nice to Mom? She's sick."

"Mother is sick?"

"Yes. She threw up all night."

"Is she going to die?"

"Are you worried about that?"

"I really don't want my mother to die," you said, in the frightened voice of a little boy. "My mother isn't going to die, *is she*?"

"No, Dad. But she needs our help. We have to be like Captain America. We have to save her."

"I don't know if I can be like Captain America, Matthew. My brain is not so good these days."

"Maybe we can be like Captain America together."

"Okay. I don't want our mother to die."

"Let's go save her," I said, and then we were in the Jeep driving back to the friendly little neighborhood of Celadon.

When we entered your house, Mom was up off the couch, but the red bucket was still on the floor next to it.

"I'm feeling much better," she declared. "Did Dad pee in the cup?"

"He crushed it. Gave blood too. He was fantastic. *Right, Dad?*"

You stood next to me smiling proudly.

"Well, Matthew," she said. "Maybe you should take your father to *all* of his medical appointments."

I got you situated on the couch with your chicken Caesar wrap, some popcorn, and a seltzer. I put on *Law & Order*, and you disappeared into TV watching.

When I asked Mom if she was feeling well enough to manage, she told me to go home and write. I didn't wait for her to change her mind. I immediately wrote up this chapter, thinking none of this would have been in the memoir if Mom hadn't gotten sick in the middle of the night. I also thought, *If helping one's demented father pee into a small plastic cup on an early Monday morning doesn't make that son a superhero, I don't know what does.* I wondered if Captain America ever did such a thing. I decided that coaching my father through the production of a urine sample was my personal version of entering into the Marvel Universe. Then I thought about those beautiful people in the Labcorp waiting room—all of them looking out for each other, voluntarily triaging with the limited seating—and I declared them everyday Captain Americas too.

17.

The other day when we were out walking here on Lady's Island, you told me how Pop Pop became a banker.

I knew Pop Pop played semiprofessional baseball as a young man, in the late 1930s and 1940s. He was a huge Philadelphia Athletics fan and had once seriously believed that he could play second base for them.

Back when he was a teenager, there was a priest in his neighborhood who worked with disadvantaged city boys. This priest formed a baseball team and would organize games against other neighborhoods. People would come to watch. The priest would charge admission. At the end of the summer, he would use the cash to rent a place on the Jersey Shore. And, in this way, the poor teenagers on the team were treated to their first-ever beach vacations. When Pop Pop talked about this priest—who was named Martin—he would get misty-eyed.

Dad, you were named after this priest. This is how you came to be known as Michael Martin Quick, only Pop Pop never told you that. I don't know why he told me instead of you. It seems weird.

Pop Pop could play second base as good as anyone. And he always had a plus .300 batting average. But for some reason, he couldn't hit a good curveball. Once a curveball pitcher figured out this weakness, Pop Pop had trouble. At the semipro, poor Philly neighborhood games, there were no scouts for the opposing teams and few serious curveball pitchers. But there were scouts in the pros. And ace pitchers.

Pop Pop never quite mastered the fine art of hitting the curveball, but he remained committed to playing baseball.

This next bit is the part you told me about on our walk—what I hadn't heard before. When it came time for Pop Pop to get a real job, he made a compromise. Apparently, a local bank had a baseball team, which was fielded exclusively by its employees. And they needed a second baseman. They told him he could figure the banking part out as he went along. He said, "When do I start?"

I hadn't known before that Pop Pop never really wanted to be a banker but had become one to keep his baseball dream alive, if only in some diminished capacity.

I have a photograph of the bank's baseball team. In his uniform, Pop Pop is seated on a bench, third man from the right. He looks tough as nails with his hand dangling between his spread thighs and a lit cigarette between his right pointer and middle fingers. Typed on the back of the print are these words:

Harry Quick,

You were the only one that played every inning and deserve the title of "Iron Man Harry."

Your batting average for the season was .367.

Ike Pennington 1947

Depending on when the picture was taken, "Iron Man Harry" is either twenty-six or twenty-seven years old. He'd already helped America beat the Nazis. He had a young son at home, Peter. You weren't yet born. But you might have begun growing in your mother's belly and would be on Earth soon enough. And Pop Pop was just barely hanging onto his dream of being a baseball player.

A little less than four decades later, you decided to coach my elementary school baseball team. I didn't yet know any of the above history, of course. I was still just a kid. I knew Pop Pop loved baseball, but that was about it. He wouldn't tell me about his semipro baseball days and Martin the priest until I was just a bit older than he was in that black-and-white photo I have of his bank team. That's when I started interviewing him about his past, maybe in unconscious anticipation of writing this memoir. In elementary school, I also didn't know that you, Dad, had already failed to live up to his high expectations when you had played Little League yourself.

No one asked whether I wanted to play baseball. You just signed me up. I did not protest, of course. Every boy in my elementary school played America's pastime. It was an unspoken requirement. I didn't mind T-ball, nor did I mind when we all advanced to someone's dad pitching to both teams. All the kids from school were there. It felt like gym class, and gym class was always all right. You weren't coaching then. Maybe you helped out a few times, but I don't remember you being in charge of our team.

That changed when I went to what was called—if I am remembering it correctly—The Majors. In The Majors, we kids pitched to each other. From the top of a concrete tower behind home plate, someone announced the games through a speaker system that you could hear all over town. There were playoffs, one team would be named the champion at the end of each season, and players could make an All-Star team. You stepped up and decided to be my coach.

I remember two things for sure: You drafted players no one else wanted, and you took the whole coaching thing dead seriously.

You drafted the only girl who wanted to play with the boys; the kid who had Down syndrome; the kid whose father was rumored to be rough and unpredictably dangerous, even by our rough town's standards; and one kid just because he was left-handed and you wanted a left-handed pitcher on the team. Even as a kid myself, I marveled at your daring and unconventional picks. Every coach automatically had their son placed on their team, so you didn't draft me.

Before the season began, you sat me down and said, "No one ever wants to be the catcher. It's a tough, dirty, thankless job. You don't hit so well, Matthew, but if you play catcher, I can justify putting you in the starting lineup right away. And you'll have a better shot at making the All-Star team at the end of the year. If not this year, then next. And your grandfather is going to be coming to these games, so I expect you to do your best."

I thought, *Oh, this is for my dad, not me. He wants to show his father that he can win The Majors.* There was no judgment. I really wanted to help you impress Pop Pop. I wanted that for you, Dad. But I didn't care otherwise. I didn't love baseball. I didn't even really *like* it. In fact, it mostly made me feel sleepy. I often felt like yawning while on the baseball field or in the dugouts. I forced myself not to. I cheered for my teammates and did everything you and the other coaches told me to do. But I was mostly thinking about whether you or Mom would give me any money afterward so I could buy something from the snack shack.

The first time I put on the catcher's equipment, I knew I was going to fucking *hate* playing catcher. The leg pads were stiff and constricting. The chest pad reeked of a dozen or so previous boys' collective body odor. And the mask was not only dusty, but it smashed my big brown glasses into my nostrils so that I had trouble breathing. The helmet pinched my ears. And I generally felt dirty, hot, and disgusting whenever I had to put on this torturous outfit.

After you taught me how to squat down into the catcher's position, you gave me a catcher's mitt and pitched me some balls. I don't think you threw your hardest, but you were an adult, so—when the baseball hit my hand—it felt like my palm had exploded.

As I tried to shake the searing pain away, you said, "Use the webbing of the glove to catch the ball," but the webbing wasn't even a third of the area that opened up whenever I displayed what you called "a target," and I didn't have the necessary skills to make the ball land in the spot where it would hurt less.

"I don't think I'm any good at this, Dad," I said.

You came off the mound, flipped up my mask, looked through the thick lenses of my glasses and into my eyes, before you said, "You have greatness in you, Matthew. Your grandfather was an excellent baseball player. He's coming to watch you play. And you are going to become the best catcher in the league."

I thought, *Pop Pop doesn't give a shit about any of this. He never even talks to me about baseball. He likes to play pinochle with me. He likes to eat ice cream with me. He likes to take me to the movies. He likes when I mow his grass or shovel the snow off his driveway. He doesn't care whether I play baseball or not.*

But you cared, Dad. And you cared *a lot*.

Our team—which was called the Lions—started winning right away. You kept the scorebook and crunched numbers after the game like it was your job. You seemed to take it much more seriously than the other fathers. Because of this, you often outmaneuvered them. And I noticed that some of the parents began to really praise you. You treated the only girl on our team just like anyone else, and she became one of our better players. Her parents, whom I knew well, were appreciative. The one father who was rumored to be dangerous, well, you sometimes let him help out with practices and coach one of the bases. And he often seemed moved to the verge of tears as he encouraged all of us. Being a tough guy, he never cried, of course, but I understood that your including the father whom other adults mistrusted was heroic of you, especially when this man proved to be an asset to the team, and all of us kids liked him. And I'll never forget the game when the teammate who had Down syndrome walloped a ball over the home-run fence and then tried to run to third base instead of first. Our base coaches straightened him out. Once he finished his trot around the diamond, we all ran out of the dugout and went crazy with our cheering. After the game—as if you were Moses and had just parted the Red Sea—his parents thanked you for including him. I felt proud on your behalf.

Pop Pop would come to our games. Whenever I saw him in the stands, he'd be frowning. I couldn't figure it out because we were usually winning. I decided it was because I sucked so bad at baseball. We had the hardest throwing pitcher in the league on our team, and my left palm would feel fractured by the second inning whenever this fireball-tossing young man was on the mound. If the ball didn't land directly in my glove, I usually didn't catch it. I had trouble throwing to second base, and teams started regularly stealing on me. I kept moving down in the batting lineup because you couldn't justify me batting any closer to the top. Other coaches seemed to brazenly favor their sons—embarrassingly so. But you wanted to win.

Regardless of whether we had a game day or just practice, you'd be the first person to show up at the field and the last person to leave, which meant I'd be there the whole time too. And as you raked the sand of the diamond or locked up the equipment at the end, you'd give me lectures about my potential. You would say you saw greatness in me, but I wasn't living up to it. "If you'd just reach out and grab that greatness," you'd say, "you could be the star of the team." I knew you were nuts. If anyone else had wanted to play catcher, I wouldn't have even been in the starting lineup and damn well knew it. But I tried hard for you.

Then I began to notice that I felt sick every time we went to the baseball field. I'd get this sensation of my nasal passages and windpipe shrinking until it would feel like I couldn't get enough air into my lungs. I also felt nauseated. I'd get these pulsing headaches that made my skull feel like it was cracking, and I'd legitimately worry that I was going to shit my pants. Whenever my turn to bat came up, I'd secretly pray that you'd pinch-hit for me. And when I'd hear, "Quick, you're on deck," all of those confidence-crushing symptoms would intensify. As I put on a batting helmet and stepped out of the dugout to take practice swings with the doughnut weight on the end of my bat, I would pray for a double play or a strikeout, whatever would end the inning. Because I didn't want to hear my name called through the loudspeaker. I didn't want to step into the batter's box. I didn't want everyone in the neighborhood's eyes on me. I didn't want to disappoint you yet again.

"You have greatness in you," you'd say, as I'd walk toward home plate with a bat in my hands. "Remember that."

I'd look over at Pop Pop in the stands, and the expression on his face seemed to say, *I'm sorry your father is doing this to you. Anyone with eyes knows you aren't a baseball player.*

And then I'd almost always strike out.

When I was catching and a man got on base, you'd also yell, "You have greatness in you, Matthew," just before a pitch would fly by me. The man on first would start running to second, I'd flip the catcher's mask off my face, knocking my glasses askew so I couldn't see, and then I would take forever to find the ball. If I eventually made a throw, the ball would almost always sail over the heads of the infielders and deep into the outfield, which allowed the kids on base to advance even more, sometimes all the way home.

I don't remember doing one single thing properly as a Lion, but I guess I couldn't have been too much of a liability because we won the league championship. I believe we did that two years in a row. Someone's dad sprayed us elementary school kids with real alcoholic champagne, which would probably get him arrested today.

I have this vivid memory of you talking with Pop Pop afterward, trying to show him the strategies you used to help our team win The

Majors. He was not just disinterested, but kind of disgusted with you. I didn't get it at the time. You had won the championship. Your father was supposed to be a big baseball fan. His lack of praise irked you, and you stormed out of his house in the middle of the conversation. I was sitting with Pop Pop at his round kitchen table.

We looked at each other, and I said, "Why did my dad get so upset?"

Pop Pop smiled sadly at me and said, "It's just a game. You don't have to play it if you don't want to."

I didn't.

Before the start of the next season, I nervously asked you if I had to play junior high baseball. I was shocked when you said it was my choice. Then I thought, *Oh, it's because he can't coach that team.* (I think it might have been coached by our gym teacher at the time.) Maybe that read is not correct. Maybe you really were freeing me from the need to play any more baseball. Maybe you saw how much I hated it. I don't know.

I also remember this one time when you asked me to have a catch on our front lawn in Oaklyn. Outside of scheduled practices, you didn't often ask me to do anything. I was excited to throw the ball with you. Maybe we were breaking in a new glove you had bought me. We spread out to the full width of our property, which was only a little more than two car lengths. And when you threw me the ball, I caught it. I felt so proud of myself, because I didn't always catch the ball back then. But when my right fingers pulled the ball out of my glove, my throat and nasal passages shrunk again, I couldn't take in enough oxygen, and my bowels shook. For some reason, I knew that I wasn't going to be able to make the ball travel to your glove.

"Throw me the ball, Matthew," you said. "We don't have all day."

When I forced myself to throw you the ball, it soared over your head by at least twenty feet.

"I'm not chasing that," you said. "Go get it."

With my heart pounding, I ran past you, across our next-door neighbor's yard, and into the street. I picked up the baseball and sprinted back, handing you the ball along the way.

You threw me another perfect ball, but I closed my glove too soon. The ball hit the outer webbing and it dropped to my feet.

"Concentrate!" you bellowed.

I didn't want you to see that my hands were shaking, so I picked up the ball and fired it back at you.

Once again, it sailed way over your head.

"What is wrong with you, Matthew? Why are you wasting my time?"

I sprinted and retrieved the ball again. I tried to hand it to you as I passed, but you said, "I know how to throw a baseball. It's *you* who needs to learn."

So with the baseball in my hand, I sprinted back to my spot.

"Now," you said, "if you throw that ball over my head one more time, this catch is over." You lifted your eyebrows and then said, *"Understood?"*

"Yes, sir," I said. Then I prayed to God, silently saying, *Please, please, please help me throw this ball into my father's baseball glove. I beg of you, God. Please.*

I stared at the target you were holding up. I concentrated. I reminded myself not to let go of the ball until my fingers were pointing at your glove. And I told myself to let my arm and hand follow through to the ground after I released the ball. I began to feel confident. I had God on my side now. So I windmilled my arm and took a step toward you. And when I released the ball, it flew thirty feet over your head.

You immediately screamed, "That's it. I'm finished. *I can't take this!*"

As you stormed your way into the house and I jogged to get the ball, I thought to myself, *You could just keep running forever and never see your father again.* But when I picked up the baseball, I only paused for a second before I came back home, went inside, and apologized to you for throwing the ball over your head.

"It's not that hard," you said. *"Every boy in America can throw a baseball."*

Many years later, when Pop Pop was nearing the end of his life, he called me on the phone. His church needed money for a new heater or something like that. He had this big plan to put together a concert. He was going to be the star singer. If he wasn't ninety at the time, he was almost there. His singing voice had been shot for years, if not decades. But he would still tape himself singing. He'd make everyone who visited him sit through these prerecorded performances while he proudly tapped the air with an index finger and sang along. A generous person might find his enthusiasm charming. But, sadly, some friends and family members became increasingly annoyed over the years. Pop Pop thought people would actually pay money to hear him sing. He thought he could raise several thousand dollars for the church just by lending his singing voice to the cause.

He point-blank asked me to write a big fat check to his church in support of his fundraising concert. Before I had even wrapped my mind around that, he said to me, "Remember when I sat through all of your Little League games? Now you have to do something for me." The comment felt like a hard slap to the ear, because all I heard afterward was a loud ringing. I thought, *I hated when you came to those games. I hated being watched. You weren't doing me a favor. All that was for my father. He was trying to impress you. He was trying to earn your love. Was your watching me play baseball*—when I was eleven—*transactional? Were you only there to bank a favor you'd call in decades later? I was a little boy. You were supposed to* want *to be there.*

But then, Dad, I recalled the look on Pop Pop's face whenever I saw him sitting in the Little League stands. He *hadn't* wanted to be there. He was embarrassed of my glaring inability to play baseball. And he was even more embarrassed of your inability to realize that you shouldn't highlight your son's lack of athletic skills by making Little League baseball into some sort of midlife quest to earn your father's respect. Pop Pop was admitting that coming to watch you coach and me play for the Lions had been painful for him. And now he wanted compensation.

This was the only time I ever felt let down by Pop Pop. And it was the first time I truly began to understand why you were the way you were. I felt so much sympathy for you that I actually told you what Pop Pop had said—how he had tried to use his attending my Little League games to guilt me into giving his church money so that he could look like a hero.

To my great surprise, Dad, you immediately called your father and told him that what he had done was despicable. You stuck up for me—and maybe even yourself.

The next day, Pop Pop called and said he owed me an apology. Then he said what he had done was wrong and that he was sorry, and he hoped I could forgive him. He said going to see me play baseball when I was a kid had been a great joy. That last part was the only false note in the conversation. Otherwise, he seemed truly repentant.

I was surprised you got involved in my first and only little spat with Pop Pop. I was initially tempted to think maybe you were more upset about his inability to appreciate your stellar Little-League-coaching skills. But I've come to believe that you knew just how much damage your father could inflict and you chose to protect me from it. Pop Pop never tried to guilt-trip me again.

The last time I ever went to see Pop Pop and Grandmom in the Lititz retirement home Alicia was with me. The four of us spent the afternoon playing cards and eating steak sandwiches and spiced gumdrops. Pop Pop probably made us watch one of his old singing performances on VHS. Maybe all four of us sang your parents' theme song—the old standard, "Side by Side," which they often performed as a duet. At the end of our visit—after Pop Pop and Grandmom walked us out to our car—he threw his arms around me and held on for longer than he ever had before.

"I love you," he said to me.

"I love you too," I said back to him.

Grandmom kissed me and told me to drive safe.

Alicia and I got into our car and buckled up. I shifted into gear and began making my way toward the road. As I drove past Pop Pop, tears were streaming out from under his big brown glasses.

"Why is my Pop Pop crying?" I asked Alicia.

"He thinks he's never going to see you again," Alicia said. "He thinks he just said goodbye to you."

"We'll be back," I said. "I'll *definitely* see him again. I promised I'd take him to see *Silver Linings Playbook* on the big screen."

But Pop Pop and I never laid eyes on each other ever again.

When he was on his deathbed, I was on a book tour. By phone, he advised me to take care of my business—saying that I had to put my burgeoning writing career first. He said I didn't need to visit him. He died while I was flying to Michigan to accept a literary award. Thirteen years later, I now see clearly that I should have disappointed the people who were honoring my work. I should have gone to see him one last time. I deeply regret taking Pop Pop's advice.

18.

Just a few days before the Christmas of 2022, an unnamed storm hit the Outer Banks.

Since Alicia and I had already ridden out named hurricanes—and our real estate agent had told us the brand-new, triple-tiered bulkhead system behind our house would last a hundred years—we went to bed unperturbed that night and slept right through all the wind and rain.

But when Alicia took puppy Kingsly out to pee the next morning, she discovered that the lowest tier of our bulkhead had been damaged almost beyond comprehension. It looked like a giant had ripped the left half of our eight-foot seawall away from our neighbors' bulkhead and dragged it six feet into the water, leaving behind a gaping wound, which had allowed most of the first tier's sand—a few thousand cubic feet worth—to vanish into the Albemarle Sound.

When Alicia reported what had happened, I ran outside to assess. I could see that the iron underground bars—which had anchored the bulkhead to the heart of our property—had snapped. Water must have gotten behind the wall and done the rest.

Around this time, I started having this recurring nightmare:

My wife and I are asleep in bed when the entire house begins to shake. I jump up and tell Alicia to grab Kingsly because we need to escape. But before we can get to the garage and drive away, our upper two bulkheads break and the whole house tumbles into the sound with us in it. Alicia, Kingsly, and I are buried alive and then drowned.

It would always be three a.m. when I'd wake up. With my heart pounding and Alicia sleeping next to me, I'd lie there in our bed, telling myself that I was being paranoid. But the terror of my nightmare started leaking into my days.

Wearing a black T-shirt, of course, I shared the dream with my Jungian analyst.

"You really need to take a symbolic view of this," Zeus advised.

"But my bottom bulkhead literally broke. That's *not* symbolic."

"And yet, your house has not fallen into the Albemarle Sound."

"But it might."

"On what do you base that leap of logic?"

"Houses fall into the ocean all the time on the Outer Banks."

"But your house is not oceanfront. Do you know of houses falling into the sound? Is that a thing?"

"No, but we live on a hill and—"

"What did the bulkhead guy tell you?"

"He said he could repair the wall and backfill it with sand. That it would be stronger than it was before."

"So what exactly is the problem?"

"I don't really know him. He was the only one who could do the work. What if he's wrong or flat out lying?"

"You have to trust the expert. He does this for a living."

"But he's only working on the bottom bulkhead, and he didn't design my house."

"Your house was inspected. It was looked over by insurance people. It's been there for almost twenty years, right?"

"I know I'm being irrational, but I seriously feel like I'm going to have a heart attack if I don't get out of this house. The sane part of me knows that our home isn't going to fall into the Albemarle Sound, but I keep having that same nightmare, and it scares the shit out of me."

"Again. What do you think the dream means *symbolically*? Why would God want you to *symbolically* leave your house? What *metaphorical* danger might you be in? What might the collapse of your house in the dream be *symbolizing*? What *symbolic* bulkhead in your life has recently broken?"

"You mean my dad's dementia?"

"Do you feel like your father's cognitive abilities were a bulkhead in your life that is now collapsing? That the metaphorical water is rushing in? Are you in danger of completely losing your father? Is his metaphorical sand slowly leaking into the great water beyond?"

"You always say I can't stop my father's dementia."

"That's true."

"So what exactly am I supposed to do?"

"Maybe the better question for you to ask yourself is this: What does my soul want? And am I going to be generous with myself?"

"That's two questions."

Zeus frowned and said, "You can continue to be in pain for as long as you wish."

"Just tell me what to do and I'll do it."

"I'm not the one giving you the dream. Something greater than me is speaking to you."

"I'm really not doing well, Zeus. I haven't felt this bad in a long time. I feel really fucked up."

"What does the house symbolize in the dream?"

"I don't know. Me?"

"You are already in the dream. The dream you is in the house."

"You think the house symbolizes my father."

"Say more about that."

"Like I've constructed my entire life in response to Dad's abuse. Now that my father is losing his mind, I feel like his demise is also threatening to destroy my sense of who I am and—by extension—my relationship with Alicia and Kingsly?"

"Interesting."

"Or maybe the sands of time are running out."

"Say more."

"Like I need to escape this house not because it is going to literally fall into the water, but because my father is going to die much sooner than I had anticipated, and this house is keeping me far away from him. I have to get out of the house. Also, it's like the dementia has broken the bulkhead of Dad's mind. His memories, his intelligence, his ability to interact with me—all of that is rushing out. And, eventually, there will be nothing left of my father. He will metaphorically be reclaimed by the water. So what do I do with *that*?"

"I would ponder that last question long and hard if I were you."

"Do you think God is making me paranoid about living here so that I'll move to Beaufort? To be with my father before he loses the ability to communicate with me?"

"I think God is definitely powerful enough to nudge your soul one way or the other. This dream is stirring up a lot of unconscious material in you. But you do have free will."

"I'm not *choosing* to have the same nightmare every single night. I'm not *choosing* to be paranoid."

"Only some unconscious part of you clearly *is* choosing that."

"What should I do?"

"What does your soul want?" Zeus asked me.

The answer to that question popped into my head immediately, but I was too afraid to verbalize it at the time.

So I kept having the same nightmare by night. And I kept getting more and more paranoid by day. Until—a month or so later—I found the courage to answer Zeus's question honestly and give my soul what it had been yearning for since the day I was born.

19.

Dad, we're getting closer to the end of this memoir. And before I sign off for good, I'm going to have to cover some rough spots in our past, much worse than what we've covered so far. So I thought before we got to all that, I'd write about the time when I first really understood that you cared whether I lived or died. It's a strange moment that's both good and bad. I want to tell you about it from my perspective.

It might have been the summer in between my eighth and ninth grade school years. That would have been the summer of 1988. You would have been forty, and I would have been fourteen. Back then—and this seems rather remarkable to me now—you used to let me bring a friend on vacation with us when we went to the Outer Banks at the end of each August. I used to bring Bart.

Bart and I decided we wanted to be surfers.

One of your customers at the bank alerted you to a bargain-priced surfboard, so you came home with a shortboard made by a company called Spectrum. When I stood it up, it wasn't even as tall as I was. Neither of us knew it at the time, but it was made for advanced surfers who knew what they were doing. It was almost impossible to learn on. That didn't keep me from paddling out into the ocean with it anyway.

Bart's parents were much older than all the rest of our friends' parents. Bart started working for the family business early on in life, so he always had serious money in his pocket, back when the rest of us were relying on measly allowances and lousy paper-route pay. He bought himself a longer, more appropriate Wave Riding Vehicles board, and then we were in the Nags Head ocean from sunup to sundown, trying to catch waves. He sometimes stood up on his board. I wiped out every single time I managed to pop my chest up off the Spectrum and get my feet onto it. I ate sand for breakfast, lunch, and dinner. It's a wonder I didn't kill myself.

We'd been hearing about a hurricane warning throughout our entire vacation, but the weather was picture-perfect and it seemed like it couldn't possibly change. Uncle Pete knew some of the locals, and they said it would be all right to ride out the storm, even though there was an evacuation happening. Despite the fact that we'd not even come close to mastering the small ones, Bart and I secretly hoped for gigantic waves, keeping our plans hidden from Mom and you, of course.

When the skies darkened and the storm approached, the family stayed indoors and played board and card games. Bart and I waited until no one was paying us any attention. When our moment came, we snuck out the back door, tiptoed down the wooden outdoor staircase, grabbed our surfboards from underneath the house, and ran through the rain to the beach.

The surf had picked up. *A lot.* We suburban boys hadn't had enough experience with the ocean to really know what that meant, so we paddled out into the beginnings of a possible hurricane hit.

As the ocean churned beneath us, I wondered if we were gambling with our lives, and I felt more alive than I ever had before. Bart and I had read enough issues of *Surfer* magazine to know that real surfers chased good waves, and good waves were often made by extreme weather conditions. But it was a struggle to duck dive under the enormous white walls of water rushing at us as we paddled out. Several times, I was thrown off my board and had to rely on the rubber leash that tethered my ankle to my Spectrum. Each time I came up, I'd look for Bart. When we'd make eye contact, we'd *yeehaw* to each other like cowboys and then try again to duck dive under the white walls rushing at us. This went on for a long time. When we approached the break, it was bigger than anything we had seen before but not clean at all. Just a massive white wall, all of it collapsing at the same time. It looked impossible to surf, which was probably why there were zero other surfers in the water with us. Yet we kept paddling toward it.

That's when I heard screaming.

I thought maybe Bart had been bitten by a shark, but when I looked over at him, he was only looking at me, making sure I was okay.

"*HEEEEEEEEEEEEEYYYYYYYYYYYYYYY!*" we heard again.

We turned and faced the beach.

We had drifted far south. Farther than I believed was actually possible. Even though we were a long way out into the ocean—and therefore had a really wide view of the beach—I couldn't see any houses anymore, not even when I looked north. I only saw sand dunes. Could we have drifted a mile? My heart started beating twice as hard as it already had been. Suddenly, I absolutely knew that we shouldn't be out in the ocean during a hurricane.

Then I saw you, Dad, sprinting down the water's edge from the north.

"GET OUT OF THE WATER!" you screamed. "GET OUT!!!!! *NOW!!!!!!*"

Each time you caught up to where we'd just been, we'd already be much farther south, which is when Bart and I realized just how fast we were drifting.

Furiously, we began paddling in. Then—on our bellies and holding on to our boards for dear life—we rode an avalanche of white water toward the shore. Then we paddled the last bit toward your screaming.

"What the hell are you two doing? You could have been killed! *Easily* killed! Do you have any idea how far you've drifted? People die in hurricanes even when they *aren't* in the ocean! I thought you were already dead! You could have been dead! Do you understand that? Don't you realize how stupid you were being?"

Your face was purple, and your glasses were spotted with rain. In between your screams, you were hyperventilating. As we hopped off our boards and walked through the knee-high surf and onto the beach, you kept screaming.

"This is so stupid! I thought you were both dead! There are no lifeguards here! No one else is surfing! Why did you do this? What were you thinking? *Why?* Do you realize the risk you took? *Do you?* It's a goddamn miracle you're both still alive!"

Bart just stood there behind his now upright surfboard, marveling at your outburst. His father never screamed like that. Never. It was like Bart was observing a lion roaring at the zoo. I think he was kind of thrilled by it.

You turned your face north again and began marching up the beach, back toward Uncle Pete's house.

Bart and I looked at each other, before he said, "The waves were shit, right?"

"Yeah," I said. "If they were good, the local surfers would be swarming this place."

"Alright," he said.

And then we were silently following you at a distance, trying to keep our surfboards pointed into the wind so they wouldn't lift us into the air like hang gliders.

Then it felt like I was being choked. My stomach was rumbling. I began to worry that I was going to shit my bathing suit. The rain started pelting us harder. The temperature dropped. I noticed that you were shivering, Dad. And that's when it hit me like a thunderbolt.

If you had really wanted me dead, you wouldn't have run down the beach screaming like a maniac.

You wanted me to be alive.

You wanted me to keep living.

The idea of me drowning in the ocean actually made you distraught.

The way you had behaved in front of Bart—not just the screaming you had done on the beach, but how you had acted all week, calling me Sundial, insulting my past girlfriends, and pinching the skin around my stomach—greatly embarrassed me.

But you'd run a mile through the start of a hurricane in a legitimate attempt to save my life.

And, at the time, that was the closest you'd ever gotten to saying, "I love you, son."

20.

A few weeks after Alicia and I moved to Beaufort in the fall of 2023, Mom started making plans to visit Micah in Pennsylvania. Your two grandsons were both born in the first week of December, and there were going to be birthday parties. Even though—according to Mom—there are better and cheaper dementia-related resources available in Beaufort and she had always wanted to live in the Lowcountry, permanently moving you here wasn't an easy decision. Micah's family was still residing in the Philadelphia suburbs. The original plan had been for Mom and you to split time between Pennsylvania and South Carolina, but when you were no longer able to travel, Mom had to pick one or the other. Megan, Isla, and Brexley were also living in South Carolina and were only a three-and-a-half-hour drive away from Lady's Island, so they could and did visit more regularly than Micah's family. Leaving Archer and Oliver behind in Pennsylvania—a twelve-hour drive from us—made Mom heartsick.

You making the trip up north was never on the table. No one knew how you would handle an airport and flying. And the last long car trip you had taken down to Beaufort did not go well. You were anxious on the drive and obsessed with monitoring the fuel gauge from the passenger seat. You tried to get Mom to fill up at every gas station you passed just to be on the safe side. During a stop, you passed out in a men's restroom, badly hitting your head on a sink. A stranger had to get you up off the floor, guide you out of the bathroom, and then help you find Mom, who was more than a little alarmed by all the blood.

After that, we'd all pretty much decided that your traveling days were done, and you seemed to understand why at the time.

When Mom asked if you'd be okay with me taking care of you for a few days, you said, "Go to Pennsylvania, Doreen. See the boys. Get your hair cut. Visit your friends. Take care of your medical appointments. I'll be fine here."

"Matthew will stay with you," Mom said. "In our house."

"I don't need Matthew to sleep in our house. I'm not a child."

"I'd feel better if he did," Mom said.

"He has to stay with his wife in his house," you said. "I don't want Alicia to be lonely. That's not right."

"She'll come visit you both every day," Mom said.

"I don't need a babysitter," you said.

"Mike, I'm not going to be able to enjoy myself if you're here by yourself overnight. Can you please just let Matthew stay with you while I'm gone?"

"I don't want to keep you from your friends and family," you said to your wife, and then it was settled.

Mom had asked me to dad-sit you for three days, but when she gave me her itinerary, it was five days long. She wasn't including the travel days. I was. I worried about how you would react to being without her for so long. She said she didn't want to be a prisoner, and we'd have to find ways for her to get breaks from being your caretaker. It was hard to argue against that. But I understood from the beginning that this was an experiment, and we really had no idea how it would go.

The first sign of trouble came when Mom said to me, "You might need to sleep in bed with your father."

"Um . . . *what?*" I said.

"He wakes up in the middle of the night and gets scared. He reaches over for me, and when he feels my arm, he relaxes and goes back to sleep. But if I'm not in bed, he'll get up and search for me. When he finds me in the bathroom or in the kitchen, he'll clutch his chest and say, 'Thank god.' So if he wakes up and I'm not in bed with him, it might set him off."

"I'm pretty sure reaching over in the middle of the night and finding another man in bed with him might set Dad off too."

"Let's ask him," she said.

We found you on the couch in the living room. You had been watching TV but immediately turned your attention to us.

"Go ahead. Ask him," Mom said to me.

"Dad," I said, "do you want me to sleep next to you when Mom's not here?"

You looked at me like I had just told an off-color joke. Then you said, "You will never ever sleep in a bed with me, Matthew. Not going to happen."

"Mike," Mom said, "you wake up in the middle of the night, and sometimes you get scared."

"He's not sleeping with me, Doreen. That's not right. No."

I raised my eyebrows at Mom.

"Just you wait and see," she responded. "You're going to be sleeping in that bed with your father."

That night in my own bed, I said to Alicia, "I think this will be good for Dad and me. And it's definitely going to be good for Mom. She needs to get away."

"Are you really going to sleep in the same bed with your dad?" Alicia asked.

"I don't know," I said. "I will if I have to."

"It doesn't freak you out?"

"Not really."

"He'll never allow it anyway."

"I'm going to take him to the movies a few times. We'll walk on the beach. We'll walk the dog. We'll watch football. Maybe go out to dinner. It'll be fine."

"I don't know. Your mom's his safety blanket."

"How bad could it get?" I said and then fell asleep feeling pretty confident.

The next morning, I drove Mom to the Savannah airport with you in the back seat. She was practically floating with grandmotherly anticipation. And she kept extroverting her schedule at us, telling us every single detail of her five-day itinerary.

From the back seat, you kept saying to your wife, "Doreen, you should see your friends and family. I'll be fine. I'm glad you're going," which made me think, *This is going to be a piece of cake. Let the father-son healing begin.*

When we dropped Mom off at the airport, you gave her a quick kiss as I got her luggage out of the trunk. Then you were climbing into the front passenger seat, and she was saying, "Just call if you need me." I gave her a peck on the cheek, and then I was driving you back to Beaufort.

Halfway home, you said, "Mom's going to visit Micah's boys, right?"

"Yessir," I said. "And we're having a man weekend, Dad."

"That's good," you said, but with far less enthusiasm. "I'm for that."

When I noticed your knee bouncing up and down, I began to feel a little less confident.

That night you wanted pizza, so I ordered a few pies from the wood-fired place downtown and invited Alicia and Kingsly over to your house, saying you and I'd go pick up the food and would be back in a half hour. Then we jumped into the car and started making our way toward downtown Beaufort.

When we approached the old swing bridge, traffic was backed up worse than I had ever seen it before.

"The bridge must be swung open," you said, "to let a boat through."

I figured you were right, but then the traffic would move every so often, which made me think there was something else going on.

As more and more time passed, your anxiety became palpable. It began to feel like someone was incrementally increasing the heat in the car while also slowly sucking out all the oxygen. As you fidgeted in the passenger seat and periodically barked, "Why aren't we moving?" I began to feel the invisible hand choking me. I was a little boy again, and I was desperately trying to figure out what your nervous system needed so that you wouldn't start screaming or getting violent.

When we hit the start of the bridge, I saw that the entire downtown was lit up for Christmas, and there was some sort of winter celebration going on. As we inched our way up the bridge and over the river, I also saw that Bay Street was blocked off by police, which meant we were not going to be able to park anywhere near the pizza place. Every cell in my body said, *Abort the mission!* But we went to Hearth all the time. Mom had made friends with one of the servers, to the point of buying her gifts for her recently born daughter. I didn't want to stiff the restaurant on an order. So we drove on.

It took us another good half hour to find a parking spot, which was probably at least a half mile away from the pizza shop. There were people everywhere. Everyone was merry and bright. Little kids in Santa hats skipped down sidewalks while holding their parents' hands. In stark contrast, you, Dad, looked like you were going to explode. Your face was drained of color. Your hands were balled up in fists so that your knuckles were glowing white. And your anxiety was strangling me.

"We'll just get the pizza and go home, okay?" I tried, as I turned the car off.

You said nothing but did get out of the vehicle.

As we made our way toward Bay Street, we heard Christmas music playing. People swarmed around us. They were laughing and singing, their hearts practically glowing with holiday cheer. You looked like you were about to reenact your father's storming of the Normandy beaches in World War II.

When we got to the downtown section, there were bouncy castles set up for kids and stages for musicians and even a makeshift outdoor movie theater for everyone to watch holiday classics. There were Christmas lights as far as the eye could see. It was all charming and delightful.

"What is all this?" you demanded to know.

"They're getting ready for Christmas."

"It's not Christmas yet."

"It's the first week of December."

"It is not."

"Okay, Dad, let's just get the pizza. Then we're out of here."

We fought like spawning salmon against the great river of Christmas mirth. When we finally entered Hearth, it was swarming with an even higher concentration of people—all of them hungry for wood-fired pizza. We had to slalom our way to the front of the bar, where we waited impatiently for the attention of the beyond-overworked bartender.

"I have to get out of here," you whispered to me. "I can't take this."

"Dad, just let me pay for what we ordered and then we're gone. We'll be home before you know it."

When the bartender got around to us, I said, "Pickup for Quick."

Once we had our pizza boxes, I stuffed cash into the barkeep's hands, and then we were fighting our way through Christmas joy once again, as you kept saying you didn't think you were going to make it through the merriment of your Beaufort neighbors.

"We're absolutely going to make it," I kept saying. "We have to."

Back in the car with the pizzas on your lap, I drove away from the masses and took the long way home, going over the Port Royal Bridge, because it was far less crowded.

"What took you so long?" Alicia asked when we walked through the back door of your home. "I'm starving."

I nodded over at you, and when Alicia saw the zombie-like expression on your face, she stopped asking questions.

We ate our pizza in silence.

When the hush got too loud, I said, "Dad, we're going to have a great weekend."

"What time is your mother coming home tonight?" you asked.

Alicia gave me a worried look.

"She's with Micah in Pennsylvania," I said.

When you stared at me blankly, I got Mom on FaceTime, and then she was thanking you for letting her go north and telling you how much fun she was already having with the boys.

After we hung up, I tried to give you your meds, but you refused to take them. Since one was for sleeping and I didn't want to be up with you all night, I said, "God told me that you absolutely must take the pills."

You said, "I know God didn't tell you that," but you took the pills anyway.

Alicia took Kingsly back to our house, and I got you ready for bed, making sure you put on your pajamas and scrubbed your teeth.

When you were actually in bed with the covers pulled up to your chin, I said, "Dad, do you want me to sleep in here with you?"

"Your mother will be coming to bed any minute now," you said.

"Dad, she's with Micah for a few days in Philly."

"That's right," you said with your eyes now closed.

"Do you need me to sleep in here with you? Because I will."

"You need to sleep in your own bed with Alicia."

"Alicia will be fine. It's *you* I'm worried about."

But you had already drifted off, so I turned out the lights and retreated to your guest room at the opposite end of the house.

I called Alicia and said, "I think this might be harder than I anticipated."

"I think you have no idea how hard this is going to get," she said. "But I'm here for you."

Knowing I needed to be well rested for our morning together, I turned out the light and went to sleep myself.

I woke up in the middle of the night with dread coursing through my veins.

In the darkness, I could feel someone in the room—that person was looking down at me, looming like a demon.

"Who are you?" a voice whispered, which forced a little scream out of me.

When I turned on the light, you were trembling by the side of my bed.

"Dad, it's me, your son, Matthew."

"Where am I?"

I jumped out of bed and started rubbing your arms. "You're in Beaufort, South Carolina."

"Where is Doreen?"

"She's with Micah in Philadelphia."

Your bottom lip started quivering, and your eyes began to brim with tears, as you said, "Am I getting a divorce? Is Doreen leaving me?"

"No," I said. "She's only visiting Micah for a few days. Then she'll be back."

"Why did she leave me all alone?"

"You're not alone. You're with me. I got you."

"I don't understand what's happening. I don't like this."

"Dad, you told Mom she should go home to Philadelphia. You said it would be good for her."

"I *never* said that! I would *never*!"

"Okay, Dad. Let's get you back in bed. Everything is going to be alright."

I put my arm around your trembling shoulders and started walking you through the living room and then the dining room and then the hallway that leads to your bedroom, where I got you in bed and started massaging the back of your neck.

"Dad, maybe I should sleep in here with you."

"No!" you screamed. "You will *not* sleep with me!"

"Okay," I said, and then just kept massaging you.

I could feel your muscles relaxing. I could feel you calming down.

"Go home and sleep with Alicia," you said, just before you fell back asleep.

I watched you for ten or so minutes, just to make sure you were really out. Then I tiptoed back to the guest room, where I lay in bed thinking, *How the hell am I going to make it through five days?*

The next morning—after I got you to take your meds and eat your breakfast—we sat down on the couch.

"What do you want to do today, Dad? This afternoon we're going to see that movie you wanted to see. But we can—"

"Why is your mother divorcing me, Matthew?"

"She's not—"

"I made all this money. Gave her everything she wanted. And she just leaves me?"

"She didn't leave you, she's—"

"I don't want to hear it, Matthew! She's left me! And now I don't have any money! *And I might as well just kill myself!*"

I took a deep breath. This was a conversation we'd had before, Dad. And one we will cover more in depth before this memoir concludes. So it was hard to know what about this current situation was dementia-related and what was just you being you.

I spent the next few hours listening to you call Mom a "bitch" and a "cunt" as I tried to reassure you that your wife was not divorcing you and you still had plenty of money. Nothing I said seemed to make any difference.

Whenever I got Mom on FaceTime, you dropped the act entirely, which was maddening. You'd tell her you were fine and were having fun with me, but just as soon as you were off with her, you'd start screaming at me again.

"I don't know what to do, Mom," I privately said to her behind the closed door of your guest room.

"I just wanted to have a few days with my grandsons," she said.

I felt for her.

I also worried about surviving the forthcoming greatest hits reel of my worst childhood memories. I was already feeling beyond retraumatized, and it had barely been twenty-four hours.

Alicia encouraged me to abandon my going-to-the-movies plan, but I had already bought the tickets for *Napoleon*. Also, you usually liked going to the movies, so I gambled.

As mentioned previously, it takes a good forty minutes to drive to the theater. With Alicia riding in the front passenger seat, you were in the back. I had hoped you'd be less insane around Alicia, but halfway there, you yelled, "I'm getting out of this car right now!"

"Dad," I said. "Don't touch that handle. We're doing sixty-five miles an hour."

"I don't care!" you screamed. "Doreen is divorcing me! And I'm done! Finished! I'm getting out of the car *right fucking now*!"

"Put on the child lock," Alicia told me.

As I hit the button, I said, "Dad, you are going to sit there with your hands in your lap. And then we're going to see the movie you requested. Do not touch that handle. Do you understand me?"

"I understand you," you said. "But I'm finished. I don't even care if your mother divorces me. *Fuck her.*"

"Okay, Dad. As long as you stay inside of the car."

At the movie theater, we got you popcorn and a soda, the eating and drinking of which seemed to calm you down. And when *Napoleon* came on, you got lost in it. I breathed a sigh of relief. But I was exhausted. Through a few scenes, I even rested my eyes.

In the third act, you grabbed my forearm and—with sheer terror in your voice—said, "Where's Doreen?"

"Dad," I whispered, "she's in Philly with Micah."

"I have to get out of here!" you yelled.

"Okay," I said and then smiled reassuringly at the people seated around us, who were now all staring. It was an older crowd, and they seemed to get what was going on right away. Most of them smiled back at me like they thought I was some kind of saint. "We can go," I told you.

But when I pushed the button that lowered your footrest, you looked to your left and saw that your neighbors' footrests were blocking your exit.

"We can't leave," you whispered.

"Dad, there's room for us to get by."

"Matthew, stop. We have to stay."

"They'll lower their footrests if we ask."

"Stop!" you yelled and then sort of froze in your seat so that it looked like you weren't even breathing anymore.

I didn't know what to do, so I decided to see what would happen if I did nothing.

You didn't move a muscle for the rest of the film and were silent afterward as we made our way out of the theater. Once we were all back in the privacy of the car, you started talking about Mom leaving you again, so I called her on the phone using the car's Uconnect.

"Hi, Mike," she said in a cheery voice while I drove.

You didn't say anything back.

"Are you worried about me?" Mom said.

You still said nothing.

"I love you," she tried. "And I'll be back soon. I'm just with Micah and the boys. Do you want to say happy birthday to your grandsons?"

You said nothing.

I think you were confused.

I told Mom we'd talk later.

That night she began looking for earlier flights home but couldn't find anything that made sense. The flights were expensive, and most of them would only shave a half day off her trip, so we made the decision to ride it out.

Then you and I did the same crazy dance for another few days. You refused to let me sleep in your bed. In the middle of the night, you'd search the house for Mom and end up scaring the hell out of me. You insisted all day and night that she was a "whore" who was leaving you and taking all of your money. I became more and more sleep-deprived and mentally exhausted. Alicia began to seriously worry about me. And Mom said she wouldn't put me in this position ever again.

On our last night together, right before Mom flew home, you once again entered the guest room in the middle of the night and woke me up. You were crying. You said you didn't want to get a divorce. You said you were so scared. I was beyond exhausted, so I put my arm around you, walked you back through your house, tucked you into your bed, lay on top of the covers next to you, and wrapped my arm around you as you cried. I just kept saying, "It's going to be okay. I promise." And, somehow, we both fell asleep like that.

When I opened my eyes, your smiling face was only inches from mine.

"I think your mother is coming home tonight, Matthew," you said. *"It's a good day."*

You were cured.

A part of me wondered if you had at least some control over your insanity. If you could so easily switch from being mad and resentful to being happy and hopeful, why had you tortured me for multiple days? But I quickly decided that was the wrong question to be asking at this point. So I got up and made sure you took your meds. And, as we were eating breakfast, you said, "Maybe we should go to that store so we can buy Mom some welcome-home presents."

Somehow I knew that in your brain "that store" meant Walmart. I was pretty sure Mom wouldn't find a pile of Walmart presents to be the welcome home of her dreams, but you were looking at me with such hope in your eyes that I couldn't resist.

Then we were walking through the Walmart parking lot, and you were saying, "I think this is only the second time I've been to this store," even though you'd been there many times before.

"What can we get Mom?" you asked, as we entered Walmart.

"Anything you want, Dad. *Anything at all.*"

I let you push a shopping cart up and down every single aisle, as you carefully considered which items would be the best welcome-home-Doreen presents. You excitedly picked out a steel device that looked like a kitchen whisk but was actually a head massager. You selected a piece of lemon cake in a plastic wrapper. You sniffed fifty different candles, and your mouth opened wide whenever you found a winner. Then you'd hold it under my nose and say, "Think Mom would like that?" Every time I nodded, that candle went into the cart. You picked out socks and an ugly Christmas sweater with a French bulldog on the front. We spent a good hour shopping for the triumphant return of your wife. You didn't once call her a cunt or a bitch. You didn't once mention divorce. You didn't raise your voice. It was like someone had come in the middle of the night and switched out the evil Michael for the good one.

Because we didn't want to risk taking you on another long car ride, Mom had a friend pick her up at the Savannah airport.

"Mom's coming home today, right?" you asked me ten billion times.

And when she walked through the front door, you wore the goofy grin of a kid who had long ago become accustomed to losing but inexplicably finds himself in the winner's circle. And I was happy for you, Dad. I was glad that you had Mom. I was glad that she had returned to you. I was glad that you were no longer suffering.

After Mom kissed and hugged you and then opened all her presents, you sat down on the couch and began watching TV, as though nothing we had been through in the past five days had ever happened.

"Guess we'll never be doing that again," Mom said, as we watched you calmly taking in whatever was on the television.

"I'm sorry I couldn't make it go better," I said.

She kissed me and said, "You made it go the best it possibly could. Thank you. It was good to get away."

As I walked back to my house, I wanted to lie down in the grass of the park, curl up in the fetal position, and then sleep for a hundred years. But I just kept putting one foot in front of the other.

You actually slept in bed with your father, I said to myself.

Before I could think too much about that, I was in the arms of my own wife, who was telling me I had done a good thing. She kissed my lips, said I needed to go to bed right away, and that she had booked me a massage.

"A massage?" I said.

"You need a fucking massage. Trust me."

"Was I *that* bad?"

"I really didn't think you were going to make it," Alicia said.

And then I was simply grateful that I had.

21.

Six months after I moved to Lady's Island, which would have been spring 2024, I was feeling depressed again, so I put on a black T-shirt and brought my melancholy to the attention of Zeus during one of our Zoom calls.

"I thought the move to Beaufort would be good for me," I said. "And in many ways it has been. But I really miss having lunch with my best Outer Banks friend, Chubis. And living around the corner from my parents brings up a lot of childhood baggage. Old wounds are being reopened."

"*Solve et coagula,*" he said.

"What do you mean?" I asked.

"You dissolve and reform. Dissolve and reform. Dissolve and reform. And, in this way, you get rid of the impurities. This is how the alchemists tried to turn lead into gold. You are dissolving and reforming too. Over and over and over again."

"So my depressions are just me melting down my lead."

"Symbolically."

"The big problem is that I'm not really writing."

"*Is* that a problem?"

"Writers write. By definition."

"You're writing Substack posts."

"No one reads my Substack posts."

"No one knows about them."

"I'm not doing any *real* writing."

"What's real writing?"

"The kind you get paid for."

"Aren't you getting paid through Substack?"

"Far less than minimum wage."

"So if you aren't making a lot of money, the writing doesn't count?"

"I need money to pay your fees."

"Always right back to my fee. Do you think I shouldn't be paid for my work?"

"Of course not. But I have expenses. I'm not making any money. And I can't write."

"Matthew, when we started working together, you were frozen solid. You were so stuck. You couldn't do much of anything except run in the woods by yourself."

"I remember."

"Then one day you started writing *We Are the Light*. You found a new publisher. Had a great experience working with your new editor. And even went on a book tour, traveling all over the country, having positive interactions with hundreds of people. You were in motion."

"But then I got stuck again."

"Then you started dreaming about your house falling into the Albemarle Sound."

"Because I was paranoid."

"Because the unconscious was trying to get a different part of your soul unstuck."

"But I had stopped writing again. Pretty much altogether."

"You stopped typing words into your laptop, but did you really stop writing?"

"I don't understand what you're trying to get me to see."

"When you started analysis, you were a shell of a human being. You couldn't face anything. You had no ego strength. Two and a half years later, the unconscious begins bombarding you with a horrific recurring dream. Your house falling into the Albemarle Sound with Alicia, Kingsly, and you in it. And within just a few weeks of getting that message from the unconscious, you begin the process of uprooting your entire life, selling your house, and moving to a different state—an eight-hour drive away. To face perhaps the three biggest psychological problems you have—the money complex, the mother complex, and the father complex—*simultaneously*. The unconscious showed you a three-headed dragon and you charged right at it. That is the complete opposite of being stuck."

"So when will I start writing about it?"

"You have to *live* it first. You have to earn the right to tell the story. You have to heal yourself. You have to see how this medicine is properly administered before you try to give it to your readers."

"You really think I'm moving in the right direction?"

"In all the years we have been working together—even in all of the many stories you've told me about your personal history before we even met—I have never experienced you moving with more speed and passion toward anything. Your job right now is to soak up as much positive father as you can possibly get. You need to heal that wounded father-hungry boy inside of you. The rest will follow naturally."

"You really think I'm on the right track?"

"The soft way you talk about your father now says yes. A big part of you hated him when we first started working together. You were boiling over with resentment. But the stories you tell me now about walking with him in Beaufort and on the beaches. Going to the movies. Watching football together. The way his sickness has softened your heart. The way you're allowing yourself to love your father for the first time in your life. The way his dementia is allowing him to love you. This is the way to cure your brokenness. You *are* doing the work, Matthew. And if you keep doing it, God will grant you opportunities to be useful to others. The best parts of you really want to be useful to others. It's all the damaged parts, all the defenses, that are keeping you from doing this. Replacing the defenses with something better is an arduous process. The work is slow. But you are definitely doing it. You are listening to the unconscious. Following the nudges that you are being given by your dreams and active imaginations. And Jung really believed that this will lead you where you need to go. I believe it. And I think you believe it too. Which is why you are in Beaufort with your father, instead of being in Hollywood or wherever else might help your career. Your soul wants to be with your father. You and your father are in a container now. We don't know what that alchemy will produce. But it is definitely producing something important."

"How do you know?"

"Because there is a lot of heat coming off you. You're cooking."

"I wish I was writing."

"That will come."

"Are you sure?"

"When you go inside of yourself. When you ask the unconscious. What does your intuition tell you?"

"That I'm not ready. But I will be down the road."

"Then you need to practice being patient. And being grateful for the rare medicinal opportunity you have been granted."

"To be with my dad?"

"To heal your soul."

"What happens when I heal my soul?"

"That's above my pay grade."

"I think I'm meant to help other people. Is that why you've given me so much free extra time over the years? Because you thought I would be useful to others down the road?"

"I already told you why I gave you extra time."

"Why?"

"Because I love you."

"Okay."

"Why is that still so hard for you to believe?"

I looked away from Zeus's face on the laptop screen. Maybe I still wasn't ready to accept love just yet. But there was a tiny fire burning in my chest, and I could feel Zeus blowing hard on it.

22.

I stared at the laptop screen for two whole days before I found the courage to begin writing this next memory. Here we go, Dad. Back to the spring of 1990.

I was sixteen and attending your alma mater, Collingswood High School. I wouldn't say I hated tenth grade. I just never really felt like I was there. I couldn't match the rhythms of my comparatively more carefree classmates, who all seemed so at ease chatting at lunch tables, and playing on the sports teams, and going to parties. I had a few intense one-on-one friendships at the time. I was dating a senior, Nicole, who had her own car. Nicole would drive me places. She would park somewhere dark, and we would make out in the back seat. She was two grades ahead of me, which in high school felt like a twenty-year difference. I had originally fallen in love with her younger sister, who was in my Sunday school class, but the sister who was my age just wasn't interested when I made my move. The older sister, Nicole—who was a good person and a lot of fun—scooped me up. And whenever she kissed me, it was easy to forget just how lonely and unloved and rejected I felt inside.

My old friends were starting to party more. You and Mom didn't tolerate even the slightest bit of drinking. Like I mentioned earlier, you two were kind of psycho about me staying pure that way. So it was mostly just church, school, and girlfriend for me. I also used to play pinochle with your parents at their house. I'd go there all the time. It was my favorite place in the world. Grandmom and Pop Pop sang out my name whenever I walked through their door, like I was the character Norm on *Cheers*.

"Matthew!" your parents never failed to exclaim in unison whenever they first laid eyes on me.

It saved me every single time.

Back then, *Cheers* was your favorite TV show. We'd often watch it together on Thursday nights. Sometimes you'd audibly laugh at the jokes, which felt like a miracle back then. You liked the Sam Malone character so much that—even though we were Phillies fans—you purchased and started wearing a satin Red Sox jacket and a matching navy-blue baseball cap. Then there was a Boston B on the center of your forehead instead of a Phillies P. I would cringe because it felt like you were betraying our home city. It also felt like a fuck-you to Pop Pop, who had originally loved the Philadelphia Athletics but became a big Phillies fan once the A's left our city. Uncle Pete used to call your father "Mr. Baseball," because he loved the game so much. And Pop Pop was mystified by your Red Sox gear, maybe because he didn't watch *Cheers*.

One night when we were watching Sam "Mayday" Malone and company, you were laughing loudly enough for me to let down my guard. The sound of your laughter was so rare back then, I'd get kind of drunk off it. And then—against my better judgment and ignoring sixteen years of lived experience—I heard myself actually voicing one of the many private thoughts that were always running through my head.

I said, "Hey, Dad, what if—when I'm an adult, of course—I were to become a bar owner, like Sam Malone? Maybe that would be a good job for me."

You instantly stopped laughing. Then you said, "Matthew, let me tell you something. That's the stupidest thing you've ever said."

I should have quit right then and there, but instead, I said, "Why? I'd get to meet lots of people and laugh all the time and watch sports. And you love Sam Malone. We both love watching *Cheers*."

"It's a *TV show*."

"I really think maybe I might want to own a bar someday."

"You don't."

"But it looks like fun."

"Don't be an idiot."

"But—"

"You're never going to be a bartender! *That's stupid!* Do you understand me?"

I was instantly furious with myself. I knew better than to tell you what I was thinking. I knew you would scream at me, no matter what I said. Even when I tried to like the things you liked. Some part of me wanted to defend my decision to voice the owning-a-bar idea. You wore the Red Sox gear all the time. I wasn't making that up. And it was because you loved *Cheers* and Sam Malone. You said so yourself when I asked how you could possibly justify wearing Boston gear when you were from Philadelphia and liked the Phillies. And you said, "I love Sam Malone." You said that *verbatim*. And you watched that show every Thursday night and laughed and smiled like I never saw you do otherwise, so I thought maybe that was the secret. That if I someday was a cool bar owner like Sam Malone, you might smile when you saw me, and sit in my bar, and laugh with me, and maybe even sing out my name whenever you first saw me—just like your parents always did—and we'd actually talk, and it would be nice for a change. I thought maybe I could find a way for you to like me every Thursday night for a half hour. That you would come to my bar, and we'd at least have that.

"Matthew, I have *one* show I like! And you ruin it! I work all goddamn day for you! So you and your siblings will have food and clothes! *And then you do this?* I'm done!" you screamed and then stomped out of our little TV room.

I sat on the floor feeling stupid and hating myself.

Mom came in a few minutes later and said, "What did you do to upset your father?"

"I have no idea," I said in monotone.

"Well, you had to have done *something*. He's furious."

"He's a fucking asshole," I whispered to myself.

"What was that?" Mom said.

"Nothing."

"He's your father, Matthew. God says honor thy father and mother. Remember that."

I was staring at the TV screen, but I was only seeing the color red.

You weren't where you wanted to be career-wise. You were embarrassed of our small home. You were embarrassed of our hometown. You used to say you couldn't tell your business associates where we lived because they would laugh at you. You mostly worked. Based on your misery, I believed you worked harder and longer than anyone in the entire world. I often wondered what your bosses did to you while you were at the office. Did they literally whip you? Did they kick you in the balls all day long? Did they pull out your hair one strand at a time for ten hours a day? Is that why you were bald on top and perpetually miserable? My friend's fathers bitched about their jobs too, but they always threw in a few smiles and laughs and many jokes. Their moods were never as heavy as yours were. They didn't scream at their sons. They didn't humiliate my friends like you humiliated me. Being around my friends' dads didn't feel like drowning.

Sam Malone was also a recovering alcoholic happily working in a bar. Teenage me never zeroed in on that bit of improbable TV make-believe. You didn't have a drinking problem, but in a few years, I sure would. So the Jungian in me is now tempted to make symbolism out of us watching a show about a recovering alcoholic, whom you loved and even paid homage to with your weekend clothing. Did I unconsciously become an alcoholic just so you would love me, like you loved Sam Malone?

Just before dinner on weeknights, the sound of you opening our front door was like hearing the hammer of an old, single-action revolver being cocked. Only you weren't playing John Wayne. You hadn't come to save us from bad guys. It often felt more like you were *Taxi Driver*'s Travis Bickle in a suit and tie. Once you were home, the pistol was always cocked. I never knew when the gun was going to go off, but I was always certain it would be fired at me. And whatever levity or play your children and wife might have been enjoying, all of that ended the second your shadow darkened our home.

It was just like that on the night I want to discuss with you in this chapter, Dad. You walked through the front door. Your gun cocked. We all gathered round the oval-shaped dinner table. You sat at the head, which was in the center of the house. As the first-born son, I sat directly across from you. Megan was on my left. Micah sat to my right. And Mom was in between Micah and you, in the seat nearest to the kitchen so she could serve us. I never appreciated the home-cooked meals she made nightly, maybe because you always made them so dreary. Our family dinners were where the day's few smiles went to die.

My memory places this particular dinner on a cold spring day. The windows were shut, but the heat had been off for weeks. Nicole and I had made out after school in her car, and I was feeling okay. She had asked me to take her to the senior prom and I'd agreed. I didn't know what going to a prom would be like. I thought it might be like the movie *Pretty in Pink*, which I had probably seen on the local cable channel PRISM. And I was a little worried that I couldn't be a character in that Molly Ringwald movie because she and the other characters were always interacting with each other in interesting ways, and I mostly just wanted to be alone.

It was hard for me to breathe around other people. Even my girlfriend. When we weren't kissing, it was tricky being around her. Not because there was anything wrong with Nicole. She was great. But I was starting to suspect there was something seriously wrong with me. Like I was broken beyond repair and my whole life was a nonstop cover-up. Every second I was around people, I had to make sure they didn't know how monstrous I was on the inside. And that was exhausting work. It felt like I had crippling stage fright and every interaction with a human was another act in my life's never-ending play. The only relief I ever got was when I was by myself; or making out with a girl; or when I was with Pop Pop and Grandmom, who loved me just because I was their first-born grandchild, which was something I could never lose.

Regarding the prom, I knew the kids attending would mostly be upperclassmen. I wouldn't know anyone there except Nicole. And I didn't have any money for a tuxedo or flowers. Because Mom was in charge of managing our finances, I was pretty sure I could count on her to hook me up with cash in a quiet way that would not draw your wrath. But I knew that I shouldn't bring up the senior prom in front of you—let alone display anything resembling pride while I was within your firing range. The positive things in my life were always best discussed privately with Mom when your cocked pistol was not around because my heart was always your favorite target.

You were forty-two and perpetually miserable. Mom would have been thirty-nine; she dutifully held the family together. Megan was thirteen; she was sweet and innocent and trusting. And Micah was nine—still a little kid.

The sounds of our metal utensils were always loud when we ate, mostly because no one was really allowed to talk except you, and if you weren't yelling, you rarely spoke. Sometimes I'd try to break the heavy, awkward silence. I used to love making Micah and Megan laugh at the dinner table—often with crude humor—but smiles and laughter after your hard day at work were almost always immediately crushed by your red-faced screaming.

If I made a fart joke, you'd scream, "Matthew, I will *not* have bathroom talk at the dinner table!"

But that scenario was preferable to me saying something like, "Hey, Dad, guess what? I'm going to the senior prom this year."

To which you would have said something like, "Where are you going to get the funds for that? You know I work hard for our money, and yet we still have to live in this stupid house in this embarrassing town. *And all so you can go have a big fancy time at the prom?* You think you're special?"

At which point, I would have said something like, "Dad, everyone goes to the prom."

To which, you would have snarled, "*I* didn't go to prom. You have it so easy compared to how I grew up. You have no idea how easy you have it, Matthew."

So I didn't bring up the prom, and I didn't make any fart jokes, even though I felt like my siblings could have benefited from me breaking the toxic silence. To me back then, the sound of Megan's and Micah's laughter at the dinner table was like manna from God.

Instead, Mom said, "So how was your day, Mike?"

You grunted and then launched into some repeat speech about how unfair work was, and how stupid your bosses were, and how no one understood just how much you were contributing, and how the system was rigged against you, and how you needed to eventually make major changes because you deserved better.

I had long ago stopped paying attention to what you were saying and was thinking about what it might be like to attend the prom with Nicole, which was already making me feel beyond nervous. I just didn't have the bandwidth that night to take on your stress too. So your words went in one of my ears and right out the other.

Would the upperclassmen tolerate an underclassman crashing their prom? Would one of them try to kick the shit out of me in the bathroom for having the audacity to attend when I was two whole grades below them?

I'd already been attacked by a senior in the gym locker room earlier that year. Buzz had grabbed me when I was only wearing boxer shorts and had thrown me against the metal lockers. And *hard*. Then he shoved me again and again. At the time, I had no idea why I was being attacked, which petrified me, and I didn't defend myself.

Buzz later told Nicole that he was trying to send some weird message to us underclassmen because he had gotten into some sort of trouble at school for picking on a kid in my grade. Earlier on the day of the locker-room incident, during a basketball game, that picked-on kid had provoked me into having a little shoving match with him. He had aggressively fouled me over and over again, until I had pushed him in self-defense. So Buzz slamming me into the lockers was supposed to prove that he was now looking out for the kid whom he'd previously harassed. Buzz told Nicole that his shoving me had not been personal. He had to do it to get out of trouble. He thought I was an okay enough guy. He hoped there were no hard feelings. He told Nicole to tell me all of that, which she did later that afternoon as I stared at the floor.

But before I knew the motives for the violence I was experiencing in the locker room—back when I was being slammed into the lockers, with a few dozen or so of our bloodthirsty classmates cheering—the experience was more than a little disconcerting. Buzz was twice my size. He was a man among boys. It would have been suicide to fight back. He had mocked me in front of the crowd, saying, "What? Not so tough now? You fucking pussy. Fight me. Fucking fight me. Hit me, pussy. *Hit me!*" And I had seen our gym teacher watching the whole thing—waiting to see what I would do—and never once trying to break up the fight. He was old-school, and his silence absolutely condoned Buzz's aggression. My best friend at the time got in between Buzz and me, and then he too got slammed into the lockers for his trouble, as I just stood there shaking and fighting tears. I was so confused. The whole thing made me feel like my home life and school life had gotten switched somehow.

But sitting there at the dining room table, as you raged at your family, I thought, *Would the teachers who chaperoned senior prom think my being there was weird, when I was only a sophomore? Was it weird? And what would happen after Nicole graduated from high school? Would she and I still date? Was that even legal in the state of New Jersey?*

I didn't know. But I also wasn't listening to you. So I was surprised—and then truly baffled—when you said, "What's that, Matthew? You have something to say?"

I looked at Micah and Megan to see if they could somehow get me up to speed, but they were staring hard at the uneaten food on their plates.

"Don't look at your brother and sister. You look at me when I'm talking," you said. "Now, do you have something to say?"

"No," I said.

"Oh, I think you do, Mr. Big Shot. Mr. I Know Everything. Over there at the other head of the table. You always have something smart to say."

"Well, I don't tonight."

"Sure, you do. And I want to hear it. So say it. *Now.*"

"Mike," Mom said.

"I'm talking to my son. This is man business. You stay out of it, Doreen. The boy has to learn how to deal with men."

"Kids, help me with the dishes," Mom said to Micah and Megan.

Even though I hadn't moved an inch, you pointed at me and said, "Young man, you stay right where you are. You and I are going to have a little talk about respect."

Mom, Megan, and Micah had the table cleared in record time, and then you and I were alone, and you were lecturing me again. I was mostly watching spit fly from your lips and wondering just how purple a man's face could turn. I could also hear you screaming about how the world works and how I didn't understand anything.

But in my mind, I just kept saying, *I'm sixteen. I'm still a child. This isn't right. This isn't normal. And if I can just once again find my way into the back seat of Nicole's car, I can escape all this madness. And it doesn't even matter if I love her. Or if I hate myself. Or if I will even live on into the future. I just have to find a way to make it hurt less, at least for a little while. I really need a reprieve. Because I'm going to crack if I don't at least mentally get away somehow. I can feel the pressure building. My cranium is already at its breaking point. All of my worst thoughts are swelling again. And if my skull cracks even a hair, I know it will explode. And there might not be anyone in the entire world who would know how to put me back together again.*

Then I thought, *I'm like Humpty Dumpty.*

I think I might have smirked here because you screamed, "You're not fucking listening to me!" Then you slammed your open palms on the wooden dining room table.

You were insane. But, to my teenage eyes, you also looked pathetic. And your wife was going to give me the money I needed for the prom. She was going to give me *your* money. Mom was my power source. It didn't matter what you said or did.

So I let out a little chuckle, leaned the entirety of my weight onto the back two legs of my chair, and then—with all the emasculating energy I could muster—I rolled my eyes.

Oh, how triumphant it felt to put you in your place. To join your older brother and father in the simple dismissal of the maniacal but generally harmless—all-bark-and-no-bite—Michael Quick. To liberate myself from your tyranny with the simple roll of my sixteen-year-old eyes. To dismiss you. To let you know just how small you really were.

As a sophomore, I was going to the prom with a senior. She had a car. With my eye roll, I was absolutely saying, *Fuck you, Dad.* I was free.

But wait.

No.

Oh, shit.

You were charging around the table at me like a rabid rhino on cocaine.

And then you were kicking my chair out from underneath me.

And the back of my head was hitting the ledge of the window.

And then I was on the floor.

And you had a knee on the center of my chest.

And your finger was poking my forehead.

I didn't know if it was the full weight of your body pressing all the air out of my lungs or if I was having an anxiety attack, but I couldn't breathe.

"You will *never* fucking roll your eyes at me *ever again*! You will *respect me* in my own house! And, until you're man enough to take me out in the backyard and kick my ass fair and square, you will do *whatever the fuck I say* when I say it! Do you understand me? *Do you?*"

The house was deathly silent.

I hadn't had a breath in what felt like more than a minute, and my heart was pounding.

My face was covered in little frothy balls of your spit, which had rained down on me like hail as you screamed.

Your finger was jackhammering my forehead.

I felt like I was starting to pass out.

"Do you fucking understand me?"

When I nodded, you took your knee off my chest. Then you stood. For a weird moment, you looked down at me like you were examining a turd you had just deposited into the toilet. Then you stormed out of the house, slamming the front door behind you.

The first thing I thought was, *Get up. Don't let Mom and Megan—and especially Micah—see you like this.*

But I couldn't move.

I was shaking.

I was crying.

And I just couldn't get up.

Then I really wanted someone to help me get up off the floor, but no one came.

I imagine now that Mom was upstairs with Micah and Megan.

I imagine now that no one knew what to do.

But, in the moment, I couldn't understand why no one came to help me.

When I was attacked in the locker room, my best friend had at least taken a hard shove for me. And when the violence was over, he had patted my back. He stayed with me as I dressed. And he was still there when all the other boys had left. "Are you okay?" he had asked. And when I couldn't answer, he looked me in the eyes and answered for me, saying, "You're okay," in a way that had felt believable.

But after the violence in my own home, no one was there to help me.

And I couldn't get up off the floor.

So I lay there for what felt like an eternity.

At first I was just so confused about what had happened.

You'd hit and humiliated me before—spanking my naked butt when I was little, grabbing me when I wasn't doing what you wanted, smacking my cheek when you didn't like the words coming out of my mouth, touching your nose to mine and screaming in my face when you were angry, pinching the loose skin around my midsection, snidely critiquing my body as it changed during puberty—but I'd never previously experienced this new level of violence and hatred.

When I looked up into your eyes, there wasn't a human being in there. It was like I had been attacked by a demon.

But it wasn't a demon, I told myself. *It was just my asshole pussy of a father.*

Then I was mad at myself for not fighting back, for not kicking your ass and taking my rightful place at the head of the table. I told myself I absolutely *could* fuck you up in the backyard. And, just as soon as you returned home, I totally would. I would humiliate you the way you had humiliated me. And I'd do it right in front of your wife. I'd smash your head open with a brick from Mom's garden. I'd kill you and free myself. Free my brother and sister too.

But I was still shaking and couldn't get up off the floor.

Get up, pussy! I told myself. *Get the fuck up!*

But I couldn't.

I just couldn't.

I was so scared.

I was so ashamed.

Then I hated you for not finishing the job.

For taking your knee off my chest.

For allowing me to suck air back into my lungs.

For failing to crack open my forehead with your terrible stabbing forefinger.

Because I didn't want to be alive anymore.

23.

The day before our beloved Philadelphia Eagles took on the Kansas City Chiefs in Super Bowl LIX, Mom dropped you off at my house here on Lady's Island for our weekly Saturday morning man walk with Kingsly. When she left to go play tennis, we strolled through our neighborhood, basking in the glorious spring-like weather, and you talked about how much you loved living in Beaufort, before you said, "Oh, the Super Bowl is on today. Maybe Mom will let us get pizza."

Since the Eagles beat the Washington Commanders in the NFC Championship Game two weeks before, you had woken up every single day excitedly thinking it was Super Bowl Sunday and dreaming of pizza.

"What are those circles that they sometimes put on pizza pies?" you asked me.

"Pepperoni?" I asked.

"*Yes*," you said.

"Do you like pepperoni? I think you're more of a barbecue chicken man."

"Oh, that's right," you said. "I am a chicken pizza man."

"Should we get barbecue chicken pizza for the Super Bowl tomorrow?"

"The Super Bowl isn't today?"

"Today's Saturday, Dad."

"What day is the Super Bowl?"

"Sunday. As in *Super Bowl Sunday*."

"That's right. I knew that."

"We can absolutely get pizza for the game," I said.

"What kind of pizza do you want?"

"When I eat one with you, we usually get a plain cheese pizza, because you don't like vegetable toppings and I don't eat meat toppings."

"Then we should have Mom get us a plain pizza pie for the Super Bowl."

"Is that what you want? I'm going to get it today because the pizza place is having a private party tomorrow. So we'll have to put one in the fridge tonight and heat our pizza back up on the baking stone before the big game."

"That's okay. I love pizza, even if it's heated back up. Whenever someone gives me pizza, I say, 'Thank you.'"

"I know you do, Dad."

As we walked on, you marveled at the feeling of sun on your skin. And you looked for turtles in the ponds we passed and said you hoped we didn't see any alligators—because you are frightened of them. You talked about your parents looking down on us from heaven and being proud. And, on that morning, I really felt they were. You told all your stories about being a named executive at a publicly traded bank. You fictionalized a better, more palatable relationship with your deceased older brother, Peter, whom you said was the "wild man" busy in the home around the corner from you here in South Carolina, writing a book about the family. You said to my dog, "Kingsly, you're so lucky to be walking out here in this warm sunshine." And, to me, you said, "I love walking with you, Matthew," and "I love living here with you in this beautiful place that your mother picked out for us," and "It's good to have you here helping me, Peter," and "I worked hard my whole life for my wife and children and now I finally get to take it easy." And each time you made such a declaration, you reached over and rubbed my back for just a split second.

In the depths of my bones, I felt that I was witnessing the great miracle of my life: Your dementia had taught you how to be grateful. And it was like a fairy tale—when the evil witch's spell is broken by the everyday kindness of the lowliest character in the story. Even though you were still mixing me up with your deceased older brother, I almost wept tears of joy.

But instead, I said, "I love you, Dad."

You said—so freely, and with an ease and quickness that felt true—"I love you too, Matthew. And I love your mother. And your sister, Megan. And your brother, Micah. And I love my parents in heaven. And Peter. And my brother Jon. And . . . and . . ."

"And your grandchildren—Isla and Oliver and Brexley and Archer."

"I do."

"And?"

"What else do I love?"

"Pizza."

After our walk, we loaded up my Jeep with the week's trash and recycling, and we then got in ourselves.

I said, "Simon & Garfunkel, Fleetwood Mac, or the Eagles?"

And you yelled, "The Eagles!"

So I put on the Eagles mix I made for you. You sang the words to "Peaceful Easy Feeling," telling me you knew I wouldn't let you down, and in my mind, I promised I wouldn't.

"The Eagles are my favorite band," you said during the guitar solo.

"And your favorite football team," I said.

"I never saw the Eagles in concert. I really wish I had," you said.

"We can listen to them every Saturday morning, though, and pretend we're at a concert," I said, but the guitar solo was over, and you were already singing again about a voice whispering that you might never see me again.

We went to the post office, where I checked my professional post office box, but no fans had sent me any letters, which made you say, "Maybe next week someone will send you something good."

"Take It Easy" came on as we pulled out of the post office parking lot and headed to the dump, and even though Glenn Frey was talking about women and not sons, I felt like you were singing the lyrics to me. And it almost started to feel like you were offering me good fatherly advice, after all these decades of waiting for you to give me any type of direction whatsoever.

I looked over at you. With the unseasonably warm highway wind rushing in at you through the open window, I momentarily saw you as the twenty-four-year-old young man you were in 1972, when the hit first came out. You were not yet a father. You were still just a carefree kid yourself—with a new pretty wife, hair on top of your head, an entry-level banking job in Center City, Philadelphia, free lodging in Great Oma's row house, and your whole unknown life ahead of you.

Through your singing, you told me to ease up. Stay sane. And hold my ground.

As we pulled into the dump, I turned down the music. You became a panicked old man again as you asked if I had my pass, because you never remember that mine is on my iPhone and is not a piece of plastic like the one Mom keeps in the glove compartment of your car.

I held up my glowing phone so you could see the digital pass—just like I do every week—and you said, "That's right. I knew that."

"Fantastic day," I said to the kind woman who scans our pass each Saturday morning.

She was wearing a surgical mask that didn't quite cover her silver nose ring. Her eyes were just about the brightest in the world.

"Always nice to see your father and you," she said to me.

"We appreciate you," I said. "Enjoy this great weather."

"I love the dump," you declared as we drove on in.

Then we pulled up to the recycle station. The many different dumpsters always confuse you, so you only carried the bags, as I put all our paper and plastic and aluminum in the different containers.

"Good job," I said, as you helped, which made you light up like the midday sun.

Since moving to Beaufort more than a year ago, I'd learned that there is a little boy deep inside of you who just wants to be useful, just wants his father's approval, and so I play benevolent surrogate father whenever I can.

"High five," I said to the little abused boy trapped deep within you.

And that little boy quickly and dutifully raised your hand, which I tapped with all the love I have. The little wounded boy in you smiled and smiled.

It's amazing how easy it is to make the little boy inside of you happy. He can make a feast out of crumbs, which, of course, makes me want to feed him the best of what I have whenever I can. He's so hungry, Dad. And I now understand just how hungry he has always been.

We hopped back into my beater Jeep and drove up to the trash and cardboard stations, where we got out again. You're always more confident here because there aren't as many dumpsters. Just trash and cardboard. Even still, when I filled your hands up, you waited until I said where each bag and box went before you moved a single muscle. And just before you threw each bag of trash or tossed a handful of cardboard, you looked at me and said, "Is this right?" And, when I nodded, you threw away what you no longer needed. Then you looked at me with your eyebrows lifted, as if you had just scored a touchdown.

"Fantastic work, Dad," I said, and then raised my hand up in the air. When you slapped my palm hard, I said, "Another victorious dump run for the Quick men."

"What now?" you said, as you got back into the Jeep.

"Home," I said.

"You're not staying here in Beaufort? You're going home?" you said with alarm in your voice.

"Nope," I said. "We're sticking together for the duration. Right here in Beaufort. We're just going to your house so you can have lunch with Mom."

"Pizza?"

"Tomorrow. For the Super Bowl," I said.

But you were too busy singing "Already Gone" to hear me, something about someone putting you on a shelf and singing triumphant songs.

When we got home, Mom had the haircutting supplies out on the counter. It had been several weeks since your last cut, so you took off your shirt and sat on the kitchen chair right by the island.

I combed the bushy ring around the lower part of your head and began cutting and buzzing and doing my best to shape. I don't really know how to cut hair, but going to the barber now makes you extremely anxious. When, a year ago, Mom first suggested that I cut your hair, you screamed, "He'll shave me bald! I don't want to look like Matthew! I want hair on my head!" But you've somehow learned to trust me since then. So you sat calmly and obediently followed my every instruction, tilting your head left and right, lifting and lowering your chin, holding really still. As I worked, I marveled at just how far we had come. You were submitting to me, letting me cut your hair. The much younger, deep-inside-my-heart versions of me were amazed. And—as I snipped and buzzed with my face mere inches from your head and my forearms brushing against your neck, arms, and back—there was this almost unbearable, wildly unfamiliar feeling of intimacy that I struggled to endure, as tufts of your salt-and-pepper hair fell to the hardwood floor and Mom moved around us with the speed of a hummingbird, trying in vain to sweep up our mess before we'd even made it.

When I finished, I looked at you and proudly thought, *This is the best haircut I've given Dad yet.* I'd done a much better job of blending so that there was no ring-around line, and my work had somehow made you look a decade younger than you had appeared just ten minutes ago.

Mom wanted me to shave your back. I asked if that was okay. And when you said it was, I began erasing the huge lung-shaped hair patches with the clippers, as you stood there obediently, and every once in a while said, "That tickles." I noted the looseness of your skin and just how much your muscles have atrophied.

When I was done, I brushed all the hair off your body with an old-fashioned broom-looking barber's brush that Mom said has been in the family for generations.

After I cleaned as much hair off you as possible, you put your shirt back on and said, "How much do I owe you?"

"Four Wheat Thins," I said, obviously joking.

But you pointed with sincerity to the snacks cabinet and said, "Take as many crackers as you want. Thank you."

So I grabbed a handful, and when I ate, I thought about communion and felt like I was being forgiven somehow.

Then I went home and told Alicia that she had to make sure I remembered to get your pizza later that day.

We drove the Jeep into downtown Beaufort and walked Kingsly around for hours, as tourists lollygagged in the intoxicatingly good weather.

On a bench swing down by the river, as Alicia and I kicked our feet back and forth and Kingsly panted between us, I said, "I think I'm really going to finish writing this memoir."

"I know you will," Alicia said.

"How do you know?"

"You're a lot easier to live with whenever you're writing well."

"Sorry," I said.

"Why? You've been a dream lately."

The historic bridge was to our left. Sailboats were floating on the water. Teenagers laughed and skipped past. Mothers and fathers held the hands of their grinning toddlers. And an elderly couple with ice cream cones in their fists licked their way by us.

"Thank you for coming to Beaufort with me," I said to Alicia. "Thanks for letting me be with my father as he dies."

"I like it here," she said.

"I know, but thanks."

My wife turned her head, looked into my eyes, and—with a dead-serious expression on her face—said, "I have something really important to tell you."

I swallowed and said, "What?"

"Don't forget to order the Super Bowl pizza for your father."

I laughed and then called the place across the street from our neighborhood.

"One large cheese pizza," I said.

The young woman on the phone told me it would be ready in thirty minutes.

Alicia and I held hands as we walked Kingsly through The Old Point, past the antebellum mansions and former movie sets and palmetto trees and historical landmarks. I felt happy to be in Beaufort with my marvelous wife and the little dog with whom I have also fallen head over heels in love.

I picked up the pizza on the way home and put the box in our refrigerator. We couldn't put it in your house. You wouldn't be able to remember that the pie was supposed to be a special treat for the Super Bowl. Whenever there is pizza within your reach, you eat every slice. And then two minutes after you've swallowed your last bite of pizza, you say, "Doreen, can we maybe order a pizza pie? I love pizza. We haven't had one in *forever*."

Lying awake that night—with my wife sleeping next to me and Kingsly curled up in his little fuzzy doughnut by our feet—I thought about how you and Mom had helped Alicia and me put our heavy, wooden, king-sized bed together when we first moved into this funky house that no one else wanted, just so I could be here with you in Beaufort. And I recalled how happy you seemed to have Alicia and me moving into a home just around the corner from you—and how your enthusiasm had made the little, scared, father-starved boy inside of me feel like he was being given food for the first time in decades.

Then I wondered if the Eagles winning the Super Bowl would be a good ending for this memoir. Since Mom had bought us the NFL Sunday Ticket, we'd watched the entire Eagles season together, right there on your living room couch. For the first time in my adult life we had watched every single game sitting next to each other. And I really think there was some medicine in that. Sometimes you would cheer and sing the fight song and chant, "E-A-G-L-E-S *Eagles*!" like in the old days. But other times you'd look at me and say, "Those guys on the TV, they're the Eagles, right?" Or "Are we in Philadelphia right now?" And when I'd say we were indeed watching the Philadelphia Eagles but here on Lady's Island, you'd say, "But we used to go to the games in Philadelphia, right? Didn't we used to live there?" And when I'd say we did go to the games together and did indeed hail from Philadelphia, I'd worry that this might be the last season of Eagles football that we'd be able to really enjoy together with any sense of you understanding what was actually happening with the team you have loved all of your life.

I recognized that there were men in Missouri and Kansas who were in equally complicated father-son relationships. A few years ago, I had done a book event at the fantastic Olathe Public Library right outside of Kansas City, and the people there were warm and kind and easy to love. I knew they all wanted to see their Chiefs win a record-setting three Super Bowls in a row. I knew some of them were even praying to their gods, asking for a Super Bowl win for their fathers and sons and nephews and grandsons and brothers and friends. Hell, maybe even their wives and sisters and daughters. A part of me realized how silly it was to pray about a football game when there were so many more important things for God to address. But, Dad, I wanted you to see your Birds win the big game one more time before your dementia took Eagles football away from you forever. And I wanted to be with you. I wanted to reverse the experience I had the last time the Eagles won the Super Bowl, when I sobbed all alone in my Outer Banks home and felt like I had completely lost my chance to connect with the only father I would ever get.

I knew an Eagles Super Bowl defeat wouldn't diminish all that you and I had accomplished together here in Beaufort, but I wanted a win anyway. I wanted it for the little abused, hurting boy in you. And I wanted it for the little abused, hurting boy in me. So I prayed to God and thanked Him for all that you and I have, Dad. I thanked God for all the healing I'd been gifted. I thanked God for letting me know I was loved. I thanked God for the second chance at loving my father in the way that all sons should love their fathers. I thanked God for Mom's lifesaving story—whether it was true or not—about you rubbing my head during Eagles games when I was a newborn baby. I told God I was grateful. I told God I was willing to use the opportunity my publisher had given me to help other hurting men, that I would write whatever God wanted me to write, that I would open my heart and allow God to move through me—"down and out" as my analyst always says—and then I asked God for an Eagles win.

As I lay there in my bed, in the darkness of our bedroom, I felt God smiling down on me—laughing at the silliness of my request—but I also somehow felt God was proud of the good work you and I have done together, Dad. And I felt as though God was pleased with our sacrifice. I didn't believe that whatever we'd accomplished together would guarantee an Eagles win the next day, but I was pretty sure that I was going to finish this memoir one way or another.

I knew that you were dying, and there was nothing I could do to stop that.

I knew I had already wasted so much time being resentful and narcissistic and human.

But I also knew that I had come to Beaufort and done what I could to remedy all that too.

Lying there in the darkness of our bedroom, in the funky little home just around the corner from you, I think I experienced what Thoreau once called "a success unexpected in common hours."

24.

Dad, this is the last hard part of the memoir. I've put it off for as long as I possibly could because I didn't want to relive what is most likely *still* the worst weekend of my entire life. I wasn't sure how to write about it. I knew it would make you look monstrous. You *were* monstrous. The worst you've ever been to me. By far. I feel as though I have to say the things that follow, if only so I don't make the same mistake you made with your dying father, when he begged you to tell him what he had done to offend you so greatly. I don't write these words to condemn you. I write them to show other men what is possible when we allow love to lead us out of the darkness—and to do that, I have to show everyone just how far you and I have come.

Maybe you'll remember the summer between my senior year of high school and freshman year of college. You had gotten me a job as an industrial roofer, working for a construction company to whom you had given bank loans. My job was a favor granted by an astoundingly wealthy man who owed you. But before any readers cry nepotism, I should probably say it was a job most people wouldn't wish on their worst enemy. And it also paid terribly. Zero benefits. I was a grunt laborer for hard men who worked like dogs and didn't particularly like boys headed to university in the fall, especially since these men had never had access to higher education themselves. Many of them were more than smart enough. They had just caught bad breaks earlier in life. So they made me pull buckets of hot tar up onto multistoried buildings. Sometimes we'd use a boom-and-pulley system. Other times we'd dangerously lean our torsos out over the edge and pull by hand.

The foreman was always more worried about me spilling tar on the side of the building than he was about me falling headfirst to my death.

Sometimes they'd make me work the kettle, which meant slipping—by hand—fifty-pound plugs of tar into boiling black lava, pinhead-sized blobs of which would jump out and sting my flesh like hornets. "Hey, College," the men would yell down from the roof high above. "Did you know that one day of working the kettle is the equivalent of smoking twelve packs of cigarettes? Sure glad it's your lungs down there and not ours."

On other days, we'd paint flat roofs silver, which effectively made them mirrors for the unrelenting South Jersey summer sun, whose endless rays never once had a problem fighting their way through the many bottles of sunscreen we smeared all over our sweaty faces and arms.

All of the roofers were initially suspicious of the college boy who had infiltrated their ranks and was rumored to be a spy for the owner of the company. They worked me good and hard. They cursed at me. They yelled a lot. They tested my ability to take it. Slowly, I earned their respect. Eventually, they started offering me bits of their food and cups of their coffee during breaks. And I swiftly learned to love these men, who respected anyone who could put in eight decent hours without adding to anyone else's already unbearable shame, which they collectively tried to hide with loud music and crude jokes and by violently attacking the day's work as if it had threatened their children and owed them money.

At quitting time, I'd leave the worksites so exhausted and dehydrated, I could hardly drive home. In bed at night, I'd pick little hardened balls of tar from my arms, ripping out the sun-bleached hairs they were tangled up in. I'd have to be on the road by six the next morning, so there was no hanging out with friends. There was only work and sleep and the quiet intuitive knowledge that I was doing what I would later hear called "ash work." I was like act-one Cinderella—the little ash girl—tasked with the lowliest job of maintaining the cooking fires, removing the ash, and keeping the cinders glowing for the more important cooks. I was the male roofer version of all that. I too had to be humbled, and I think you understood that, Dad. You made sure I did my humbling young-adult ash work. And I'm now exceedingly grateful for that.

The worst part was that my girlfriend at the time, Lisa, who was a year younger than me, was in Argentina for a good portion of the summer, via some type of student exchange program. I thought I was in love with this young woman, enough to marry her. But I, of course, was still a boy. I could only ever offer Lisa the love of a boy—and a broken one at that.

At the end of every August back then, our family went to the Outer Banks for two weeks. Nags Head, North Carolina. Since I hadn't seen Lisa all summer, I didn't want to leave South Jersey just as she was returning from South America. But I knew you'd never let me stay home for love, so I pitched earning two extra weeks of money by working through the family vacation. I argued that I could pay for more of my food and books at college. Because you always prioritized money, you went for that. Then I was home alone. While I did enjoy spending time with my girlfriend, I also started feeling like an orphaned boy in an adult world. For the first time in my life, I was waking up and coming home at night to a silent, empty house. I had greatly anticipated my liberation from the family, but my first taste of freedom felt eerie—like I was living through a tiny apocalypse.

When Lisa came home from Argentina, she seemed different. As far as I was concerned, she might as well have been to Mars. All I really knew was Philadelphia and South Jersey. I'd spent two weeks each year on the Outer Banks, only because Uncle Pete had built vacation houses there. Otherwise, we never left home. I'd never even been to New York City, which was only a few hours away by train or car. Back then, I couldn't imagine what going to South America for weeks might have been like. I got the sense that my girlfriend found my lack of imagination disappointing upon her return. Oh, I'm sure I asked her questions about her trip and took an interest, but I think we both knew that she had begun to advance into adulthood in a way that I wasn't quite yet able.

On the day you and Mom and Megan and Micah drove me to college, you allowed Lisa to come with us. It was a strange morning for me. It felt like being pushed over a bridge that would instantly crumble just as soon as I was on the other side. I didn't really want to go to college, but going also felt suspiciously exciting. Yet leaving behind our little family of origin—as crazy as it often was—made me feel like a traitor.

Before we left that morning, I paced around the exterior of our small green Oaklyn home, doing endless circles.

Who would make Micah and Megan laugh at the dinner table? Who would be there to draw your fire away from them? Who would Mom talk to about how she felt? Who would take long walks with her? Who would make her feel less alone when you were working all the time?

I asked myself these questions until you, Dad, came outside and said it was time to go.

On the drive to La Salle, it felt like I'd simultaneously swallowed lots of baking soda and vinegar, and my stomach was exploding.

As we moved my stuff into my dorm room, I was drawn to the buzz of boys slowly filling up the hallway. I felt guilty about that. Megan and Micah were wide-eyed as they got a glimpse of their futures. Mom seemed proud, maybe because she never got to live in a dorm and wasn't able to finish her undergraduate degree. But you, Dad, were cold and distant, like usual. You didn't have any words of advice for me. You didn't express anything resembling pride or happiness. You just seemed kind of annoyed and burdened by the whole thing. I imagined that the cost of college would force you to work even harder at your job, which would only increase your misery. And—even though I had never asked to go to college and you yourself had made it mandatory—I felt more than a little guilty about your having to sacrifice on my behalf, because college seemed shockingly expensive to the part-time industrial roofer making nine dollars an hour before taxes.

But the craziest thing was this: I think some loyal part of me was really going to miss the only life I had known and the people who had populated it. I wanted to hold onto all of you, even though I knew on some level that not leaving home would have been a perversion of the growing-up process. And, as we finished transporting all my stuff from the family minivan to my dorm room, it felt like someone had sunk an axe blade into my chest.

Then I watched all of you driving away, leaving me with strangers in a part of Philadelphia I didn't know.

That night, as I lay in bed, in my dark dorm room—with another boy I had only just met that day sleeping no more than twelve feet away from me—I understood why there were iron bars on all our windows.

Gunshots went off in the surrounding inner city all night long.

I heard, *Bang! Bang!*

Pow! Pow! Pow! Pow! Pow!

Bang!

Then silence, which I imagined meant that someone had won the gunfight.

And, lying in my strange new bed, I wondered if some poor soul out there was dead, or headed for the hospital, or if, by some miracle, no one was hurt at all. I never knew, of course, but I always hoped for the best.

I was not prepared for college. I'd often ask my new peers how to write a term paper or use the library or even how to spell the simplest words or answer basic grammar questions, and they'd always say, "Where the hell did you go to high school?" and "How did you even get into college?" because they all knew so many things that I did not. But there was this infectious all-for-one-and-one-for-all, Peter-Pan-and-the-Lost-Boys-type camaraderie on our dorm floor, and—much to my great surprise—a few of the question-answering people actually became my friends. They helped me catch up. I'd play tackle football with them down on the muddy field behind our dorm. We'd play video games in our rooms, staying up late into the night. We watched the Eagles Gang Green defense dominate other NFL teams on our secondhand TV sets. We'd all talk and bust balls and laugh and play practical jokes on each other. Slowly, I began to like living there. I started to believe that I was taking baby steps into my adulthood.

Not having to worry about setting you off anymore felt like heaven. You weren't there to scream at me when I laughed, or tell me I didn't know anything, or make me feel small, or pin me against a wall, or pinch my belly, or psychologically torture me.

My girlfriend, Lisa, was still in high school. I'd call her on the phone and write her letters, but I felt her drifting away. A part of me suspected I wasn't the type of person who went to Argentina and did cultural exchanges with foreign students. Lisa wanted to sail the seas of life, and I was a dropped anchor, but I pretended that if I loved her enough it wouldn't matter. Looking back now, I can see that I didn't really love *Lisa*. She was more like *an idea* that I thought might be able to save me. I was drowning, so she looked like a life preserver, which wasn't fair to her, of course. Lisa was a good person. A terrific soul. And as I started to sink deeper into what I would later learn was mental illness, the best parts of me knew that she had to get herself away from me and enjoy her senior year of high school. That knowledge was so devastating that I hid it deep at the back of my consciousness for almost two months.

When my nineteenth birthday rolled around at the end of October, I decided to go home for the weekend. I thought some face-to-face time might help us patch things up. Lisa wanted me to go to the high school football game. I didn't want to. It wasn't that I was now too "college." I think I was just too *shaky*, especially being back in your world, Dad. And I wanted to spend time alone with my girlfriend.

Lisa and I ended up at her house, where she gave me a birthday present. As I removed the wrapping paper, it became overwhelmingly obvious that she didn't want to be with me anymore but was too kind to say so. She didn't do or say anything to tip me off. I could just feel the emotional distance between us.

When I couldn't take it anymore, I said, "What's going on here?"

She opened her mouth, but no words came out.

"You want to break up, don't you?" I said.

"Let's just celebrate your birthday, okay?"

"So it's true?"

Lisa swallowed and then said, "I really, really, really didn't want to do this today."

It felt like she had taken out a pistol and shot me between the eyes.

For a few seconds, I couldn't see. Then I felt like I was going to puke.

"Are you okay?" she said.

I flashed on the handwritten letter she had given me when she dropped me off at college. It had promised that we'd find a way to stay together. I was young, so I had believed her.

But I also knew we were now living in radically different worlds. The breakup was, of course, inevitable. Pretty much everyone in my dorm who had come to college attached to someone who wasn't also a La Salle student had already gone through their very predictable split.

"Just a matter of time," they had told me. "Might as well get it over with now." But I had insisted that my situation was different—I was in love. I was going home for my birthday, my girlfriend absolutely wanted to see me, and it was going to be beautiful.

As I sat there on my birthday staring in disbelief at my now ex-girlfriend, Lisa kept explaining herself in this rehearsed way that made me realize she had wanted to end things for a long time but had just been too kind to do it—maybe because she knew how much it would hurt me.

When I tried to leave, Lisa made me agree to a diner meal the next night so we could have one last nice chat and remain friends. She was sweet. She was gentle. She was more compassionate than she needed to be. And all that made me feel so much worse about the loss.

The next day, this other girl I knew—who used to cut my hair and had graduated high school with me but didn't go away to college—offered to hang out. Tammy picked me up in her little car and drove me to a secluded park in another town. She spread out a blanket. Then we sat behind a bush near a lake. Tammy was tall and voluptuous and had the free spirit of an artist. I had often wondered what it would be like to kiss her. And, as we sat there all alone together on my birthday weekend, I wondered if kissing her might give me some relief from the unbearable breakup pain. So I told her all about getting dumped on my birthday and tried to elicit some sympathy.

When I finished my tale of woe, Tammy's eyes flashed. "How would the girlfriend of your dreams act if she was sitting across from you right here, right now?"

As the electricity passed between us, I answered, "I'd want her to make the first move on me."

Tammy smiled and then she started kissing me. Her mouth tasted like the tuna-salad sandwich she had eaten for lunch. But, in my memory now, her long, thick hair smells like peaches.

I was just about to let go of everything and sink into the obliviousness of lust when my heart started racing and I couldn't catch my breath. I could see the concern on Tammy's face right away, so I blurted out as a sort of explanation, "People can see us."

She made a show of looking left and right and behind her and behind me. Then she put a soft hand on my face, stared deep into my eyes, and, in the most reassuring voice, said, "There's nobody here. We're all alone."

Then Tammy began kissing me again. Her lips felt thinner than I expected them to be, and fragile as flower petals. A large part of me wanted to disappear into her, to accept her female medicine. But my heart wouldn't stop punching the inside of my rib cage. And then I couldn't breathe at all.

I jumped up into a standing position and blurted out, "I can't cheat on my girlfriend."

"Lisa dumped you last night, right? *And on your birthday*," Tammy said while looking up at me with an amused look on her face. "So this definitely isn't cheating."

"I have to go home. *Please take me home.*"

She laughed as if she thought I was joking. Then she smiled, patted the bit of blanket next to her thigh, and said, "Sit down. Relax. We don't have to do anything. Let's just talk. We're friends, right?"

"I really, really have to go home," I said and then realized I was shaking. *"Please."*

She clocked my trembling hands, frowned, and then drove me home.

Just before I got out of her car, I said, "I'm sorry."

In the split second we made eye contact—before I hopped out and ran to our front door—I couldn't tell if Tammy was disappointed, angry, disgusted, worried, or all of those emotions at the same time. But whatever that look was on her face, it made me feel even more ashamed.

That night at the local diner, I was unable to look Lisa in the eyes. I wanted to confess that I had kissed another girl that afternoon and ask for her forgiveness. I wanted to beg her to continue being my girlfriend. I also wanted to get up from the booth, walk out of the diner, and completely erase her from my memory. And as these thoughts went round and round in my mind, I began to feel like the diner was spinning. Someone played R.E.M.'s "It's the End of the World as We Know It (And I Feel Fine)" on the jukebox, and the opening drumrolls entered my ears like machine-gun fire. Lisa looked worried. I don't remember eating any food, but I absolutely remember thinking that I would never again let myself fall in love. I vowed that I would not allow love to destroy me a second time. Love was for masochists. And I didn't want to hurt myself like this ever again. The worst part was that I could tell Lisa was really enjoying her senior year of high school. She was happy. More at ease than I had ever remembered her being before. And now that I was out of the picture, her life would be even better.

At some point, we both got up and left the diner. We probably hugged awkwardly. I wasn't able to be the bigger person that night. I hadn't been able to thank her for all the good memories. For helping me get through the end of high school. For taking me as I was for a few years. For being a friend. For making me feel less alone. For tolerating all of my wounded young man bullshit—all of the self-loathing and fear and shame. Instead, anxiety and paranoia flooded through my bloodstream, making me feel as if I were in some sort of surreal nightmare, while the rest of the world was just enjoying regular life. Lisa promised that we would always remain friends. But I have no memory of ever speaking to her again.

I don't remember what happened the next day, Dad. Maybe we went to church as a family. Maybe we had Sunday dinner at Pop Pop and Grandmom's house. Maybe we ate in our little green Oaklyn home. In my mind now, I see lit candles sticking out of one of Mom's homemade apple pies and our little family singing the birthday song to me. But I was so dazed from the breakup, I wasn't really there any-more. I was somewhere deep inside, hiding in the darkest recesses of my soul. Mom probably gave me a card full of money that she had earned working one of the many jobs she had over the years: flower shop worker, family doctor receptionist, garage sale organizer, restorer of trash-picked furniture, etc.

Then you and I were alone in your car and headed back to La Salle University. You didn't say much as we made our way out of South Jersey and over the Ben Franklin Bridge. I felt numb and dreaded walking into my dorm, where everyone would immediately ask how my birthday weekend with my girlfriend had gone. I contemplated lying and saying it was absolutely fucking amazing, but I knew that would only increase the truth-telling difficulty down the road, and I was too shattered to pull off believability anyway.

Of course, I would have loved for you to have said, "Hey, son, you seem down. What's up?" And to have meant it. If you had been the type of dad who asked empathetic questions and really listened to the answers, I probably wouldn't have been in the bleak reality I found myself inhabiting. Because it was the dark broken thing inside of me that seemed to repel everything good in my life. And I was pretty sure you, Dad, had put that dark broken thing in me.

At least Dad's not yelling at me, I thought. *At least there is no insane and demoralizing lecture tonight.*

But once we hit the Schuylkill Expressway—and the Philadelphia Museum of Art and Boathouse Row rushed by the passenger-side window—you said, "Matthew, you and I need to have a talk."

I could tell by the icy tone of your voice that this was not going to be a surprise pick-me-up, father-son, heartfelt chat that would make me feel a little less shitty. I had no illusions about you saving the day. I knew there wouldn't even be any throwaway platitudes, like "There are many other fish in the sea," or "It's better to have loved and lost than to have never loved at all," or "You have your whole life ahead of you." You probably didn't even know that my girlfriend had broken up with me. Mom knew because I had told her, but I didn't think she had told you yet. I certainly wasn't going to trust you with such sensitive and weaponizable material.

But maybe you did know that I'd gotten dumped. If so, that makes what follows much worse. I choose to believe that you didn't know that I was already heartbroken and feeling worthless, although a simple turn of your head and a glance at my face should have clued you in.

Either way, you were strangling the steering wheel, knuckles white as light bulbs. "It's nice that you're having such a fine time at college," you said. "But I'm exhausted. I don't think I can stick around anymore."

We were doing sixty miles an hour. A little internal monster told me to take off my seat belt, open the car door, and just fucking roll to my death. But I didn't do that, of course.

Instead, I said, "What do you mean, Dad?"

"I've done all I can to support your mother and you kids. I've worked myself almost to death. I've given up on my dreams. But does your mother appreciate these things? *No.* Do you and your siblings appreciate my sacrifices? *No.* Nobody appreciates what I do. *No one.* So I think I'm just going to disappear."

It became harder to breathe.

I felt my internal organs popping like balloons on a dartboard.

I turned my head and saw your contorted face lit eerily by the dashboard light. You looked possessed. I knew I was outmatched. I was also completely out of ammo. In elementary school, I had tried being a good boy. In junior high, I had tried sarcasm. At the start of high school, I'd tried belittling you, mirroring your cruelty. Then I'd tried ignoring you. I'd even tried submission. But your demons were undefeated.

I had no idea what to do.

Then I heard a voice in my head saying, *Maybe I can save my father with love. Maybe—if I can utilize all that I have learned in church and manage to be Christlike—I can cast the demons out of my father. And maybe, if I can be my father's Jesus Christ, maybe then Dad will stop hurting me. Maybe he will beg for forgiveness. Maybe he will even wash my feet. Maybe he will finally start loving me. Maybe then I'll be able to breathe. Maybe I will actually begin to enjoy my life. And Dad will begin to enjoy his life. For once.*

So I tried to sound loving and Christlike. "What do you mean by *disappear*?"

"I think it's time for you to step up, Matthew. Be the man of the house. You can earn all the money and support your mother and brother and sister. Because I'm not going to be around much longer."

The voice in my head kept saying, *The demons are making him suicidal. I have to take on all of his sins. Allow myself to be willingly crucified. Die for him. Micah and Megan and Mom need Dad to make the money. They won't survive without him. He can't die. Only I am expendable. I can't make family-supporting money because I'm still a child. I must cast out my father's demons. Take them into myself, if need be. Even if it kills me.*

"What are you saying *exactly*?" I asked.

"You're probably never going to see me again," you told me. "When I disappear, you're going to have to take care of the family. They can't take care of themselves. It's on you now. Because I'm ending things."

The sound of your car engine was all I heard for a minute.

"Dad," I said. "We all appreciate everything you do for—"

"Bullshit! *Bullshit!*" you screamed as you banged on the steering wheel and dashboard. "None of you appreciate *anything* I do! And I'm fucking done! I'm tired. I'm out. It's over. I'm going to disappear. Do you understand me, Matthew? *Do you?*"

In the small, enclosed space of your car, your screams and the sound of your angry fists were too much for me.

That's when I absolutely knew that I was not your Jesus Christ, Dad.

I was just a pathetic boy who had been dumped by his girlfriend.

I was the idiot who was too afraid to kiss the attractive young woman who had tried to take his breakup pain away.

I was just a coward whose hands shook all the time.

Whose throat was always closing.

Who was constantly on the verge of tears.

I was a piece of shit whose own father hated him.

With my voice quivering and my words sounding like an SOS, I blurted out, "Dad, are you saying you're going to kill yourself?"

"You better figure out how to support a family, Matthew," you said. "And quickly. Because I'm done. *Fucking done.* I don't want to be here anymore! Can you understand *that*?"

"Dad—"

"*I don't want to hear it!* There's nothing you can say to change my mind. You just have to figure out a way to support the family. It's on you now. So figure it out. Your mother's depending on you, Matthew. It's your problem now. *Understand?* Because I'm done! *Fucking done!*"

Dad, I was pretty sure you were not going to kill yourself but were just going to go home, sleep next to Mom, get up the next day, brush your teeth, shower, eat a bowl of cereal, go to work, and continue doing what you always did. This talk about disappearing was just a mind game you were playing with me, mostly because some dark part of you understood how susceptible I'd be to it. That dark part knew I would instantly feel all of the self-esteem-murdering things that you were experiencing. All the pain. All the shame. All the helplessness. You wanted me to carry it for you. You were loading me up with your worst baggage. I didn't have the psychological insights, let alone vocabulary, to voice all that when I was just nineteen, but I felt the truth of it in my gut. I knew that you had sensed how wounded I was, how defenseless I was feeling, and so you sized up the moment and extroverted all of the worst things you had inside of you, forcing them down my throat and into me, your first-born son. At the time, the only thing I could come up with to explain why exactly you would do such a thing—other than you were possessed by demons, which I wasn't even sure was actually a real thing—was that you believed I was a piece of shit. Just something inconsequential for you to smash when you were hurting. And the pain of that sudden realization—that even my own father thought I was excrement—split me in two.

When we pulled up to my dorm at La Salle, you said, "It's up to you now to take care of the family. You'll never see me again, Matthew. I'm disappearing. This is it for you and me. *Understand?*"

I leapt out of the car, grabbed my bag, and ran into the dorm, ignoring all of the concerned faces I passed and their kind questions about my birthday weekend. "What happened? *We want details,*" everyone cheered, as I passed like a storm cloud.

I furiously keyed into my dorm room.

My roommate was sitting on his bed doing schoolwork, nodding his head to the beat of some pop song coming out of his boom box. He looked up at me with such a foreign expression on his face. At first, I couldn't make out what it was. Then I realized it was joy.

"How was the big birthday weekend with the girlfriend?" he asked, before registering the horror on my face. Then he said, "Hey, are you okay?"

I didn't know what to say, so we just stared at each other.

My eyes were brimming with tears. "I really need to be alone. Can you please leave?"

He didn't know what to do. He was a kind person with a big heart. I know he wanted to help me, but I also think he wasn't quite sure what scene we were in. And he was only eighteen years old.

"Please!" I yelled, because I didn't want him to see me crying, and I was about to explode with tears. "Can you just *leave*?"

His eyes grew wide, before he turned off the music, gathered his books, and then left without saying another word.

Just as soon as the door locked behind him, an ocean flooded out of me.

I screamed into my pillow.

I sobbed for an hour.

Then I lay there in the darkness, just looking up at the ceiling and feeling nothing.

It felt like I was already dead.

I don't remember my roommate coming back that night, and I don't think we ever talked about what happened. I was sorry that I made him leave the room. Looking back now, I suspect he would have tolerated my crying quite well and would have done his best to comfort me. But I was raised to believe that men don't cry. I was also raised to believe that I was not worthy of compassion.

In the morning, I showered and put on an "I'm fine" mask. Then I told all my La Salle friends about getting dumped on my birthday, passing it off as a funny story, which earned me much respect and sympathy.

"On your *birthday*?" everyone said, in a way that suggested I had absolutely won the shit lottery, and my peers were at least going to give me the notoriety I deserved. After what you had put me through the night before, Dad, I was taking just about anything I could get.

In a pack of boys, I left the cafeteria midday and walked down the busy main street that runs through the heart of La Salle's campus—Olney Avenue. For some unknown reason, I pulled out my Zippo lighter, spun the flint-grinding wheel with my thumb, saw the flame begin to dance in the breeze, and then held it under the brim of my friend's baseball hat, which he was wearing at the time. He defensively swatted my hand away from his face, which sent the Zippo flying out into the street. Without looking, I sprinted into traffic and scooped up my lighter. But when I turned around to run back to my friends—

Brakes squealed.

The scent of burning tire rubber filled the air.

Then I was flying.

I landed on my hands and knees and slid down the road.

Just as soon as I came to a stop—ten or so feet from the front of the car that had hit me—I popped back up onto my sneakers and declared, "I'm fine."

The driver got out of the car and started to apologize.

"I'm fine," I repeated, waving the driver off.

Traffic had stopped.

My dorm buddies had surrounded me.

"Dude, look down," one said.

When I did, I saw that my jeans were shredded and bloody.

My hands were bloody too.

My right thigh muscles felt locked; I couldn't bend my knee.

"I'm fine," I said again and then started to limp away.

"Don't you want my information?" the driver said.

"I'm fine," I said once more over my shoulder.

Some La Salle employee—maybe a nurse—arrived and said I had to go to the hospital.

When she gently put her hand on my arm and begged me to sit down, I yelled, *"I'm fine!"*

She removed her hand.

As I resumed limping down the sidewalk, I heard the nurse tell my boys, "He could be in shock. You have to make him go to the hospital. He needs to see a doctor."

When I glanced back, I saw they'd gotten in between the nurse and me. I heard one of them say to the driver, "He said he's fine. No harm done. We'll take care of him."

The nurse continued to yell after me, but I limped away as fast as I could, and when my friends caught up, they shook their heads in admiration and said I was "tough as balls."

We went back to my dorm room, where I hung my bloody shredded jeans up on the wall. People would see them hanging there and say, "You never even went to the hospital?" And I'd say, "Pffff. What? You think I'm a pussy?" And then everyone would laugh and we'd talk about something else.

I limped for a week or so.

Then I connected with Shannon, a girl in my lit class whom I now suspect saw how badly I was hurting on the inside. Shannon had attended a top high school before coming to La Salle. She took me to the library and, over the course of a few weeks, officially taught me how to use it. Then she taught me how to write a research paper. College was easy for her. I think she kind of took me on as a project to fill up her spare time. We started kissing in our dorm rooms and that eased the pain you had inflicted. But I forbade myself from falling in love with her. Shannon dressed kind of sexy goth and was smart and so full of life. She extended the outer corners of her eyes with black eyeliner so that she looked like Cleopatra. She felt edgier than any girl I had dated before, made all the moves on me, and seemed way out of my league. Friends even let me know just how out of my league she was. I had no idea why she liked kissing me. I even tried to gently discourage her from time to time, saying I wasn't looking for a girlfriend. But, for some unknown reason, that made her try even harder to infect me with her vitality—to save me, to initiate me into life. When I wasn't with her, I often was alone in my dorm room smoking unfiltered clove cigarettes and feeling depressed. But Shannon had a knack for showing up when I was just starting to feel my worst. Whenever she kissed me, I'd feel better. And in many ways, I now think she might have begun to save my life that year. But when she asked me to meet her family, I remembered the vow I had made to myself and refused. *Never love again*, I'd think. At the end of freshman year, when she said I had to commit exclusively to her or else she was moving on, I told her I would never again commit to anyone.

So Shannon moved on, and—as I returned to the hellishly hot industrial roofs of South Jersey and took shit off roofers who called me College—I wore my "I'm fine" mask enough to continue earning the respect of these father-aged men with whom I sweated and worked. But deep inside, I could feel the old lonely horrors making me depressed and anxious again. I'd worry about falling off the roofs all the time. I'd even ask my coworkers about the few men who had fallen off roofs in the past. And they would always be eager to tell me about how some dumbass had broken an obscene combination of arms and legs because he had been stupid and fallen through or off a roof—but no one had any fatalities to report. I feared I'd be the first. Maybe because some dark part of me wanted to be.

But there was also something good fighting inside of me, and it always gripped the ladders tightly and got extra careful around the roof edges and liked to listen to the men tell stories about their childhoods; and their wives and kids; and their youthful backpacking trips across Europe; and their secret plans to someday quit the construction company and start building something for themselves, instead of the mega-rich dude who employed them and borrowed money from the bank where you worked, Dad. And that good part of me would light up whenever these rough men would smile at quitting time and say, "Hey, College, you weren't *complete* fucking shit today," or "Don't crash your car on the way home, okay? Because, this late in the summer, we can't get another young dumbass to do our shit work," or "Go read a fucking book tonight or something so you won't get stuck here in hell with us forever." I loved working with these gruff men because I knew if I pulled my weight, they would at least treat me fairly—and after I had put in enough time, some of them would act fatherly to me and say things like, "Hey, kid, you still dreaming of being a writer after you graduate? You think you can pull that shit off? Because I got a story or two for you to put in your books."

When I returned to your house every night, Dad, you usually said nothing to me whatsoever. And so, during the long summer days, I'd try to squeeze as many words out of my roofing fathers as I could. But it was a tough few months, and I continued to sink deeper and deeper into depression.

Of course, I met the real love of my life at the beginning of my sophomore year at La Salle. That would be Alicia. She was seventeen, with this amazing mane of brown curly hair, a knockout smile, killer legs, and—after a beer or two—a wicked Massachusetts accent. She had a calming disposition, an infectious curiosity about life, and an ability to make me feel like maybe good things were in my future after all. When she first kissed me, it shook me to my core. Looking back now, I think we instinctively took all of her broken parts and all of my broken parts and—with that first electric touch of our lips, with all the love we had at the end of our tricky teen years—we forged ourselves into one barely functioning thing. At first I was afraid of committing to her too, but she somehow broke through the worst parts of me and made it easier to start believing in the good parts again. It was kind of like the middle bit of that Gordon Lightfoot song "If You Could Read My Mind." Alicia began to resurrect the good in me. And that's when I really began fighting my way back up from the internal darkness and into the rest of my life.

Thirty years after that sadistic birthday weekend car ride, I told Zeus everything I've written in this chapter, and he said, "Do you think maybe running out into traffic was an unconscious suicide attempt?"

"I was retrieving my lighter," I said.

"The flame of which you held up to the brim of your friend's ball cap."

"Are you saying some unconscious part of me intentionally created that scenario so I could put my own life in danger?"

"Why else would you try to light your friend's hat on fire?"

"We were just stupid boys doing stupid things."

"Your friend didn't do anything stupid in that story. Only you did," Zeus said.

"I don't think I was trying to commit suicide," I said.

"Isn't the timing at least noteworthy?"

"What do you mean?"

"Your father asks you—who was still psychologically a child—to hold his suicidal fantasy, and the next day, you unconsciously invent a reason to put your life in harm's way."

"So you're saying I tried to kill myself?"

"I'm wondering if your suicidal feelings are yours or your father's."

"Maybe my father's suicidal feelings were actually his father's," I said. "And then it's turtles all the way down. What difference does it make? It sucks to feel suicidal any which way."

Zeus nodded a few times and then said, "But knowing which feelings actually belong to you and which feelings belong to others—feelings that might be colonizing you—makes a huge difference."

"Why?"

"Because you don't have to feel your father's feelings, especially now that you are an adult. You have a choice. You can use what you are learning in Jungian analysis as a psychological vaccine. You don't have to tolerate being infected by your father's fantasies. You can liberate yourself."

I felt something shift deep inside of me because I had never before thought of your miserable madness as a contagious virus. I had never considered that you, too, had caught this virus when you were just a defenseless boy. And your father before you. It was a powerful thought.

For decades I had hated you for putting the fuck-you exclamation point at the end of my nineteenth birthday weekend. But how could I hate you for being infected by something against which you hadn't ever received inoculation? One might argue that you should have sought treatment as an adult, but that wasn't really an option for much of your life, especially for men who grew up long ago in blue-collar towns, in the shadows of fathers who scoffed at the mere idea of mental health being a real thing, let alone something you should actively address. When I lived in your house, in a lower-income town—again, long ago—I would have rather died than risk anyone knowing I was entering into therapy. Not because I didn't think I needed help, but because it would have felt like dropping a nuclear bomb on the already fragile social support system I had back then. I knew my support system was inadequate and failing, but any port in a storm, right? My boat definitely had a few holes in it. And the rough workers on the dock where my ship was tied up said, "Just plug 'em any which way you can. Man the fuck up. Period. End of story."

Sitting there with my analyst, I thought, *I better get my own infection under control so I won't inadvertently infect anyone else. And if I can someday cure and then inoculate myself, maybe I can also find a way to lessen your suffering too, Dad.*

Later, I would think, *Maybe I can even help many other men get their infections under control. Maybe we can inoculate the masses. Maybe we can stop the spread of such a devitalizing contagion.*

25.

I woke up on Super Bowl Sunday LIX to the smell of Alicia's oat and cornmeal pancakes wafting up from the first-floor kitchen. Instead of getting out of bed, I picked up my phone, looked at the Eagles website, and played their Super Bowl hype video. It's narrated by Bradley Cooper, who, of course, starred in the movie adaptation of *The Silver Linings Playbook*. In some ways, he was playing a metaphorical version of me in that film. Long ago—on set and during the promotion of the movie—I'd had a few brief interactions with Bradley. I once heard him say my name and plug my novel on *The Howard Stern Show*. I'd had a really nice chat with him backstage at Katie Couric's TV show. You and I, Dad, had both seen him sitting with the owner of the Eagles on TV and at games.

In the hype video, Bradley takes us through the entire Eagles 2024 season and the 2025 playoffs. The few lows and many highs. He talks about people dismissing the team and the team responding. He shows us the most violent hits and amazing catches and, of course, Barkley's insane backward leap over a Jacksonville defender. He talks about "the hunt." And he takes us back to the Eagles previously losing Super Bowl LVII to Kansas City, before allowing us to briefly relive Super Bowl LII, when Nick Foles won it all. Mr. Cooper ends by saying, "It's our time now." Then these words are displayed on the screen: "See ya Sunday."

Even though she was only downstairs—and with a giddiness that belied my age—I texted Alicia a link to the hype video and then leapt out of bed, ready to face Super Bowl Sunday.

Downstairs, as Alicia finished cooking, I asked if she was going to watch the hype video, and she said, "Um, no." When I asked why, she said, "I don't need Bradley Cooper to get me ready for the big game. I'm ready, baby."

We ate our breakfast at the table while Kingsly sat in his bed trying to contain his whines so he could earn a bite of pancake, which he eventually did.

He loves Alicia's pancakes.

Then I went into my office and wrote four thousand words of this memoir. I've been writing with the speed I once had as a young man. I've been feeling as though I'm writing with a purpose again.

Two nights before, when Zeus had asked me to describe who I needed to be in order to write something that other men would find useful, I was surprised to find that delivering my answer required a good thirty minutes. It mostly underscored the importance of humility and gratitude and being ready to serve. The whole time I was talking, Zeus smiled paternally and nodded his head in agreement.

In the afternoon, I went for a long run. I passed a dead deer on the side of Sams Point Road and thought about ephemerality. Then I thought about how you, Dad, were dying, and I felt really old.

I was listening to my Los Campesinos! mix. Los Campesinos! is a guitar-driven, emo-pop band from the UK. Being a Gen-Xer, I think of them as a post-punk indie-rock band. You would hate them, Dad. Alicia *truly* hates them. (Yours and Alicia's musical tastes overlap in shocking ways.) But I love the music of Los Campesinos!, mostly because it produces *big* emotions in me. I have a writing friend who also loves Los Campesinos! He and I used to have coffee together every Friday. After I left South Jersey, we used to talk on the phone every Friday morning for two hours. He also has struggled with mental health issues. But at the height of my alcoholism, I'm not sure I was the best friend to him. We abruptly stopped talking on the phone around eight years ago. I'm still not quite sure why. We've been texting lately, and that has been healing—at least for me. He's been through some shit. I've been through some shit. And I think we now do our best to love each other through our text messages. I hope to someday resume our phone conversations and feel we are building back up to that. We've been text bonding some over our ailing fathers because his father is in decline too. As I ran, I wondered if my old Los Campesinos!–loving friend would read this memoir someday and understand that my journey has been complicated and that I have made a lot of progress. I fantasized that maybe he'd learn to trust me again and we'd eventually even resume our phone conversations. Fantasizing gave me a lot of hopeful fuel.

Next I thought about my old college buddy Erik, who now runs a major TV station in Philadelphia. If the Eagles won, he would have a lot of work to do, covering the celebrations and the parade. Historically, Philly championships have been marred by drunken fans and stupid violence. Shortly after you and I had that traumatic 1992 conversation—when you were dropping me off at my La Salle dorm after my birthday weekend home—Erik and I had bonded over being let down by our fathers. His dad had also disappointed him that semester. And more than thirty years later, Erik and I are still talking to each other about our father issues, albeit with the recent benefits of my having been in analysis and him having been in therapy. I thought about how much he had encouraged me over the past few years and how he had been brave enough to be vulnerable with me in a way that reinforced my long-held suspicion that there were other men out there who are also starving for the types of conversations that you and I are now having, thanks to this long-form nonfiction piece I'm writing here.

The Los Campesinos! song "5 Flucloxacillin" came on. It's an upbeat tune mostly about depression, or at least that's the way I hear it.

But the chorus talks about victory and humility in a way that seems ironic, given all that I had been thinking. Basically, it points out how losers often say they would have shown more humility than the winners managed, but there is never a way to prove it, because the losers have, of course, lost. The thing I like so much about this band is their unrelentingly aggressive musical cheer, even as they sing the bleakest of lyrics. And for people prone to depression, there is something liberating about singing and chanting with almost childlike glee at the worst of the world.

And then I was running faster than a fifty-one-year-old man has any business running.

Victory.

Humility.

Victory.

Humility.

After a fast shower, Alicia, Kingsly, and I made our way to your house. I had the pizza box and a heavy baking stone in my hands. Alicia carried the end of Kingsly's leash and a plastic bag containing my Perfect Pushup circles so that I could do seven push-ups before each quarter of the football game—one push-up for each beat of the Eagles chant: "E-A-G-L-E-S *Eagles*!" This ritual had been first thought up by yours truly to at least *appear* to be combating the sloth of watching football on the couch all day, but it had also turned out to be good luck so far, so it just couldn't be skipped.

We found you on the couch scrolling through news feeds on your iPad.

"Super Bowl, Dad!" I yelled as we entered the living room. *"It's finally here."*

"What?" you said, without looking up, sounding more than slightly annoyed.

Mom was in the kitchen making a salad with olives and hot peppers and pickled onions. We got the oven going, and then we were heating up the pizza on the baking stone.

I went back into the living room and asked, "You ready for the big game?" Then I began massaging your shoulders.

"The Super Bowl isn't on yet, I don't think," you said, with little enthusiasm.

"But soon," I said. "And we have *pizza*."

"I like pizza," you said, but with almost no emotion, which is when I realized you were sundowning, meaning your dementia was kicking into overdrive at the end of the day, after you had already used up all your brain's rest from the night before. I pretended that it didn't matter, that you would get a second wind, that the father-son Super Bowl of my dreams was imminent.

The lucky Eagles Santa figurine that I had bought you earlier in the year—Kris Kringle in a white and Kelly green Birds uniform, with a wrapped present in his hand instead of a football—was on the mantel in his lucky spot, but you were in the wrong sweatshirt.

When I said something to you about forgetting to wear your lucky Mitchell & Ness throwback sweatshirt, you went to your bedroom to change but reappeared wearing a green pullover sweater, which Mom immediately told you to take off because she didn't want you getting pizza sauce on your good clothes. A rebuked, betrayed expression spread across your face, which made me wish I hadn't said anything about the lucky sweatshirt.

At dinner you ate your pizza with little joy. When I asked if you were happy to be having pizza, you said yes, but in a way that was unconvincing, although you did eat three slices, in addition to a chicken salad.

After dinner Mom got you into your lucky Mitchell & Ness throwback Eagles sweatshirt with the old-school, flying, Kelly green eagle spread across your chest. Then we made our way back into the living room to watch the pregame, during which you really seemed out of it.

"Super Bowl, Dad!" I kept yelling, trying to pump you up, but got no response.

I sat in my lucky seat at the exact center of the couch. You sat in your lucky seat to my left. Mom sat on my right. And Alicia and Kingsly sat in the leather chair to the right of Mom.

From Pennsylvania, Micah sent pics of Oliver and Archer dressed in Eagles green for the game. From Greer, South Carolina, Megan sent pics of Isla and Brexley also clad in Eagles green.

Bradley Cooper introduced the Eagles before they came out, and you said, "Who is that guy?"

"He played the main character, Pat, in the movie adaptation of my book," I said, but you didn't seem to understand.

Micah's wife, Kelly, sent a little video of your grandsons standing with their right hands over their hearts during the playing of the national anthem. Mom loved that bit of patriotism. I smiled at the boys' earnestness.

Your brother, Jon, texted us. Megan and Micah texted, *Go Birds!* And the men who have been supporting me through my ups and downs these past years, the men in whom I often confide, began to text me love. My boys: Kent Green and Matt "Chubis" Huband and Erik Smith and Mark Cecil and Nick Butler and Adam Morgan and Scott Snow. My in-laws, Barb and Peague, sent supportive messages. My nephew Conor surprised me by chiming in from Massachusetts. I heard from Eric Zimmer and Matt "Eddie" Woolford and Scott "Mr. Canada" Caldwell and Dr. Corey Shagensky. They all said they were rooting for the Eagles to win. Not all of these people were fellow Eagles fans. Some weren't even football fans. But they knew I was watching with you; and they knew about your disease; and they knew how much I'd been hurting over the years; and that time was running out. Many of the men listed above had their own father issues, so they understood the heightened significance. They loved me. I loved them. And I loved you. So they loved you too.

Even still, I was feeling anxious, so much so that Mom joked about giving me one of your emergency CBD gummies. It felt like someone was tightening several loops of rope around my chest. I had a hard time breathing through my nose. I don't think I was worried about the Eagles' performance so much as I was worried about what this night would mean to you, to me, to the memoir—and how all that might or might not illuminate the path forward into the rest of my life. I simultaneously hated myself for building up this moment so much in my imagination *and* firmly believed that it might be the most important night of our father-son relationship—at least symbolically.

"Will the Eagles win?" I asked you.

"I hope so," you said in a flat voice that made me worry you didn't really understand that the team you had passionately loved for more than seventy years was playing in the Super Bowl.

And then the game began.

Dad, the Eagles absolutely slaughtered the Chiefs. They murdered them. Gutted their dynasty. It was an awesome thing to behold. Perhaps the most dominant ass-kicking we Eagles fans have ever witnessed the Birds dole out. It was magnificent. Almost flawless.

But all through the first half, while I cheered and jumped up and down, you kept asking me if legendary Philadelphia sports radio host Angelo Cataldi was still on the air. I kept saying I thought he retired, and you kept saying, "All the old guys are gone." You were somewhere else—lost in the past.

When the second quarter ended, the Eagles were up 24–0.

You lemon-faced squinted in bewilderment at Kendrick Lamar's halftime show.

"I'm not sure the Eagles will win," you said as the third quarter began.

"Dad, it's twenty-four to nothing."

"They've choked before," you said with the same unbelievable pessimism that I had often experienced when I was a child.

When the Eagles went up 37–6, I asked again if you thought they were going to win, and you sniped back, "I'm just watching."

I tried to remember what it felt like to have you rubbing my head for good luck during Eagles games, back when I was a baby.

I wanted to live out that feeling in the present moment.

I'd never wanted anything more in my entire life.

"The Eagles are winning, Dad. They're going to win the Super Bowl. *This is real*," I said and then gave you a big hug and a kiss on the forehead, but your body was stiff, and you didn't say anything back to me.

When our team actually did win the Super Bowl, I hugged you again and said, "I love you."

You echoed my words in monotone. I could tell you were beyond exhausted and desperately needed sleep. It was hours after your regular bedtime. And your disease had robbed you of the ability to really be with us.

I knew it was the dementia, but you being easily within arm's reach and yet still inaccessible, well, that felt like every second you and I spent together during my entire childhood.

Mom and I told you it was okay to go to bed if you needed to, but you wouldn't. Instead, you sat there blank-faced. When they played the Eagles fight song, you quietly clapped offbeat, with a vacant look in your eyes.

I think Mom could sense my disappointment, because she said, "He'll rewatch the game in the morning when he's fresh. And he'll rewatch it every day for the next six months, thinking it's live. He'll get to enjoy it. Every day will be an Eagles Super Bowl win. Do you want to know what he'll say each and every time I put the game on for him?"

"What?"

"Your father will say—with panic in his voice—'I have to call Matthew. He should be here.'"

"How do you know that?" I asked her.

"Because that's what he says every single day when I replay an Eagles game for him and he thinks it's live. He always wants you with him. Just like when you were a newborn baby."

I looked away.

Even after all these years of practice, it was still hard to swallow Mom's medicine.

The Eagles were awarded the Lombardi Trophy. Coach Sirianni thanked God and Jesus. When he was named the Most Valuable Player, Jalen Hurts also thanked God.

Then Mom and I put Eagles Santa back into his original packaging so I could store his luck safely, to help us again next season.

As Alicia and I walked Kingsly home through the crisp winter South Carolina air—passing under the live oak trees' long Spanish moss beards—she said, "Your team won."

"Yeah, but Dad seemed really out of it."

"He asked about Angelo Cataldi six times in the first quarter before I stopped counting."

"The win didn't feel like I thought it would."

"It's just a game."

"I know."

"And I love you."

"I love you too."

When I went to bed that night, I felt deeply sad, Dad. Our time together watching Eagles football was over for this year and maybe even forever. I was glad that we got to see the Birds win the Super Bowl while we were together again on the couch, but as I lay there in the darkness of my bedroom—with my wife sleeping to my right and my dog snoozing by my feet—I felt the old depression trying to fight its way up from deep inside of me.

I didn't pray before I fell asleep. I just let the sadness have its way with me.

Then, in the middle of the night, I felt someone standing next to the bed, looking down at me.

When my eyes adjusted to the darkness, I saw a man. Dressed head to toe in camouflage, he was petting Kingsly, who had abandoned his fuzzy doughnut bed and was now sleeping snug against my side.

"Uncle Pete?" I said.

"Quiet, pretty boy," he whispered. "I don't want your ugly mug wakin' up that gorgeous wife of yours. And Kingsly needs his beauty sleep too."

I gently moved my snoozing dog to the other side of me. Then I slid out of bed and followed Pete into the hallway, slowly pulling the bedroom door closed behind me, doing my best to make sure it didn't bang and wake up Alicia.

At the top of the stairs, Pete smiled and said, "I don't have much time. I have to go back soon."

"Go back where?"

"Where do you think, genius?"

"They let you wear camouflage in heaven?"

"If you get into heaven, God lets you wear whatever the fuck you want. That's why it's called heaven, girly man."

"I've really, really missed you," I said. Then I hugged him.

Pete pounded a fist on my back three times, broke away, and then said, "Okay, enough of this bullshit. So you're almost done writing the new little book. Memoir this time, huh? Lettin' your nuts hang out for all to see. *Badass.* You've almost completed the current mission. God likes that."

"He does?"

"Why the fuck else do you think I'm here?"

"Did you know that the Eagles won the Super Bowl?"

"Yeah, we got TV in heaven. Up there, we got everything you can possibly think of."

"Don't you care that the Birds won? They beat Andy Reid. He coaches the Kansas City Chiefs now."

"You and I got more important things to discuss here."

"Like what?"

"Like your ugly ass walkin' down these steps. And quietly," Pete said, "so you don't wake up your better half. I like Alicia. *A lot.* She loves dogs more than anyone I ever met. Well, besides yours truly, of course. Because I love dogs even more than I like people. So you do the math, girly man."

"Sometimes the thought of publishing this memoir terrifies me," I said to Pete. Then I added, "I want to be brave. *Brave like you.*"

Pete smiled proudly and then said, "Until you make it up into heaven, just remember, there's an entire ass-kickin' army of hard motherfuckin' men inside of you." Then he poked my chest with enough force to make me take a step backward. "*I'm* marchin' with 'em. And I ain't never fuckin' afraid. Neither are the other men in our army. *And we are many.* Remember that, pretty boy. But you really gotta walk down these steps now."

"Why?" I said.

"Finish the mission," Pete said while he turned my shoulders around so that I was facing the stairs. "And then I'll see you up above. Eventually. *Now fuckin' go.*"

I walked down the steps as quietly as I could.

When I made the turn at the wall, I saw Grandmom standing at the bottom of the staircase with a huge smile on her little wrinkled face and her arms spread wide. I ran down the last flight. When my feet hit the first floor, I bent down to meet her tiny four-foot-eight-inch frame, and then I fell into her embrace.

"Matthew!" she said as she kissed both my cheeks. "I've told God about all the funny greeting cards you used to send me at the old folks' home. That I loved getting your mail. Every week I'd get something good from you. And I still pray for you every single day. You can keep right on praying in heaven after you die."

I was so happy to see her, I couldn't even speak.

"You know," she said to me, "after your Pop Pop passed away, your father, Michael, would come and sit with me. He brought me Starbucks coffee almost every weekday. And your mother and father took me to church every Sunday. They were living in Pennsylvania then. And I was back over the bridge in good old Collingswood, New Jersey. In the Methodist home. So it was a long drive with the city traffic. After he retired, Michael came almost every day. *Every day.* No matter what the weather was, he never missed. And we'd just sit there drinking coffee and tea and talking for hours, getting all the problems behind us. Your father was very good to me at the end. Made sure I had whatever I needed. Paid for everything I wanted and couldn't afford. And he took me to your big *Silver Linings* movie premiere in Philadelphia. I got to see the Quick name up there on the silver screen. Those Hollywood stars dancing at the end of the film. *I just love dancing.* Then, when the movie ended, there you were standing next to that famous director. I was so proud of you. And your father also took me back to the Outer Banks when I thought I'd never see it again. And all you men blocked the crashing waves with your bodies and got me out into the gentler water, where I could float on my back with my tootsies sticking up in the summer air. *In my nineties.* And now you do that with your father. I see you in the ocean watching out for him, just like you used to watch out for me. And I get so happy whenever

I'm looking down from heaven at you and your father swimming out there in the sea."

"I think about you and Pop Pop every single time I float over a wave," I said. "I really miss swimming with you. Sometimes I feel like I can't keep going without you and Pop Pop and Uncle Pete here. I feel lost. Like I was left behind. And I don't always know what to do."

"We only get as much as we need at the time we need it, Matthew," she said, holding my face in her hands. "God doesn't always give us luxurious extras. But getting what we need is better than a kick in the pants. *And you had better believe that.*"

I laughed at her favorite old-timey saying. Then I said, "I still need you."

"You're on the other side of needing now," Grandmom said. "Time to give. People need you."

"Need me for what?" I asked.

"Well, for starters, your grandfather needs a word with his first-born grandson," she said.

Dad, that's when I saw your father standing by my front door. He was wearing an old Eagles sweatshirt and the blue and gold La Salle baseball cap I had given him in the early nineties. His huge stomach still bulged out over his belt, and his signature big, brown-framed glasses covered a good third of his face.

He was weeping.

"Pop Pop, what's wrong?" I said, as I rushed over to him.

He covered his face with his spotted wrinkly hands and said, "I owe you another apology."

"For what?" I asked. "You were good to me. Your love probably saved my life when I was a teenager. I loved you more than I have ever loved any other man."

Your father began trembling, and then he was sobbing so loudly, I thought he might pass out. So I wrapped my arms around him; and said he was okay; and that everything was fine; and that Mom and I were taking care of you, Dad, as you slowly succumbed to dementia; and that you and Jon had already made peace; and Uncle Jon and I were writing letters; and that I was even starting to get back in touch a little with Jon's three daughters, Rebecca, Sarah, and Rachael; and that I talked to Megan and Micah all the time; and loved my nieces and nephews the best I could; and that I was once again attempting to be the glue of the family, just like Pop Pop had taught me.

"I really tried to do my best," Pop Pop sobbed. Then he said, "And I loved every one of you with every drop of my ability. I'm confident about that. But I grew up so poor; and my mother was always losing all our rent and food money playing bingo; and my sisters had to drop out of high school and work to support me; and then the war happened and I had to do horrendous things that you can't even imagine; and my best buddy in the whole world parachuted out of a plane over Europe and was never seen or heard from ever again; and I never got to play professional baseball; and had three boys before I could blink; and I had to feed and clothe them and get them through college; and after, I never even had the guts to earn a college degree myself; and the only three things I ever had to sell were a smile and a joke and a firm handshake; and I read the dictionary, trying to learn all the big words, but I couldn't ever make any of them change my station in life; and I was always trying so hard to appear proud when, privately, I was ashamed; and, in many ways, I failed your father; I didn't treat him like I treated you because, when your dad was a boy, I was young and ignorant and trying to forget the war; and people wanted me to pretend to be a hero—like I was General Patton himself—but I was only ever a scared boy whose own father was simple and couldn't hear so well and didn't know how to make his way in the world. So, you see, I was only ever guessing and pretending otherwise; and I used to call your father Michelle; and I hit him *a lot*; and I made him feel small;

and belittled his dreams; and forced him to live out mine; and now I see my mistakes so clearly; and I see you trying to fix it all; and I see you crying so much every day as you write the memoir; and I see how much these things have hurt you; how much my failures have always crucified you, even when you were a little boy; and I'm standing at the foot of your cross with a handful of nails and a hammer. I'm just so, so, so sorry and . . ."

I held onto Pop Pop and rocked him like a baby, as I just kept repeating, "I know, I know, I know, I know, I know, I know, I know . . ."

And when I woke up in my bed the next morning, the pillow I was hugging was soaked with tears.

26.

"I've been thinking more symbolically about Jesus," I said to Zeus.

This was toward the end of a Friday night analytic session in June 2025. Dad, I was, of course, wearing my black T-shirt. And even though I was not drinking alcohol in real life, I'd emailed Zeus a series of dreams I'd recently had about breaking my seven years of sobriety.

I'd also been addressing my editor's editorial letter, revising this memoir. He loved the first draft—even the title. "Triple entendre!" he joyfully proclaimed on a phone call earlier in the week. He also said, "We have a hell of a story on our hands." Despite the fact that he wanted me to cut more than a hundred pages and write forty new ones—"Think of it as a math problem," he suggested—I learned that we were going to publish in a year, which was much faster than I had previously anticipated. My editor said he believed in my book. He said he believed in me.

"Tell me more about symbolic Jesus," Zeus said.

"Well," I said, "Jesus comes to Earth as the Son of God. But He flips the money changers' tables and hides from crowds. And He gets mad at his disciples for betraying Him. Jesus asks God the Father to take away the very task Jesus was sent down to Earth to complete. When He is crucified, even though Jesus knows the plan, He yells at His Dad and asks why God has forsaken His only begotten Son. That's the needy-son mentality right there. But through the crucifixion, the needy-son mentality is tortured out of Jesus, and then He is able to put on the giving-father mentality. He takes on the sins of everyone freely, even though we don't deserve it. Jesus stops whining about His needs and simply gives. I think the story of Christ is a metaphor for reaching masculine maturity. The needy-son mentality has to be crucified out of boys if they are to become men."

"I think that just might be an original idea," Zeus said. "You should put that in the memoir."

"Do you think my memoir will help men?" I asked. "My editor thinks it will help a lot of hurting people. Might I finally become someone who gives as much as he takes?"

Zeus paused to collect his thoughts, which usually meant something mind-blowing was about to come out of his mouth. Then he said, "Helping many others is the fantasy you needed to justify reintegrating your trauma history, which you split off as a child so you could survive. Feeling all the difficult emotions—which you couldn't afford to feel as a teenager because you needed to survive living in your father's house—took courage. Since your sense of self-worth was so low, you couldn't justify doing it for yourself, so you told yourself you were only doing it to help others. And now you are using the same fantasy as a psychological defense against the pain of publishing your memoir. If you are helping many people, you can justify the torment you are feeling. But what I want you to understand and eventually *believe* is that the well-being of your own soul is enough justification for enduring the necessary agony required to heal yourself. Regarding everyone else, God doesn't need your help, Matthew. God wants to help all of us. God wants to help *you*, regardless of what you are or are not doing to help others. It isn't necessary to publish a memoir to justify your own salvation."

"I actually do *want* to publish my memoir," I said.

"And doing so will be painful in ways you don't even understand yet."

"But don't you think God can use my story as an instrument of change? Surely my words can nudge other trauma survivors toward forgiveness and healing."

"*Listen to me.* I really want you to hear what I'm saying. This is important. You do not need to save anyone—let alone the world—to prove your soul's worth. To be worthy of being healed, you didn't have to save your siblings, you didn't have to save your students, you don't have to save your father and mother, and you don't have to save your readers," my analyst said. "You are already important enough just as you are. You don't have to earn salvation. You never did."

"I know."

"But do you really?"

I stared at Zeus, not knowing what to say.

"In an effort to heal your soul," he continued, "I tried to get you to privately write about your trauma *for years* so you would finally allow yourself to feel what you were not strong enough to feel when you were younger—what you numbed with all the alcohol for decades. You got quite angry with me when I pushed you to write about the shelf-falling incident. Remember? You flat out refused to explore your trauma in writing for hundreds of sessions, until all of a sudden you signed a contract with a major publisher and agreed to tell the entire world. I think it was the fantasy of helping others on a large stage that gave you the strength—and quite frankly permission—to help yourself. Because you didn't think you alone were worth helping. It's a psychological work-around. One that you no longer need, now that you have done the hard work of facing the full horror of your trauma, which has massively helped to heal your soul. I hope it has also given you an appreciation and a love for who you innately were before the trauma with your father happened, who you still are, and who you will always be."

"Are you saying I *shouldn't* publish my memoir?"

"You're an artist. You deserve to get paid for opening a vein and allowing others to watch. You need to thrive financially. All perfectly reasonable. But that has nothing to do with the souls of others or your own."

"But I really do want to help other people. So many books have helped *me* in the past. I believe in the healing power of story and so do you."

"You're not hearing me, Matthew. *God doesn't need your help.* Thinking that you are helping God heal other trauma survivors is a defense against the shame and guilt you are currently feeling. God is doing all sorts of things, over which you and I and everyone else have absolutely no control. You keep dreaming about drinking for a reason. Your feelings of shame and guilt surface, and then you drink in your dreams at night. Those drinking dreams picked back up right when you learned that the publication is really happening and much sooner than you thought."

"Do you think I'm ashamed to be telling my secrets? Does making my father look bad produce guilt?"

"Your shame and guilt stem from the fact that you couldn't stop the abuse, and it went on *for decades*. It's inappropriate shame and guilt. None of it was your fault. But you have to work through it all before you publish this memoir so that you won't start drinking again. It's important work. We're going to do it."

I nodded because I knew Zeus was speaking the truth.

"There could be millions of people reading your memoir next year," Zeus said. "Millions of people reading about what you kept hidden for half a century."

"I should be so lucky."

"There is no time now for childish superstition."

"I couldn't just let *millions* hang in the air."

Zeus gave me a stern look here.

"Okay. What should I do?"

"First, you need to let your mom and siblings read the entire memoir just as soon as you finish editing. Let your family, especially your mother, react in privacy and then acclimate to the fact that this book is actually being published. Mom, Megan, and Micah are going to have to learn how to live with this memoir being out there in the world. People are going to ask them about it. Your dad is obviously a different story."

I swallowed hard and looked at the reproduction of Henri Rousseau's *Carnival Evening*, which hangs in a gold frame opposite my writing desk.

"You didn't do anything wrong," Zeus said. "You needed to claim your truth. You needed to work through your trauma."

"But I didn't need to publish a book about it."

"You're a writer. It's what you do."

"I still think publishing my memoir can help others."

Zeus smiled and then said, "Writing the memoir has done more to heal your soul than all of the many analytic sessions we've done in the past five years. You absolutely needed to write it. You told your truth. Of that, I am certain. And it really *has* mended your soul. That's an extraordinary, transcendent thing. Publishing is just your job. Again, it's a fine job to have. But God cares about your soul, not your career. And *I* care about your soul."

"It really doesn't bother you that readers won't know who you are? That I've changed your name and disguised your identity?"

"I don't want to be famous. Your memoir isn't about me."

"You're the hero of the entire story."

"I'm your analyst."

"You're more than that and you know it. You plucked my heart from the Titans' slaughter and regrew me in your thigh."

"We have a year to prepare your soul. You're going to have to talk publicly about your worst traumas. You and I have a lot of psychological prepping to do."

"Can I ask you something that's been bothering me for a long time?"

Zeus nodded.

"Have you really not noticed that I wear black to every single session?"

"You already know the answer to that irrelevant question," Zeus said and then looked deep into my eyes.

As I sank into his warm gaze, it felt like our souls were hugging through our computer screens.

And then I was no longer fixated on my clothing.

For what felt like a few minutes, we held eye contact.

With my mind, like I was telepathic, I told Zeus that I loved him.

The corner of his mouth curled upward for the briefest of seconds. Then he said, "Matthew, we have to finish up for the night. We'll talk more on Tuesday morning."

And I said, "Thank you," like I do at the end of almost every session.

27.

Dad, we made it. This is the final chapter of the memoir.

If it isn't obvious by now, let me officially state for the record that I forgive you for all the times you weren't at your best, for having limitations, for being wounded, and for not always possessing what I needed from you. No one can give what they don't have. I understand that now.

I hope you will forgive me too, for not being able to forgive you sooner, for wasting so much time, for wanting you to feel all of the worst that I've felt in my life, and for not always being able to love you in the way a good son should. I don't know how much time we have left together, but I'm with you to the end—or as you like to call it "the duration."

Thank you for picking such a dedicated wife to be my mother; for bringing me into a world ripe with possibilities; for providing me with such a loving sister and such a loyal brother; for working so mind-numbingly hard to put a roof over my head, clothes on my back, and food in my belly; for making sure I got a college degree; for worrying about my financial security and my ability to afford health insurance; for making me a Philadelphia Eagles fan; for paying my dental bills when I was trying to become a fiction writer; for reading every single one of my books; and for all the warm, sunny times we've had in Beaufort, South Carolina, where you made loving you so much easier, where you allowed me to hug and kiss you, where you were cordial to my wife and dog, where we walked the beach and swam in the ocean, where you told me the entire story of your life and gave me a fuller and more honest glimpse into your soul.

Before I sign off, ending this long letter, I'd like to thank you for the following scene that Mom, you, and I played out in the summer of 2024. Maybe in your mind here—while you take in the following little movie—you'll start hearing your favorite tune, "Desperado" by the Eagles, which you've often called your personal theme song. Are you picking up the opening piano notes? Is Don Henley's raw, vulnerable voice working its magic? Let all that be our soundtrack as we acknowledge the many gifts God put on our table. In a way, what's below is the beginning scene of this entire great corrective to our long, bumpy relationship. Because your demented brain doesn't remember it at all—and, also, so it will be recorded forever—here we go:

It starts with me walking to your house. "This isn't a walk of shame," I keep telling myself, but I can't make myself believe it, as I traverse the one block and small park that separate Alicia's and my home from yours and Mom's. The soupy air slows me down, but, like always, the journey still only takes two minutes. The palmetto tree in front of your home looks exactly like the one on the South Carolina state flag. As I pass it, I remind myself to breathe. I remind myself that I'm not a little boy anymore. I've been alive for more than half a century, and, lately, things really have been different between you and me, Dad.

I grit my teeth on your front porch for another two minutes before I manage to gin up the courage to knock on your door.

"Did something happen?" Mom asks when she sees my face.

"What's wrong?" you say from the living room couch.

"Can we talk?" I ask.

We all walk through air-conditioning to the screened-in porch attached to the back of your home. Then we sit down on the chairs and couch that surround your outdoor tabby fireplace. Under the haint blue paint above, the bronze-colored ceiling fan pushes muggy air down onto our heads.

"My editor doesn't think the novel I wrote should be my next book, and my agent says I shouldn't send it to another publishing house," I blurt out. When Mom asks what that means, I try to put it in terms you'll both understand, saying, "I worked for three years and won't get paid a single penny for it."

The pain of creative rejection is abstract to you, Dad, but the loss of potential income is as hard as one of your all-time favorite Eagles football players, Chuck Bednarik—aka Concrete Charlie, just in case your dementia has also erased him from your memory.

"Do you need money?" you ask without hesitation.

"No," I say, even though my recent inability to earn has been edging me toward another nervous breakdown.

"What can we do to help?" Mom asks.

I take a deep breath before saying, "My editor suggests writing—*today*—the book I thought I'd write ten years from now. A memoir. About my alcoholism and my Jungian analysis and moving to Beaufort to help with Dad's . . . *situation*."

You and Mom are both silent, like I knew you would be.

"What about the screenplays you've written and the famous actors and directors you've been talking with?" Mom says.

"They haven't been returning my texts, calls, or emails."

"Why?"

"Honestly? I have no idea. I did everything they asked me to do. But it's Hollywood, so hardly surprising. And I really think I need a break from all that. I actually believe the memoir could be my best book yet. My closest writing buddies and Alicia agree. Plus, just the thought of writing it gives me an anxiety attack. And I'm always telling up-and-coming writers to write the books they're afraid to publish. *So.*"

You're frowning.

Mom's chewing her lip.

My stomach churns like a washing machine.

"Listen," I say, when I can't take the silence anymore. "If you don't want me to write a memoir about us right now, I won't. But I'm going to write it eventually because I need to heal, and storytelling has always been my medicine. So, one day, I *will* be writing nonfiction about personal things. My childhood. Dad's disease. Our difficulties in the past. I'm going to have to tell the truth as I see and imagine it. I'm sure it won't be as you see and imagine it. I'm going to have to write things that might make all of us look bad. I'll be undressing the family. People will absolutely judge us. Right now, I feel like we're all just starting to be okay again after not being okay for decades. I don't want to ruin this good time we're having in Beaufort, especially with everything we have going on. To even consider the opportunity that's currently on the table, I'd need you to say that no matter what I wrote, the three of us would still be good. That you won't hate me for telling my truth. For digging into the past. For showing people our secrets. I'll be fine if you decide you want me to wait ten years. I can tell my editor that now is not the best time. My agent will understand. But I think fate might be calling. I really might *need* to write this book now. Not for the money. Not to advance my career. But to figure out exactly what my truth is—maybe for the first time in my entire life. My analyst says it could be very good for me. I won't lie. I'm scared. And I don't want to hurt either of you."

I can't make eye contact with Mom or you.

I catch myself chewing the inside of my cheek.

My knee is going up and down.

The whirl of the ceiling fan is deafening.

Dad, I'm a middle-aged man who has published nine novels, the first and most successful of which was very much against your wishes. I haven't asked your permission for anything since I was a teenager. Since I've moved to Beaufort to help care for you, my relationships with Mom and you have been on the mend. This is the best we've ever been. But you both have grown old and no longer feel unbreakable. And my caring about your fragility makes me feel vulnerable—almost like a child again.

My heart pounds.

The old invisible hand begins choking me.

Your silence is painful.

It has always been so terribly painful.

When I can't take it anymore, I say, "It's okay. I'll tell them no. We have to stick together now more than ever."

Another long moment of silence.

Then Mom asks, "Who do you think would play me in the movie?"

"I don't know that there'd *be* a movie," I say.

"Of course there'd be a movie," Mom says. "You're a *New York Times* bestselling author. Your books are turned into Oscar winners."

"One book. *Singular.* A long time ago. And I don't know that I'd want *anyone* to play either of you in a movie adaptation. Hollywood might lampoon you. Turn you into cartoons. And I wouldn't be able to live with myself if—"

"Write the memoir, Matthew," she says.

I search her blue eyes.

She nods.

I turn toward you and say, "Dad, are you okay with this?"

"To become a named executive at a publicly traded bank, I did a lot of things I didn't want to do," you say. "I lived all alone in a hotel for years. Ate every meal out. Got fat. Got prostate cancer. And now my brain's all messed up. You have to do whatever it takes to make money."

"*Again.* It's not for the money. It's not for career advancement. But I am going to have to explain why I became an alcoholic. Why I've had so much anxiety and depression. I'm asking for carte blanche," I say. "You both probably won't like what I write about you."

"We *never* like what you write about us," Mom says and then smiles. "You're always making us look awful. We've gotten pretty used to it over the years."

"I know I'm the dad in *The Silver Linings Playbook*," you say. "And the book, not the movie."

I look at you.

I look back at Mom.

And then I look at you again.

"So," I say. *"We're actually doing this?"*

Mom kisses my cheek, hugs me, and says, "God gave you a gift. Who are we to keep you from using it?"

"Dad?" I ask.

You close your eyes, press your lips together until they turn white—it's like you're praying—and then . . .

Acknowledgments

For a quarter century, I repeatedly tried and failed to write nonfiction about my father. Turns out, fifty-one years of pain, six and a half years of sobriety, and four and a half years of intense Jungian analysis were the necessary costs I first had to pay.

My wife, Alicia Bessette, blazed our sobriety trail by completely giving up alcohol five months before I did. When I got 100 percent sober, she nobly endured the bumpy aftermath. As you have witnessed many times in this memoir, Alicia is the true heroine of my life. Since 1993 she's been helping me find the necessary strength to be vulnerable on these pages. She was the first to read this manuscript. She was the first to edit it. She greatly improved it. And she encouraged me to put it into the world. I love Alicia most of all.

Zeus, my analyst—whose real name shall remain hidden until our work together is finished—is one of the wisest and most generous men I have ever known. He has many times endured—with astounding patience and poise—my absolute worst. He has also faithfully drip-fed my soul medicine for years. On a symbolic level, Zeus is absolutely my father. This memoir would not exist if he hadn't reparented me with the mysterious and wondrous alchemy of Jungian analysis. I love him too.

My mother will tell you that she endured the worst pain of her life to bring me into this world. I'm grateful to be here. Mom has often given me what others couldn't. And, as we've dealt with my father's dementia, she and I have become even closer. I love my mother. I appreciate her permission to speak my truth. What a gift.

My father and I have done a lot of healing since dementia began altering his brain. As I've said earlier, I'm grateful for all the many things he provided. Spending time with him in Beaufort has been some of the best medicine I've ever received. I love my father now more than ever.

My sister, Megan, talked me through a few difficult memories and encouraged me to say what I had to. She also gave me two phenomenal nieces, Isla and Brexley, whom she regularly brought to Beaufort throughout the writing of this memoir. I love the three of them with all my heart.

My brother, Micah, has always been loyal and supportive. He also brought my amazing sister-in-law, Kelly, into my life. Together they created my two fantastic nephews: Oliver and Archer. During the writing of this memoir, all four of them made the long drive from Pennsylvania to coastal South Carolina once every season. I love them like crazy.

My uncle Jon and I have been enjoying a late-blooming uncle-nephew relationship. In addition to sending me many letters, Uncle Jon has frequently driven from New Jersey to South Carolina just to spend time with Dad and me. His efforts to promote inner peace and forgiveness—as he shows my father grace—are nothing short of heroic. Positive masculinity. In a bid for intimacy, Uncle Jon also sent me his short, unpublished memoir, *My Story Is*. Reading it helped me understand the difficult spiritual work he has done on himself. It also helped me fine-tune the thesis for this memoir. I love my uncle Jon.

Without my uncle Pete, Pop Pop Quick, and Grandmom Dink, I would not have made it through childhood. They were all big early supporters of my writing. In many ways, they're still supporting me from beyond the grave. RIP. I will always love them dearly.

My in-laws up in Massachusetts, Peague and Barb, always send love. They also visited us in the Lowcountry while I was wrapping my head around this project. I appreciated it. I love Dr. Bob and Barb Bessette.

On any given late afternoon during the writing and editing of this memoir, you could have found me running or walking around downtown Beaufort while talking on the phone with my best Southern friend, Matt "Chubis" Huband. Whenever I was at my lowest, Chubis would never fail to say—and with great conviction—that something good would break for me soon. His warm Southern accent and eternal optimism are quite the tonic. Whenever I hear his voice, it feels like home, because he is my brother. I love Chubis. Shout-out to Boo Boo and Big Daddy for bringing Chubis into this world.

Once a week during the creation of this memoir, I spoke to my fellow two-man movie club cofounder, Kent Green. We discussed a different film each call. Kent also listened to me work out this memoir in real time. He encouraged me to keep writing. He was not only a brother, but also a convincing fan, telling me weekly that he couldn't wait to read the Matthew Quick memoir. His enthusiasm helped some deep part of me start believing long before the rest of me really bought in. I love Kent Green.

Erik Smith has been my brother since our freshman fall semester at La Salle University, back in 1992. He and I also talked a lot during the creation of this memoir. We discussed what it means to be a man in midlife, helped each other heal our father wounds, and supported each other as we made our journeys through therapy and analysis. This helped colossally. Erik also greatly encouraged me to write this book. I love Erik Smith.

The gifted novelist Nickolas Butler encouraged me—with tremendous passion—to write about my father. Nick believed in this project long before I did. He and I talked at length about modern masculinity, as well as what it means to be a male writer these days. Nick also provided warm, smart advice while I was revising the prologue. It all improved this memoir. I love Nick Butler.

Back in 2022, the eternally positive novelist Mark Cecil interviewed me on his podcast, *The Thoughtful Bro*. We've since become phone-call and texting friends. Being a wildly optimistic man, Mark often pushed back on my darker thoughts and became an ardent apostle for this project. We've spent hours on the phone talking about modern masculinity, midlife, and fatherhood. I love Mark Cecil.

Talented Canadian novelist Andrew David MacDonald and I also spoke by phone about modern masculinity, mental health, midlife, and the importance of male mentorship. He also saw the necessity of this project and really championed it. I love Andrew David MacDonald.

My supportive friend Adam Morgan kept me laughing via text while I worked on this project. I love Adam Morgan.

My brother in introversion and long philosophical discussions Scott Snow and I texted during the creation of this memoir. The few phone conversations we had covered such topics as father wounds, positive masculinity, and the need to author one's own life. All of these talks were epic and treasured. I love Scott Snow.

And I love all the people below too:

My ace literary agent, Doug Stewart, has been in my corner since 2007. He's never once stopped believing. Thanks also to everyone at Sterling Lord Literistic. My mensch film agent, Rich Green, started representing me shortly after Doug did. Without Doug's and Rich's hard-earned business acumen, I would not have had the necessary time and resources to pause, reflect, heal, and grow—which, of course, means this memoir would not have existed. I'm eternally grateful.

While I wrote this memoir, the fabulous Ellen Goldsmith-Vein championed my work around Hollywood, keeping that dream alive. Her efforts are appreciated.

Tenacious producer David Thwaites also battled hard for me in LA and has my gratitude.

My maestro editor, Jofie Ferrari-Adler, added the necessary oxygen and fuel to get this father-son memoir blazing. I'm blessed to have his faith in my work. Through the editing process, he improved this manuscript in every way possible. He's a hell of an editor and has my gratitude and loyalty.

At Jofie's request, Carolyn Kelly did a line edit of this book that led to numerous upgrades. Carolyn's contributions are gold.

Thanks also to everyone at Avid Reader Press.

During the writing of this manuscript, I met famed literary agent and wise woman Marly Rusoff. Marly and I had several chats in her lovely Lady's Island home, where she showered me with encouragement, tossed relevant books at me, told me a lot about Pat Conroy, and tried her best to get gourmet snack food into my belly. Marly introduced me to Robert Bly's poem "Keeping Quiet" when I most needed to read it. Our friendship feels fated.

Just before I really started moving on this memoir, my former student, current writing-life colleague, and fellow novelist Brigid Duffy popped back up in my life with a timely reminder that teaching others with an open heart is a sublime way to heal oneself. She also reminded me that seeds planted and forgotten decades ago might yet bloom when you least expect.

Former literary agent Bess Currence encouraged me back in 2007 when I was first trying to find representation. Without her cheerleading, I don't know that I would have endured the querying process long enough to find Doug. During the writing of this memoir, Bess and I began emailing again about mental health, writing, and religion. It all felt timely and was a gift.

Shout-out to the brilliant novelist Ron Currie for letting me use his sage quote about male writers and their fathers.

Thanks to Deborah C. Stewart, Lisa Marchiano, and Joseph R. Lee of the *This Jungian Life* podcast for being my auditory on-ramp to the great Jungian freeway. An extra shout-out to Mr. Lee for his illuminating insights into masculine psychology.

Thanks also to Jason E. Smith for sharing—via the *Digital Jung* podcast—his wise thoughts on the symbolic life. Throughout the writing of this memoir, on my afternoon runs and walks, I binged Mr. Smith's fascinating Jungian lectures.

Many people read and funded my Substack adventure, which allowed me to dip my toes into the scary waters of this big memoir plunge. Every paid Substack subscription, every like, every heart, every comment, every handwritten letter snail-mailed, and every email was a vote for me to write what you are reading right now. Thanks to all who voted while the ballot boxes were still open.

Robert Bly's seminal book *Iron John: A Book About Men* was my primary gateway read into Jungianism. It also long ago alerted me to and gave me language for my wounded masculinity and father hunger.

Robert A. Johnson's *The Fisher King & The Handless Maiden: Understanding the Wounded Feeling Function in Masculine and Feminine Psychology* helped me comprehend my father's and my own psychological wounds.

William Wharton's book *Dad* helped me wrap my mind around writing—and build up the courage to write—about my own father. Thanks to my fellow Philadelphian writer. RIP.

I first saw *The Prince of Tides* film adaptation in the Eric Westmont Theatre, back when I was a high school senior living in southern New Jersey. It moved me greatly. A decade later, while I was teaching English at Haddonfield Memorial High School, fellow teacher John Duffy slipped Pat Conroy's *My Losing Season* into my teacher mailbox. Inside the book was a note from Duff that began with these words: "To the next Pat Conroy." I devoured Conroy's memoir and then immediately read and loved all of his novels. I related strongly to the father issues so boldly on display throughout Mr. Conroy's work. Of course, I had no idea that I would someday move to Pat's part of the world to deal with my own father issues. Often, while spending time with my dad in and around Beaufort, South Carolina, I've thought to myself, *Your life has become a Pat Conroy book.* Tales of Pat abound here in the Lowcountry. And every time I see sunlight dancing on the waves of Hunting Island State Park, or someone is kind enough to take us out on a boat to cruise through the tides and observe the wildlife, or Alicia, Kingsly, and I stroll past the antebellum homes of downtown Beaufort, I think of the literary father I never met—the writing king of the Lowcountry, Pat Conroy—and I feel grateful for the early introduction that his work gave me to this magical place. I also appreciate the chance to follow in his giant footsteps, if only in my small way.

As mentioned in the manuscript, the late Dr. Meyers, professor of sociology at Albright College, saw the potential in Dad when he was a young man and loved my father in the way that he needed to be loved, initiating Michael Quick into manhood. I might owe my existence to Dr. Meyers. He has my gratitude.

My former Furley Street neighbor Johanna Zagursky Nicholson emailed me pictures from the seventies and provided details about the first few years of my life in Philly. When she was a teenager and I was a toddler, our row home bedrooms shared a wall, on which we'd knock hellos back and forth from our separate houses. Her late father, Joe Zagursky—aka Joe the Scoop—often held me when I was young. All of this helped enormously.

My aunt Cheryl also lived with us on Furley Street in the seventies. At my request, she wrote me a letter about it. It was appreciated.

My old Philly photographer Dave Tavani and I exchanged several philosophical emails while I was working on this memoir. These examinations of religion, midlife, and masculinity helped me work out a few of the ideas you have just read.

Eric Zimmer of *The One You Feed* podcast occasionally spoke with me by phone about mental health, midlife, and what it means to be a man these days. That was also appreciated.

Thanks to Wallace Wilhoit for twenty-plus years of steady friendship.

Thanks to Kalela Williams for her support and friendship.

Thanks to Liz Jensen for sharing the hard-won wisdom she acquired by publishing a deeply personal memoir herself.

Thanks to Maddee James and Riley Mack of xuni.com for keeping my website running and looking good.

Thanks to Dixie Keyes for her unwavering encouragement over the years.

Back in the mid- to late eighties, my Sunday school class earned a reputation for being disrespectful and unteachable. Our bad behavior forced several men to give up on us boys, and then no one wanted to take us on. Mr. Dunn showed up with a box of doughnuts and a Christlike attitude. His kindness, patience, and selflessness won us over right away. He never had a problem with us, and we never had a problem with him. He fed us doughnuts every Sunday morning, he invited us to his house for dinner, he taught us Bible stories, and he loved us like sons. During the writing of this memoir, I wrote to Mr. Dunn, after having lost touch with him back in the nineties. It was a long overdue thank-you. We traded several letters. Getting back in touch with my old Sunday school teacher helped me live out and sharpen the message of this memoir.

Thanks to everyone in the Celadon neighborhood who has welcomed and been kind to Mom, Dad, Alicia, Kingsly, and me.

There are two fetching houses across the street from our funky little home here on Lady's Island. One is occupied by the former bookstore owner and current all-around excellent human being Chris Stanley and her adorable little white dog, Ellie. During the writing of this manuscript, Kingsly went to their house every day at three p.m. for a doggie playdate. Chris always sent Alicia home with two Werther's Originals, which became my little treat at the end of each writing day.

The other house across the street from us is occupied by Pat Conroy Literary Center docent Cathy Palmer, who never fails to brighten my day with her endless cheer and heavenly South Carolinian accent. Thanks to Chris, Cathy, and Ellie for making us feel so at home here on our little strip of Lady's Island.

Throughout the writing of this memoir, twice a week my father attended a day care program organized by the Alzheimer's Family Services of Greater Beaufort. A saint of a woman named Diane Naus ran an additional support group every Monday, where those dealing with cognitive disabilities could discuss their experiences. Diane would also take my dad and two of his colleagues out to lunch every other Thursday. A saint of a man named Don Rowe offered to take my father golfing once a week. Don's generosity and patience has extended Dad's ability to play the game he loves most in the world. These kindnesses have greatly helped my family.

In your neighborhood indie bookshop, in your public library, and in your local classrooms, you'll find more saints fighting the good fight. Some of these saints have championed my work for the better part of two decades. To them, I say thanks a million. To everyone else, I say: Please keep supporting local bookstores and libraries. Tell the good teachers in your schools that you value them. Tell their bosses too. Keep these treasures from vanishing.

Last but not least, I appreciate you who are reading these words. I'm sending you love. *Right now.* That's what this entire memoir is: an act of love. If you are a person with a trauma history, you are not alone. If you know someone with a trauma history, please be as gentle with that person as you can psychologically afford to be. Do whatever you have to do to protect yourself, of course. But also remember that there is usually something good in the heart of every human being, no matter how damaged they might be. And sometimes—when we can hold that good part in the right way—miracles become possible. I never thought I'd make peace with my father, but I have. I hope you will be able to make peace with the difficult people in your life too—however that looks for you. I don't think there is a one-size-fits-all solution. But I love my dad now. And for most of my life, I swore that loving my father was impossible. Declaring things impossible was bad for me. It made me sicker than I had to be for decades. I hope having read about my many mistakes will help you and the people in your life. I wish you and yours all the redemption that life has to offer.

And if you love someone, please tell them.

About the Author

Matthew Quick is the *New York Times* bestselling author of *The Silver Linings Playbook*—which was made into an Oscar-winning film—and eight other novels, including *We Are the Light*, a #1 Indie Next Pick and a main selection of the Book of the Month Club. His work has been translated into more than thirty languages, received a PEN/Hemingway Award honorable mention, was a Los Angeles Times Book Prize finalist, a *New York Times Book Review* Editors' Choice, a #1 bestseller in Brazil, a Deutscher Jugendliteraturpreis (German Youth Literature Prize) 2016 nominee, and selected by Nancy Pearl as one of Summer's Best Books for NPR. *The Hollywood Reporter* has named him one of Hollywood's 25 Most Powerful Authors. Quick lives with his wife, the novelist Alicia Bessette, in Beaufort, South Carolina.

Avid Reader Press, an imprint of Simon & Schuster, is built on the idea that the most rewarding publishing has three common denominators: great books, published with intense focus, in true partnership. Thank you to the Avid Reader Press colleagues who collaborated on *Dad, Love, Me*, as well as to the hundreds of professionals in the Simon & Schuster advertising, audio, communications, design, ebook, finance, human resources, legal, marketing, operations, production, sales, supply chain, subsidiary rights, and warehouse departments whose invaluable support and expertise benefit every one of our titles.

Editorial
Jofie Ferrari-Adler, *VP and Co-Publisher*
Alexandra Silvas, *Editorial Assistant*

Jacket Design
Alison Forner, *VP and Art Director*
Clay Smith, *Associate Art Director*
Sydney Newman, *Art Associate*

Marketing
Meredith Vilarello, *VP and Associate Publisher*
Kayla Dee, *Associate Marketing Manager*
Katya Wiegmann, *Marketing and Publishing Coordinator*

Production
Allison Green, *Managing Editor*
Hana Handzija, *Managing Editorial Assistant*
Jessica Chin, *Senior Manager of Copyediting*
Vanessa Silverio, *Production Manager*
Carly Loman, *Interior Text Designer*
Hannah Lustyik, *Desktop Publishing Assistant*
Cait Lamborne, *Ebook Developer*

Publicity
Rhina Garcia, *Senior Publicist*
Eva Kerins, *Publicity Assistant*

Subsidiary Rights
Paul O'Halloran, *VP and Director of Subsidiary Rights*
Fiona Sharp, *Subsidiary Rights Coordinator*